THE IMPACT OF INSTITUTIONS IN APPALACHIA

*Proceedings of the
Eighth Annual
Appalachian Studies Conference*

Edited by:
JIM LLOYD
and
ANNE G. CAMPBELL

Managing Editor:
JANE SHOOK

APPALACHIAN CONSORTIUM PRESS
Boone, North Carolina

The Appalachian Consortium Press is a division of the Appalachian Consortium Incorporated, specializing in the publication of carefully produced books of particular interest to Southern Appalachia. The Press is controlled by the Publications Committee and the Board of Directors, the members of which are appointed by the Chief Administrative Officers of the member institutions and agencies of the corporation.

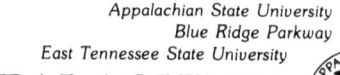

Appalachian State University
Blue Ridge Parkway
East Tennessee State University
N. C. Division of Archives & History
Southern Highland Handicraft Guild
United States Forest Service
Lees-McRae College
Mars Hill College
Mountain Regional Library
Warren Wilson College
Western Carolina University
Western N. C. Historical Assoc.

APPALACHIAN CONSORTIUM

ISBN: 978-1-4696-3687-0

Copyright © 1986 by the Appalachian Consortium, Inc. all rights reserved.

Table of Contents

INTRODUCTION, *Anne Campbell* i

TRIBUTES TO CRATIS WILLIAMS
    Loyal Jones 1
    David Williams 3
    Grace Edwards 5
    Charlotte Ross 7
    James Gifford 11

I. HEREAFTER EFFECTS ON THE HERE AND NOW: RELIGION AND REGION
    Passing Over Yonder, *Howard Dorgan* 14

II. GOVERNMENT AND TECHNOLOGY: CHANGE AND EFFECT ON A REGION
    Some Thoughts on Science and Technology in Appalachia, *Ron Willoughby* 24

III. CAPITALISM AND COAL: A REASSESSMENT
    Capitalism, Patriarchy and "Mens Work": The System of Control of Production in Coal Mining, *Mike Yarrow* 29

IV. WORDS AND PHOTOGRAPHS: ENDURING IMAGES OF APPALACHIA
    Early Regional Photographers: Margaret Morley and William Barnhill in Western North Carolina, *Richard Straw* 48

V. JOCKS AND JUNKETS: COME PLAY AND STAY
    Sports and Play in Southern Appalachia: A Tentative Appraisal, *Robert J. Higgs* 57

    Appalachian Documentaries: Hyping the Myth, *Sharyn McCrumb* 68

Appalachia: A Tourist Attraction?,
Melinda Bollar Wagner, Lynn Batley, Kai Jackson,
Bill O'Brien, Liz Throckmorton 73

VI. BEFORE THE YELLOW BUSES: THE QUEST
FOR EDUCATION
Settlement School Goes to the People: Pine Mountain
School's Community Centers at Big Laurel
and Line Fork, 1919-1940, Nancy Forderhase 88

VII. ISSUES OF THEORY AND METHOD
IN REGIONAL RESEARCH
Class and Gender: New Theoretical Priorities in
Appalachian Studies, Sally Ward Maggard 100

Beyond the "Traditional Mountain Subculture":
A New Look at Pre-Industrial Appalachia,
Mary Beth Pudup 114

VIII. ETHNICITY AND MOBILITY
Blacks: An Invisible Institution in Appalachia?,
Wilburn Hayden 128

Moving On: Recent Patterns of Appalachian
Migration, Philip Obermiller and Robert Oldendick .. 148

IX. FREE AT LAST?: VIEW OF
APPALACHIAN HISTORY
Impact of the Company Town on
Traditional Life, Dean Herrin 166

X. REALITIES AND MYTHS: MOUNTAIN POLITICS
Hubbard's Branch of Mill Creek—1964-1984:
Twenty Years After the War On Poverty,
Warren Brunner and Tom Boyd 175

INTRODUCTION

The Appalachian Studies Conference first met in Berea, Kentucky in March of 1978. Since that time scholars, teachers and regional activists have continued to participate in an annual conference at which ideas and research, as well as personal experiences and concerns are shared. These meetings are composed of many facets — sessions which introduce research findings and theories; panel discussions with community and academic participants; creative presentations that highlight regional artistic endeavors; keynote speakers who share insights, observations and experiences; displays and exhibits which feature publications and programs offered by individuals, institutions and regional organizations; social gatherings where friendships are formed and renewed. These annual events have been held at state parks in Georgia and West Virginia; on campuses in Kentucky, Tennessee and Virginia; at a 4-H camp in West Virginia; and at the Blue Ridge Assembly in North Carolina.

The return to Berea College, host of the initial gathering seven years ago, indicates that the Appalachian Studies Conference continues to be of value to those who participate in its annual activities. By rotating the site each year, the Appalachian Studies Conference Officers, Steering Committee and Program Committee attempt to feature specific locales and encourage attendance from neighboring areas.

Each year the Program Committee selects a theme for the conference. The 1985 Program Committee chose to direct attention to the impact of institutions in Appalachia. Few people and regions have been as greatly effected by institutions as those in Appalachia. Whether it be religion, family, education, land development, culture, craft guilds or government agencies, all have contributed to shaping Appalachia and influencing its people. While the Committee planned the conference program with this overall theme in mind, we broadly interpreted the concept of institution. Thus the program offered a variety of topics and approaches which included a panel discussion on international perspectives relating to Appalachia, papers on turn-of-the-century settlement institutions, as well as contemporary assesments of capitalism and coal.

The papers in this publication are a sampling of those presented at the Berea meeting. Hopefully, these offerings as well as future programs of the Appalachian Studies Conference will continue to provide a forum for exchange, dialogue and understanding, and will contribute to the future of Appalachia.

Anne G. Campbell, Chair
1985 Program Committee

1985 Program Committee

Anne G. Campbell, Chair

Alan Banks
Carol Barrier
Andrew Baskin
Malinda Crutchfield
Rosemary Goss

Judi Jennings
Loyal Jones
Jim Lloyd
Sue Thrasher

Pictures Courtesy of Morehead State University

Pictures Courtesy of Morehead State University

Cratis Dearl Williams
1911-1985

When the tributes to Cratis Williams were presented at the Appalachian Studies Conference, Cratis lay ill in the Charlotte Memorial Hospital, after bypass heart surgery and a pacemaker. He had thought to be present, and because we knew Cratis, that he would be with us if it were physically possible, we half expected him to appear. But of course he didn't, although David, his son, was a part of the program. We put together a slide show of photographs of Cratis in different periods of his life and in his many roles. We played excerpts of his speeches, conversations and concerts. Then, some of his friends talked about him for a while, not always reverently, and we looked forward to greeting him and honoring him in person when the Appalachian Studies Conference meets in Boone next March. But Cratis died in May, and so our tributes to him now become our memorial statements. In fact three of us spoke at his memorial services.

For years you could mention the name of Cratis Williams to those who knew him, and the immediate response you would get would be an appreciative smile, or perhaps a grin. Although we like to say that everyone is unique, we can describe most people by saying they are "like" so-and-so. Not so with Cratis. He was not like anybody else, and, furthermore, we know of nobody who can carry on his very special work in the world. No one else can explain the Appalachian character as he did, or reflect on or sing a ballad in his distinctive way. And speaking: whether his subject was Appalachian speech, folklore, cultural history, material folk culture or whatever, he was a lecturer without peer, with a precision and vividness of language and facial expressiveness that both amused and fascinated listeners.

Already we're thinking that we shall never again hear such good stories in the night, told in that careful but sparkling and Chaucerian way. We don't look forward to attending the Appalachian Studies Conference with the scholarly tedium unrelieved by late-evening sessions with Cratis and his clusters of admirers.

Cratis published his first regional essay when he was 17; called "Why a Mountain Boy Should be Proud," it appeared in the Louisa (Ky.) *Louisian* on December 12, 1927. Many other works were to follow: a master's thesis on folksongs of Eastern Kentucky; his New York University doctoral dissertation (1,650 pages), *The Southern Mountaineer in Fact and Fiction*, the definitive work on the subject of Appalachian literature to 1960 (once, showing this imposing work to a friend, Cratis remarked: "I just wanted you to admire the magnitude of the SOB"); a series of insightful and colorful essays on Appalachian speech; and numerous articles on a variety of Appalachian subjects.

Although most of us knew him as a writer and lecturer or speaker at some notable event, to a great many others he was a teacher and administrator. His educational career included teaching in a one-room school, a high school, being a high school principal, a university English teacher, graduate dean and chancellor. Those who served with and under him spoke of his wisdom and vision.

To me, Cratis was an ideal man, representing the essence of Appalachian culture combined with the best in the tradition of liberal learning. He was both erudite and earthy, at once profound, entertaining and delightfully honest in thought and language. We wish we could have just a few more of his insights and a few more stories in the night.

Loyal Jones

Remarks at the Tribute to Cratis Williams

Loyal Jones remarked earlier that Cratis Williams is many things to many people, and from my vantage point that certainly has a ring of truth about it: he does indeed do many different things and, to that extent, is many different things. But from my unique vantage point, he is predominantly one thing. He is family. He is Papa. And it is as Papa that I shall speak of him tonight.

Perhaps I should offer an explanation of why I find it important to speak of him as Papa. Those of you who have heard him tell the tales of our ancestors in Eastern Kentucky will recognize the almost magical qualities generated by the bestowal of familial titles upon the characters. Thus, instead of hearing about my ancestors as men named David or Jake or women named Mandy, I always heard about larger-than-life characters with magical names such as Pa Dave, Grandpap Jake, and Granny Mandy. For me, as a young listener to the family stories, the family history was transformed into legend, and the teller of the stories was not the man Cratis Williams but rather a larger-than-life participant in the legend, Papa. Perhaps someday he will settle into the family narrative as Pa Crate, but for now he remains simply Papa.

It is, I suppose, somewhat awkward to have a roast without the body present. Papa has considered that dilemma and, in a sort of optimistic fatalism which I have heard described as characteristic of the mountaineer, has concluded that perhaps it is just as well that for this roast, the body could not be present. Since we are at Berea College, which awarded an honorary degree to "Daddy" King as well as "Papa" Williams, perhaps it is appropriate to summarize Papa's reflections upon not being able to attend his roast by recalling, and misapplying, famous words of Martin Luther King, Jr.: in the cool captivity of his hospital room, Papa feels safe from the searing flames of withering justice which this roast has produced.

In actuality, modern technology in a sense has allowed Papa to be here. The roast has been video-taped, and one of those tapes is destined for Papa's eyes and ears. Thus, while the body is absent, the eyes and ears are present. See, I have only been speaking of him as Papa for a few moments and already he has assumed larger-than-life proportions. And, in conjunction with that, I would remind the roasters that next year's Appalachian Studies Conference will be in Boone, which should give Papa a year in which to prepare his rebuttal.

He warned me before I came that he was sure that there was going to be "a lot of meanness" said about him. And, with that characteristic twinkle in his eye, he assured me that after reviewing the videotape he would clarify for me what was fact and what was fiction, what was accurate and what was meanness. In the spirit of Orwell's Winston Smith, I await such clarification.

Papa asked me to convey to you some news of his status and progress in the hospital. He reports that the operation and the drugs have whittled him down to a plucky 115 pounds. Those of you who know him know that that is quite svelte. It is, in fact, exactly what his weight was toward the end of his sophomore year in high school. The weight loss has fatigued him a great deal, and he does not currently have the energy that has been spoken of tonight. His spirit, however, has not been dampened in the least, and he is happy to report, in his impish way, that while he lacks the energy and stamina to charm the female nurses in any active manner, his new physique seems to have prompted them to pay greater attention to him.

He should be out of the hospital next week. He is progressing well, but more slowly than anticipated. His optimism, however, remains irrepressible. He is very sorry that he could not be here tonight. He had hoped even as late as last week to be able to attend, but he is not yet able to travel.

He sends to all his greatest appreciation for this tribute. He conveys his love to the Appalachian region, the Appalachian people, and the scholars of Appalachia. This is, I think, in the end not so much a tribute to him as it is a tribute to you, the people and scholars of Appalachia, for what you see and admire in Cratis Williams is a reaction to who he is, and he is, in his own words, a complete mountaineer. What you see in Cratis Williams, even in the many different things which he can be to different people, is then a reflection of the Appalachian experience and of you as Appalachian people. This tribute in that sense is a tribute to you, the people and scholars of Appalachia, and that is the spirit in which he hopes that you will reflect upon the tribute.

David Williams

Tribute To Cratis: A Student's View

Once upon a time, long, long ago, a child went out into the world to seek a fortune. The child's footsteps were directed toward the mountain and after climbing and climbing, and climbing at last she reached her destination. Although she had scaled seemingly dizzying heights, she found herself still at the foot of a mountain, Howard's Knob to be precise. "Wait here for instruction," she was told. Soon a parade of faces marched before her shouting out dates and times and places and calculations and formulas, babbling in Spanish, showing off in Chaucerian English, demanding, commanding, pushing, shoving, pulling. At the height of the chaos, out of the rabble emerged a single face, calm and kindly. The voice that spoke sounded like home, "Follow your *own* path, child. I will show you the way."

And so she followed him, for his face was real, and not a mask, and his voice was true, not false. They traipsed through the New England woods that fringe Walden Pond and heard Henry David Thoreau talk about "stepping to the beat of a different drummer." They sat in the parlor of Ralph Waldo Emerson's house and listened to the philosopher say again and again, "Trust thyself." They watched shy Nat Hawthorne tell the story of the fallen woman who wore the scarlet *A* with dignity. They even rode the high seas on Herman Melville's *Pequod*, traveled through Europe with Henry James' *American*, returned to their own country to raft down the Mississippi with *Huck Finn*, and at long last came home again to the Southern Appalachian Mountains.

To the child's amazement, a treasure trove awaited her even in her own land. The master of kindly face, calm manner, and familiar voice spoke, "You have seen the wonders of the world and the literary masterpieces that extole them. Now look at the riches around you." And he began to spin a tale about a boy named Jack and then to sing a song about a girl named Barbary. Those stories and those songs, just like the master's voice, sounded like home. The child felt good to know that someone else shared the entertainments she had grown up with, and more importantly, valued them. For she had labored under the mistaken notion that only customs and manners different from hers mattered—to the rest of the world. The master said again, "Follow your *own* path, child." And suddenly, she knew the way.

Though her path was not free of brambles and briers and though it sometimes plunged into murky gloom, she followed it steadfastly, for the master was always there when she needed him to encourage and compliment and spur her onward. Just as he had promised, she found rubies and diamonds along the way, riches in her own land and among her own people.

The story has no end, for the child is still following the path and the master is still encouraging her. This is where fact blends with fiction. In case you haven't identified the characters in this story, the **master is Cratis Williams** and I am the child. He has truly been my teacher, advisor, mentor, and friend for over twenty years now—in fact, from the moment I first walked into his classroom as a scared, shy college student at Appalachian State Teachers College. I have taken something like ten courses from Dr. Williams over the years, from undergraduate to graduate to post-graduate days. I have pursued a career that happily intersects with his. I have called on him for advice and help time and time again. Always he responds promptly, fully, generously. But he doesn't wait to be *asked* for help. He inspires through his letters, that come, unexpectedly, like treasures themselves. Most recently he wrote from his sick bed to offer congratulations for something he had read about. Every now and then, a colleague, a student, or a reporter asks me, "How did *you* get interested in Appalachian Studies?" I always answer with a name—Cratis Williams.

Grace Edwards

Remembering Cratis Williams

Once and only once he spoke to me of the inevitability of this day, and he said that I was to wear a bright dress and tell all the people to smile and be happy. And he said this: "Remember me with joy and laughter, or don't remember me at all."

He said that if anyone gathered here today had a good memory of him, it would be all right to tell it to Libby or David or Sophie or to someone in this fine extended family of Williamses and Lingerfelts. The folklorist in him understood that there is no finer monument to any man than good memories well shared.

He wanted me to speak today because he knew my memories were happy ones. Sometimes two people meet and discover that they share the same magnificent obsession. Both of us had as young children become obsessed with the time and place into which we were born, with these mountains and the people who inhabit them. Each of us had studied Appalachia for many years before we met. The day we met, Cratis correctly placed my accent within twenty miles of my home, and I fell in love with him forevermore.

He was my friend and mentor for seventeen years. I loved him as one loves a parent or only the rarest, only the very greatest, of teachers. For the next few minutes, I wish to share with you some of my great joy in remembering Cratis Williams.

I remember Cratis pausing each morning to sniff the air, to take the measure of the new day, saying, "We do live in a pretty part of the world." I remember Cratis tramping through woods still wet with snow to see if the sarvis, that first harbinger of the mountain spring, was blooming yet. I remember Cratis stopping his car so suddenly that four cars nearly collided behind us so that he could glory over a Mail Pouch, tobacco sign painted on a West Virginia barn. I remember Cratis savoring good whiskey both here and abroad; and if it was homebrew, he'd shake the jar and watch the bead form, and turn to the crowd which had gathered to watch his antics, and taste, and say, "Now that's fine, finer than frog hair." I remember Cratis calling me in the early A.M. anguish he often knew with the dreadful news that the Red Bird Mission School had burned, or that Bill Plemmons was worse, or that we had lost that good man, Jesse Jackson. And I remember Cratis forever watching the faces of passers-by for evidences of the mountain heritage. "That looks like an Etheridge," he'd say. "Go and call him over here, Charlotte, for I want to know him." Once he stopped a woman on a Philadelphia street saying, "You have an Eastern Kentucky face." And when her shock abated, she told him she was from Harlan County, U.S.A.

I remember him as always moving: bouncing across a footlog near my home in North Georgia, hurtling through Eastern Kentucky, skidding on gravelly coal near Neon, Kentucky, discovering that he had no brakes as we sped through the Cumberland Gap with Cratis yelling "Whoa, dammit, Whoa!" to his Chevette. I remember his foot slipping through a rotted board on a swinging bridge in West Virginia, and I remember him wading the Pigeon River with plastic garbage bags over his pantlegs so that I could show him an old graveyard on the other side. And I remember him always moving during that magic five-week trip we took together in England, Ireland, Scotland and Wales: riding the ferries with the spray in his face in the Outer Hebrides, buying tweeds in Scotland, sampling the pubs in Ireland, walking the Roman Wall dividing Scotland and England long after night had fallen, looking north toward Celtic lands.

I remember him as always talking. When he got into a car and perched on the passenger seat, it was as if a switch had been turned. He could talk nonstop for hours as long as the car was moving. Mostly, he talked about Appalachia; some of his best informal teaching was done in these circumstances. But he also talked to people everywhere: to waitresses, and schoolchildren, and to old men on the courthouse steps, and to people in the street.

When he wasn't talking, he was singing. His greatest disappointment in me was that I cannot carry a tune, so mostly, he sang to me. I remember one day of sheer serendipity in the lowlands of Scotland when Cratis Williams sang the English and Scottish ballads for nearly six hours.

I remember him as the consummate teacher. He was always observing his own culture, always asking the hard questions, always setting me tasks to enrich my understanding. Like all truly great teachers, he expected that the student should surpass the master. "Else what's a teacher for?" he'd say. His mind was analytical and his interests wide-ranging. Yet, his style was always narrative and anecdotal, for that is the Appalachian way. What I seem to remember most is the highly personal nature of his teaching.

I can still hear his voice asking me to sing that verse from "Lambkin," the one about the false nurse, or laughing at me because I'd never thought to ask why cedar trees grew in straight lines on the hillsides. He would taste old paint to see if it was made with lead or buttermilk. He reminded me that only the rear doors of old cabins were ever painted, for blue paint kept the devil out.

He taught me to observe the people of the region closely. "That's the Appalachian body type there." "Looks like Ernest Hartley." Or, "You must remember that family name; they came down the Holston on a flatbed raft and later fought at King's Mountain." He wanted me to know the places of legend and history. When he was able, we'd walk the historic landscapes together: whole sections of the Wilderness Road and of the Great Wagon Road from Philadelphia, the twists of Dark Hollow in Surry County where the pioneers veered southward into Carolina and the Yadkin country, and the old route from Wolf Cave south along the Holston to the Watauga settlements. In later years, he'd take his afternoon nap in the car while I made my way along the river looking for the place where they found Jenny Wiley, or edged along under the cliffs seeking the place where Indians tortured Boone's son, or found the site of some forgotten treaty. And it was always just as Cratis had said that it would be.

For seventeen years, assiduously, he taught me. It was the most intensive educational experience of my life, and easily the most personal and the most exciting. There was such glory in his giving, and he was always teaching.

I will remember Cratis most for the thing he did the best. He was consistently, obdurately, and unrepentantly Appalachian. From the day we met until the day he died, I never once saw him waver from the Appalachian point of view. He was the original autochthonous Appalachian; his very blood and sinew were sprung out of the ground that bred him. And his mind was like a clear spring of water bubbling upward through limestone. He was the perfect exponent of Appalachian culture in the last half of the nineteenth century, though he was born in the twentieth. He was Cratis Williams, mountaineer, and he was Appalachian to the fourth power.

You have to admire that kind of singularity of purpose, that consistent vision. Cratis though that lives lived without passion were uncommon dull, and he was never dull. The secret of his charm was that his life was dedicated to the study and explication of his culture, his people, his mountains. He sorrowed for those whose lives had no such center, who seemed to be always searching for identity.

If he had a fault—and he admitted to one—it was that he couldn't understand why this viewpoint was not universal. He could not comprehend why anyone, particularly one of his blood, would live in flat country. "What," he would demand of me, "do they rest their eyes upon if there are no mountains?" Several times a year he would leave some meeting or other in the strained silence which in him passed for high dudgeon. After a silence of a few miles he would turn to me and say, "I was not born to the middle class, nor do I aspire to it." "A thing like that could purely stultify a man's soul." "They do not have our values."

There are certain images and sounds which will always evoke his presence. I will remember Cratis whenever I see the leaves on the trees turning their backs to the wind as they did on the August day when he first came to Boone in the year that I was born. I will remember Cratis whenever I see a man cutting spring onions into cornbread or digging new potatoes. I will remember Cratis whenever I see the first bloom of spring upon the mountainside. I will remember Cratis whenever I hear any of the five sounds which he thought just might be the very essence of Appalachia: the sound of fiddle music on the night air and the accompanying stomp of a barn dance, an Appalachian tenor with that high lonesome sound, an old woman singing ballads to the rhythm of her churn, hounds running foxes up the mountainside, and the sound of the human voice rising and falling, telling the old stories.

Once, operating on some internal radar, for all the road signs were down, he found Ossian's grave in an Ulsterman's pasture. He stood for a long while in the soft rain. The next day in Belfast during an interview for the BBC, he spoke about the experience. He said that it was a very fine thing to be buried in a grave on a hill overlooking a beloved country.

Now, the ashes of Cratis Williams begin the final journey home to a grave on a hill in the Williams family cemetery—Caines Creek, Lawrence County, in the kingdom of Eastern Kentucky. And some of us will remember him always.

When I first knew him, I loved him because he was all our yesteryears. Now, I know that remembering him will color all of my tomorrows. And I will love him for all enduring time.

Charlotte T. Ross

In Memorium

Cratis Williams was born April 5, 1911, on Caines Creek in Lawrence County, Kentucky. In 1924, his father took him by wagon to the county-seat town of Louisa and enrolled him in high school there. After becoming the first from Caines Creek to graduate from high school, Cratis was awarded a tuition scholarship and a workship by Cumberland College in Williamsburg. After a year at Cumberland, he returned to Caines Creek to teach a one-room school.

With a broom in one hand and a bucket packed with chalk, erasers, dipper, and a record book in the other, Cratis walked the five miles from Blaine to his home, proud of his accomplishments and excited about his future:

"I was now a teacher," he later recalled, "I remember the cool, dank stretches of the sandy road beside Blaine Creek and the dust on the tall weeds and the leaves on the sycamores, willows, and water birches as I strolled along. Occasionally, I would be blinded by the dust kicked up by a car, but after I turned up the Caines Creek road I saw no more cars. The afternoon was hot. Poison ivy along the fence rows and the trumpet flowers that dipped from the Virginia Creeper growing on posts were still and dark in the hot sun. I thought of my trip up the creek in the wagon a year and a half before when I held proudly on my knee the loving cup I had received at the high school commencement and how pleased I had been to find on the front page of the *Big Sandy News* a week later my picture and a writeup that Earl Kinner had prepared. I remembered the trip in the wagon less than a year before when my father brought me to Blaine to find a ride to Louisa where I left by train for Cumberland College. That had been a hard but pleasant year, for all of that. I had made good grades, earned extra credits, and felt confident that I would teach a good school. I had also felt more keenly the pinch of poverty and recognized more deeply than ever before that I was depressed much of the time. The running sore on my thigh had never healed. My left leg tired easily. But I also knew that I felt irrepressible joy, especially with other people, and that I would go on to the University of Kentucky where I would have the money I had earned as a teacher to support me without having to try to work and go to college at the same time."

His approach to one-room school discipline was unique. He assumed "that all thirty-three of the children were capable, eager, and industrious." Proceeding on that assumption, he laid down no rules, as one-room school teachers before him had always done. Rather, he referred to "the desire of everyone to be thoughtful and considerate of others and to have others return thoughtfulness and consideration." With this as a guide, he observed, "we would most certainly get along well and enjoy school." Cratis was so successful in presenting his basic guidelines for conduct that it was not necessary all year to whip a child with a switch, the "traditional terminal punishment" for misbehavior in one-room schools.

Cratis's keen sensitivity to other people's feelings and his compassion and appreciation for others became personal trademarks. As a one-room school teacher, he had "three little tow-headed girls" who could not buy toothbrushes for their oral hygiene class, and so Cratis asked parental permission to buy the brushes as presents. "The father and mother looked at each other for a moment. Tears came to the mother's eyes as she nodded her head slightly."

The father said that he would like "for his girls to be able to do what the other children did," and he told Cratis that the children quoted him as the "pure Gospel." The father offered to repay him, but Cratis told him that he had not come to urge him to go into debt for the brushes, that he liked his little girls and they were doing so well in school that he wanted to give them the brushes...but did not want to run the risk of hurting (the parent's) feelings," and so he sought and received their approval. On his way back home, Cratis stopped at the country store and post office and bought three toothbrushes, a green one, a blue one, and a red one so that everyone could participate in the toothbrush drill.

Throughout his career, Cratis extended this kind of loving help. I first met him in the summer of 1977 at a Berea College workshop in Appalachian history and literature. I had heard of him long before I met him, but, unlike many living legends, he equalled his advanced billings and exceeded his reputation. He enthralled audiences with his knowledge, and he captivated individuals with his charm. Not surprisingly, I was eager to involve him when I came to Morehead State University in 1978 to develop an Appalachian Studies Program.

The following fall (November 28-30, 1979) Cratis served a consultancy at MSU's Appalachian Development Center. As always, he kept a hectic schedule gracefully. He met with the Appalachian Studies Advisory Committee, delivered a public lecture one evening, addressed several classes, and met informally with interested students and faculty. Afterwards, he submitted a detailed and extremely beneficial set of guidelines that provided intellectual, curricular, programmatic, and developmental cornerstones for our emerging program. His greatest effect, however, was on the individuals he encountered. One faculty member wrote to him: "Words have not the power to convey either my joy from or the positive effect of your three-day visit to our campus...I am delighted to have met a person with your knowledge of our cultural heritage and zest for sharing it with others. I eagerly await your next visit to Morehead." Another wrote that his lecture to her literature class "provided one of the finest academic experiences that our students could ever have."

In June of 1980 and 1981 and again in 1984, Dr. Williams served as Scholar in Residence for MSU's annual Appalachian Celebration. I was impressed with the quality of his wide-ranging knowledge and appeal and with his enormous personal charisma. Again, his contribution were enormous and far-reaching and the positive effects of his visits reverberated throughout the area long after he returned to his home in Boone, North Carolina, where he remained actively "retired" as a special assistant to the chancellor of Appalachian State University. On September 17, 1981, Cratis made the first presentation in MSU's "Our Mountain Heritage" lecture series. He maintained a regular interest in and support of our Program.

Cratis's contributions to Morehead State University exemplify the type of assistance he gave throughout Eastern Kentucky. He worked closely with Ron Dailey and Mike Mullins at Alice Lloyd College and with the late Leonard Roberts at Pikeville College. He regularly taught in Berea College's highly regarded summer workshops. He served on the Board of Directors of the Hindman Settlement School and as Chairman of the Alumni Board of Cumberland College. His contributions to Eastern Kentucky institutions illustrate the service he provided throughout Southern Appalachia.

Yet, it seems to me that his greatest contribution was his positive influence on individuals. Cratis had an uncanny ability to become a part of peoples' lives. Like a modern day Johnny Appleseed, he went about The Southern Mountains planting wisdom, and joy, and good advice, and whenever he returned he found lifelong friendships in bloom. Cratis was consummately human. He revelled in a well told story, a good party, a hearty chuckle, or a mischievous giggle. Yet, for all his down-to-earth qualities, he transcended his humanity and became a mythic and heroic being. All of us are children at heart; all of us once joyously looked forward to a visit from Santa Claus or the Easter Bunny. After we got older, we looked forward to a visit from Cratis.

Life is a series of beginnings and endings. I do not think Cratis would want us to view today as an ending, rather I think it is the beginning of a new phase of our relationship with him. We can no longer seek his advice and we can no longer draw strength and comfort from our visits with him, but we can do the things he would want us to do and we can rely on both memory and the written word for his guidance and inspiration.

Like Tennyson's Ulysses, Cratis became a part of all that he met. The part of us that is Cratis is now more than a gift—it is a responsibility. Although he received many honors and awards, (including honorary doctorates from Morehead State University and Marshall University) his most significant awards are not inscribed on plaques or printed handsomely on diplomas or books; they are written with love and admiration on the hearts of hundreds of people like me who are forever grateful for his friendship, advice, and good company. Cratis made his mark upon the immortal mind! He set fires of love and learning that will brighten to all eternity.

James M. Gifford

HEREAFTER EFFECTS ON THE HEAR AND NOW:
RELIGION AND REGION
   Convenor: Chester R. Young, Cumberland College
Frontier Baptists and Changing Values, 1821-1910
   John L. Bell, Jr., Western Carolina University
Impact of Church and School in Black Communities in Jackson County
   Victoria A. Casey, Sylva, North Carolina
Passing Over Yonder
   Howard Dorgan, Appalachian State University

Passing Over Yonder
by
Howard Dorgan

When Old Regular, Regular, Primitive, Union and some Missionary Baptist associations print minutes of their annual sessions they include obituaries for members who died during the previous year. This isn't an honor reserved just for leaders of the association or for leaders of the affiliated churches. Instead, all members—and sometimes nonmembers—may have their obituaries printed in these pages. It's just a matter of someone in the family composing the document and submitting it for publication. The cost of printing is borne by the association, with only a small charge to families wanting to include a picture of the deceased. Placing an obituary in the association's minutes constitutes a final tribute and farewell too important to overlook, and Old Regular families in particular are quite diligent in this duty to the deceased. In this subdenomination, the document is often read at the funeral, and once the statement is published, it is preserved in the family papers as an important memorial for the deceased. It will be read and reread in years to come.

Occasionally, an individual will write his or her own obituary, with some member of the family then updating the document at the actual time of death and adding whatever sentiments seem appropriate. Such was the case for Alice Belcher, who on July 24, 1980, authored the following statement about herself:

> I will now try with the help of my good Lord to write my obituary. I was borned February 10, 1899. At Lookout, Ky. I was the daughter of the late Dave Mercer and Alfire Castle Mercer.
> I was married (to) Bowes Belcher, June 8, 1920. To this union was borned six children. One boy and five girls. The boy and

was borned six children. One boy and five girls. The boy and one girl were still borned, leaving four girls. Vivvan died in 1970....I have eight grand children, eleven great grand children. One sister Mrs. Viola Hall of Manchestor, Ky. I love them all very much. I wount all my Brothern and Sisters to pray for them all.

I joined the Old Regular Baptist Church at the Little Hattie Church in May 3, 1950. I was baptized by Elder Jim Green and Fon Bowling. I all ways love to go to church. I love all my brothers and sisters.

I fell and broke my hip and did not get to go. I prayed to the good Lord to let me get well so I could go. I could not get off the porch with out help. I set at home by my self so many long days. I hope this life will soon be over. I wont have to suffer and set alone.

Cheldren remember the good council Mother gave you. Be good to each other. Read the bible. It will not tell you anything wrong. I hate to leave my family, but God is able to take care of them, if they will only listen.

Have mine and Daddy picture put in minutes. My husband has been gone for sixteen long years. I miss him so much.

Written by Sister Alice Belcher, Wife and Mother.

By God's help, I love you all.

Mother passed from this life February 4, 1984. At the age of 84 years, 11 months and 25 days old. Mother was a devoted mother and a loving grand mother. A dedicated Sister in the Church for over 33 years.

She has fourteen great grand children now. Daddy passed from this life October 4, 1964. We miss them so very much. But we know they are together up in heaven (where) there will be no more sorrow, truble or pain to bare.

If we take mothers advice, by the grace of God we will meet them in Heaven some sweet day.

With all our love, Her Daughters. Phyllis, Etta, Geraldine.[1]

Small associations, such as the Senter District Primitive Baptists and the Little River Regular Baptist, devote only a few pages to obituaries, but the Union Baptist Association and the Sardis Association of Old Regulars run twenty to twenty-five pages of memorials, while the Union Association of Old Regular Baptist regularly publishes fifty or more pages of these farewell statements. My attention is directed at the Sardis and Union associations of Old Regulars.

Written by "left to mourn" husbands, wives, children, or other loved ones, these obituaries serve not only as farewells to deceased brethren, but also as opportunities for writers to make summation remarks about life, to affirm basic beliefs, and to call other family members to needed repentance and change. For the most part, the statements are unsophisticated and straightforward defenses of the "earthly life" contributions of respective Brothers or Sisters, augmented by calls to the living to remember and emulate. Frequently, eulogies make pointed reference to individuals who must change their lives "if they are to follow the deceased into heaven," and occasionally the statements become apologias for the deceased, as if to say, "This individual was a person of goodness and worth: God should take note of the stars in his or her crown and open wide the gate."

A basic format seems to be followed in these obituaries. First, there is the traditional opening statement, usually a comment about the personal pain involved in writing the document, along with a suggestion that the eulogist feels himself or herself inadequate to the task at hand and thus must call upon God for inspiration and guidance. Next, there is a succinct review of the departed's life, with particular emphasis upon the family left behind. An account of the deceased's descendants is usually provided, and pride seems to be taken in the extensiveness of the list of children, grandchildren, and great-grandchildren. Then, statements are made about how important the individual was to family, friends, neighbors, and church; and it's particularly necessary to note how much the deceased will be missed:

> All us children can say that Papa (Elbert [Ebb] Fuller) was the best example we could follow for our lives. We have lost something so Precious that can never be replaced here on earth. We all hope the Good Lord will strengthen us and help us take care of our dear mother. Papa and Mommy were so good to each other that all Mommy has to worry about is the loss of Papa which will be hard... I had a good papa here on earth. Jesus took him to heaven. He knew what he was worth.

> Sister Fannie (Hale) was a pillar in the Church for the 61 years that God blessed her to spend in the Church. She baked the bread to be served in our Communion meetings from the time I first can remember until these last few years when her health wouldn't permit her to continue. She seemed always present when her name was called. Her warm felt, kind and sweet spoken words of counsel would be good for each of us as we journey through this lane of life.[2]

Near the close of an obituary there traditionally will be a statement to the effect that the departed has merited redemption and the rewards of heaven. This passage serves as a final note of assurance to loved ones that all is well with the deceased's soul. Often it will be supported by some brief narrative illustrating the departed's own awareness of imminent death and subsequent passage to "glory":

> So many times we have heard Mom (Dollie Barley Ratliff) tell of her experience as she would cast her eyes toward Canaan's Land. She led a good Christian life, and her influence will continue to give faith and hope to the ones who knew and loved her... The night before her passing, even while enduring severe pain and suffering, Mom continued to quote verses of scripture from the Bible. She seemed to know that the death angel was near and sincerely believed in God's mercy and goodness... (Mom is) resting in Ratliff Family Cemetery awaiting the coming of Christ, and to go home with Him to live forevermore in that country where sorrow and trouble are unknown.[4]

Occasionally a church member will compose an obituary for a deceased friend or loved one who was never church affiliated or ever baptized. Motivated by a desire to give his friend or loved one the best send-off possible, or by a wish to assuage fears of the family, this obituary writer will find something that projects a glimmer of hope for the departed.

The 1983 minutes of the Union Association of Old Regulars, for example, contains a memorial statement for Thestil Edward Slone, killed in a coal mining accident at the age of thirty-three. Written by the deceased's uncle, Elder David Slone, the obituary notes that the nephew had been divorced from his first wife and had remarried, producing two children by each union. Although no details are given for the divorce, this termination of the first marriage may have been the basis for Elder Slone's remark about his nephew doing wrong; for Old Regular churches generally exclude from their memberships all divorced individuals, "except those who have put away their companion for the cause of fornication."[4] At the point in the obituary when Elder Slone ordinarily would have given assurance of the deceased's eternal salvation he had the following to say about his nephew:

> Although he did wrong things in life, we all have sin(ned) and come short of the Glory of God. He never joined any Church, I have told him you must be Born again. Many times, he would ask me questions concerning the Bible what Jesus said. If he made Peace with Jesus before he died, he is better off, than any of his family and friends left here on earth... To all the family and friends of Thestil Edward be good to one another, and when you can't do any thing good for one, please don't do them any wrong, and make Peace with Jesus while you have life and opportunity.[5]

One common way obituaries are closed is to turn the discussion away from the deceased and to direct an urgent admonition at remaining members of the family, particularly the children. This admonition will call upon these "left behind" individuals to straighten out their own lives so they will be able to reap the same rewards claimed for the deceased:

> I want to say to Bob and Louise and all the other children if you get to where I feel Mother is you must repent and be born again. To do that when Jesus Christ reveals himself to you, you must believe in him and obey his spirit....He'll deliver your soul from the dead state to a lively hope in the Lord Jesus Christ....My hope is that you will repent and be born again and we'll all live together in a land where there is no more dying, but peace and love, joy and rejoicing.[6]

Reflections On Life

These obituary writers believe the pleasures of life to be centered in the circumstances of family, community, and church, with establishment of warm or loving interpersonal relations taking priority over other accomplishments—such as building careers and massing estates. When "good" things of life are mentioned they are noted as being found in the family setting, in relationships with friends and neighbors, in traditional activities of the church, and in a personal conviction of spiritual salvation. The "bad" things of life are centered in hard and drudging work, in travails of poverty, in sufferings of ill health, in pains of losing loved ones—particularly children and spouses, in worries over unconverted loved ones, in struggles for personal salvation, in loneliness of old age, and in the slow movement of time when one is ready to "pass over yonder."

In general, "Mom" is lauded for the wonderful nurturing she gave her children, for memories she left in the minds of these children, for spiritual guidance she provided, for loyal devotion she accorded her husband, for the abundance of friends she had, who subsequently mourned her death, for service she gave her Brothers and Sisters in the church, for her faithfulness in church attendance, and for the "joy" of her singing, shouting, and other forms of religious expression. "Papa" is lauded for years of hard work, for diligence in being the family provider, for firm and righteous counsel, for love of his children, for dedication to his wife, for ability to endure hardships, for faithful service to the church, for generosity to family and friends, and for his personal religious testimony.

> Mother and Poppy (John and Margaret Raines) will be remembered by all who know them for what they were, hard working, honest, praying, God Fearing people... The old home doesn't seem like home without Mom and Poppy sitting on the porch.

porch. No one could tell a story like Poppy and no one understood like Mommy. All her children were tender and beloved in her sight. She wouldn't leave home for anything if she was expecting any of the children to visit... Some of the children would travel hundreds of miles to be with them whenever they could, if only for a weekend... The family gatherings won't be the same now, with vacant seats at the long table where mother had prepared hundreds of meals for the family, friends and the church.[7]

Little is said in these obituaries about careers. Work is sometimes mentioned, but usually not in any detail. A father will be praised for having worked hard all his life, and frequently a man will be identified as a retired miner, farmer, mechanic, poultry raiser, etc. Often mention of a life's work will be made only in reference to hardships endured: A mother is praised for years of struggle to raise eight children, five of whom survived; a dad is lauded for thirty-one years of service to the furniture industry; and a son's early death is attributed to a coal mine accident that broke his back.

The dominant image of labor, as depicted in these obituaries, however, is not a negative one. In fact, labor is probably more frequently mentioned as a dignifying factor than as something to the contrary, and there are occsional glimpses of lives that have been particularly fulfilled by labor:

> Bob (Williams) had resided at this farm for about 50 years and worked very hard, he and his wife, to raise their children, and continued to work after the children left home, raising a garden and canning and freezing so we and our families could have fresh vegetables and country meat when we visited the farm to see Grandpa and Grandma, and they insisted everybody take some back to the city. He achieved self satisfaction and pleasure from his long weary hours on the farm, something very few of us accomplish.
>
> Dad was a team driver by trade, I suppose the men in his profession called him a Mule Skinner, that was many years ago when logging and lumber was the largest industry around Virginia and Kentucky, and when coal mining became the primary industry, he worked several years at Harmon Mines on the tipple and then retired from public works to live out his remaining years swapping and bartering and farming which he truly enjoyed, because it required running around the country in his pick up truck and meeting and talking to the people. Most everybody around in that country knew him. Daddy loved to listen to the old time singing in the Old Regular Baptist Church, and he liked the preaching, but he had his preferences of preachers.
>
> He died from a heart attack, while cutting briars on his farm

in the late afternoon and we truly believe he would have wanted to go this way.[8]

The overall perspective on life presented in these obituaries is strongly positive but romanticized. There are allusions to hard work and references to personal sufferings, but the broader image is one of perseverance, happiness, and love. Real hardships of life seem forgotten when these final summations are recorded, and deceased individuals are depicted as having made it through this temporal life with courage, fortitude, and joy, while providing inspiration, strength, and loving counsel to those fellow travelers of lesser talent, experience, or grit. Life, therefore, is pleasurable if lived well, with particular emphasis upon one's personal duty to family and church. Furthermore, a clear sign that you have indeed lived well is the multitude of loved ones and friends left behind to speak highly of you and to mourn your passing. Have you been an inspiration to your family, friends, neighbors, and fellow church members? Have you suffered bravely, prayed fervently, sung joyously, loved generously, and struggled diligently? If you have, then people will remember your example and thus be strengthened themselves. When your name is called out in future memorial services there will be good things to mention about your life. The elder will stand before the church, read aloud your name, and then stop and say: "He loved to sing the old songs of Zion"; "She thrilled us with her joyous shouting"; "He always had a kind word for each Brother and Sister"; "She suffered her hardships bravely"; "He was a favorite with all the children and young people"; "She maintained a warm, loving home, and kept it open to her neighbors and church brethren"; "He was poor in earthly goods, but rich in spirit"; "She was a witness to all her children and grandchildren"; "He served as moderator of our church for twenty years"; "She always baked the communion bread"; "They always filled their seats in church."

Reflections on Death

One ironic characteristic of these obituaries is that they generally communicate the idea that life, though often troubled, is basically good, but that death is even better. In one way or another, these farewell statements proclaim the passing of the loved one to be something positive, not of course for those left behind, but for the individual who "departed this world." There is the pronouncement that death has removed the deceased from a painful existence, either of a physical, emotional, or psychological nature. There is the judgement that death is allowing a reunion with loved ones gone on before, frequently with the prayer that the "circle be unbroken." There is the conclusion that death is bringing "rest" to one whose life was marked by long, hard, and continuous work. But most important of all, there is the declaration that death is opening the door to a kingdom of eternal joy, peace, beauty, and union with God.

The death of an infant or child, however, presents a difficult problem for rationalization. If the deity calls us to death, just as he calls us to redemption, why does he occasionally call so early? In relationship to the whole scenario of life, sin, redemption, death, and eternity, where does the stillborn infant—or the child who dies before reaching the age of accountability—fit?

The only rationales emerging fairly consistently from these farewell statements are (1) that the supreme being occasionally sees a new life that is suffering and decides to take that individual directly into heaven and (2) that sometimes the supreme being wants infants and small children as angels to round out or "decorate" his kingdom:

> (Stacey Wayne Deel) was born February 26, 1980 at the Appalachian Regional Hospital at 2:20 a.m. and God called his precious soul to come to be with him at 3:35 a.m... .The doctors said he didn't get the right kind of blood circulation to develop right. His lungs weren't developed and he couldn't breathe on his own. They kept him alive as long as they could. But the Lord told him "Come home and live with me where you'll never have to suffer and can breathe."[9]

There is some confusion in these obituaries concerning the precise sequence of the events through which the redeemed go to make it to heaven. Some statements clearly depict the deceased as already being in heaven, both in soul and body; others speak of the dead as having simply gone to a resting place to await the final judgment; and still others suggest that the soul has gone to heaven, while the body is remaining in the grave to await judgment day:

> If Brother Charles (Ramey) could speak back now he would say—Children it's so beautiful up here, lay everything down and strive for this heavenly land where no sad news ever comes.

> Now all we can say is "Sleep on Daddy (Sugar Slone) and take your rest until that great day when God shall awake the dead, then we can all go home with him where trouble will always be a stranger."

> I believe that he (Charley Hopkins Deel) is now resting from all his labors and his soul is taking that sweet rest in the city of God, waiting for the Great Resurrection Morning when that soul and spirit will reunite with that body that is sleeping in the earth. Then the Lord will give him a long white robe and a crown of

Glory that will never fade away. He will go to a heavenly home where troubles and sorrow will all be done away with, where all is peace and love forevermore.[10]

This last excerpt apparently best represents the formal beliefs of the Old Regular Baptists relative to death and resurrection. Elder Edwin May, Moderator of the Sardis Association of Old Regulars, has told me that confusion develops in obituaries relative to this issue simply because the writers of these documents generally are not the elders of the church but are laymen who get their "beliefs all mixed up." The correct doctrine of Old Regulars, he said, is that at death the soul of a redeemed individual goes directly to heaven, while his or her body remains at rest until final judgment when all of the souls and bodies of the redeemed will be reunited.[11]

I find myself liking the idea of giving the deceased this kind of farewell. I like what it does for the family and what it apparently does—before the fact—for the person who dies. A member of the Old Regular faith knows that he or she will be memorialized in a minimum of three ways—the funeral, the annual memorial services, and the obituary. In addition, families may elect to stage yearly individual memorials for their departed loved ones, either in the home or in the church.

All of these memorials, I assume, produce in the minds of church members the conviction that they will never be forgotten. After all, every year at the regularly scheduled Memorial Day service an elder will position himself behind the "book stand" and read the name of every deceased member of the church, pausing occasionally to comment on the virtuous accomplishments of a particular Brother or Sister. In addition, there will always be that obituary in the association minutes. These factors alone will constitute a form of immortality.

END NOTES

1. *Minutes* of the Union Association of Old Regular Baptists (Johnson City, Tennessee: Interstate Graphics, 1984), 45.

2. *Minutes* of the Union Association of Old Regular Baptists (Johnson City, Tennessee, 1979), 64; *Minutes* of the Sardis Association of Old Regulars (Published by the Association, 1983), 35.

3. *Minutes* of the Union Association of Old Regular Baptists (Johnson City, Tennessee: Interstate Graphics, 1980), 58.

4. *Minutes* of the Sardis Association of Old Regular Baptists (Published by the Association, 1983), 9.

5. *Minutes* of the Union Association of Old Regular Baptists (Johnson City, Tennessee: Interstate Graphics, 1983), 66.

6. *Minutes* of the Union Association of Old Regular Baptists (Johnson City, Tennessee: Interstate Graphics, 1984), 31.

7. *Minutes* of the Union Association of Old Regular Baptists (Johnson City, Tennessee: Interstate Graphics, 1981), 44.

8. *Minutes* of the Union Association of Old Regular Baptists (Johnson City, Tennessee: Interstate Graphics, 1982), 57.

9. *Minutes* of the Union Association of Old Regular Baptists (Johnson City, Tennessee: Interstate Graphics, 1981), 30.

10. *Minutes* of the Union Association of Old Regular Baptists (Johnson City, Tennessee: Interstate Graphics, 1980), 52, 63, and 59.

11. Interview of Elder Edwin May, February 15, 1985.

GOVERNMENT AND TECHNOLOGY:
CHANGE AND EFFECT ON A REGION
  Convenor: Tyler Blethen, Western Carolina University
**Government Regulations and their Effects
on the Grade C Diary in Southwest Virginia**
  Ricky Cox, Radford University
Producing Old Handicrafts with New Technology: An Example
  Pat Meisel and Bob Hughes, Georgia Southern College
Some Thoughts on Science and Technology in Appalachia
  Ron Willoughby, Radford University

Some Thoughts on Science and Technology in Appalachia

by
Ron Willoughby

The theme of this conference is "The Impact Of Institutions In Appalachia." The use of the word "in" rather than "on" is appropriate because it allows us to discuss some aspects of Appalachia's relationship to the rest of the world that we don't always appreciate. It is widely recognized that the rest of the United States has had a great impact on Appalachia, but Appalachia has also had a major impact on the rest of the United States, and indeed the rest of the world, for within our region have occurred events of great scientific and techological significance. In this paper I will discuss in general terms the subject of science and technology and give examples of how, through science and technology, Appalachia and the rest of the world have impacted on each other.

Let me begin by distinguishing between science and technology. Science is the pursuit of knowledge of the physical world, without regard to whether or not that knowledge might have some "useful" application. Technology is the application of the knowledge science has created to purposes that human beings deem desirable and/or necessary. Together science and technology are the carrot and the stick of change in human society. Science lures us with the promise that knowledge is power, and technology fulfills that promise by giving us some measure of control over our environment.

Science and technology exist in a symbiotic relationship that has proved amazingly successful. In its infancy science was done using only the human senses. As our knowledge expanded it became necessary to extend our senses by the use of various types of devices such as the telescope. Technology provided those devices, and scientific knowledge continued to expand, requiring ever more sophisticated devices. Increased knowledge allowed technology to provide those more sophisticated devices. It has never been a smooth progression, but it has been one that works, and it continues today. The technological impulse has been so pervasive throughout man's history that it is perhaps the distinguishing characteristic of homo sapiens. Our penchant for technological applications has given us a competitive edge in the struggle for survival, and has in recent years allowed us to live in such comfort as was unimaginable only fifty years ago. But this very success has created an uncritical attitude toward technology, an attitude that whatever can be done should be done. The result is a juggernaut which rushes forward faster and faster, like a man running downhill, until *the very technology that has assured our survival is now, ironically, the greatest threat to our survival.*

There are also symbiotic relationships among technologies. The Tennessee Valley Authority (TVA) was established to build a series of flood control dams in upper East Tennessee. The dams were also equipped with water turbines to produce electricity from the water that flowed through the dams. The availability of cheap electricity attracted industry to the area, which meant cash in the pockets of the people. This cash, along with the availability of cheap electricity, created a demand for consumer goods, including electrical appliances. As prosperity spread, the demand for electricity eventually outran the ability of the hydroelectric plants to produce it, and TVA began building coal-fired steam generating plants. This produced a greater demand for coal, and the coalfields boomed. But as metallurgy and manufacturing technology advanced, sophsticated machinery was developed that gave us the ability to mine coal by stripping off the tops or sides of mountains instead of tunneling into them. The result was a cheaper way to mine coal, by use of a smaller work force which kept the cost of electricity down and fulfilled a growing demand.

We can see from this example how different technologies feed off one another, each giving impetus to the other. But there is more to the picture than this. There is the question of how the relationship between technologies affects people. Large institutions, such as governments and large industries, evaluate nearly everything on the basis of short-term, large-scale statistics, usually economic statistics. On this basis the electric power-coal mining symbiosis, illustrated by the TVA example which is common across the country, has worked well. On the average, most people are economically better off because of the availability of cheap coal. But when one looks beyond the averages, beyond the short-term economic aspects, at more subtle questions, it is obvious that the blessings are mixed. On a local scale, for instance, increasing mechanization in the coalfields increased production and profits, but decreased employment. Leaving stripped land unreclaimed kept coal prices down, but did serious damage to the environment both visually and physically and reduced the quality of life in these areas. How does one balance the well-being of the minority against the well-being of the majority? Must there always be a group that suffers in order that a larger group (or a more powerful group) may prosper?

These are the fundamental questions that create a tension between those who wish to go "forward" without hindrance and those who would go slowly, if at all. Generally it is a healthy tension, tending to exert restraint on technological development but not smother it. It forces us to consider more carefully than we might otherwise do, the effects of technological enterprises. But even after we have considered them, the course of wisdom is seldom clear, and wisdom is something that neither science nor technology claim to produce. The difficulty of reaching wise decisions is obvious in the dilemma posed by strip mining in Appalachia. If reclamation is required, the cost of coal will go up and demand will drop. What then will coal miners do for a living in a one-industry region? But if reclamation is not required, what will the area look like, and be like, at the turn of the century? Either way, do the children in coal mining Appalachia have a future in the region?

Beyond the borders of Appalachia, the increased use of coal has meant a higher standard of living for virtually all Americans, through jobs in industrial plants and/or access to cheap electricity. Steel production and cheap energy are often cited as the backbones of American industry. But if coal is essential to the production of steel and is used to produce the major portion of electricity used in this country, what are we to conclude about the importance of coal and Appalachia to the United States?

While coal usage is vital to America's economy, it has at the same time contributed to at least two serious and wide-spread threats to the environment well beyond Appalachia: Acid rain and an increasing concentration of carbon dioxide in the earth's atmosphere. These are subtle, long-term threats of the type that our political system finds particularly difficult to deal with. But problems they are, of current and continuing concern, and they must be dealt with. Like the benefits of coal usage, they are a part of Appalachia's impact on the rest of the country.

If coal is one of mankind's oldest energy sources, nuclear energy is one of the newest. It is not entirely coincidental that Appalachia harbors both, for Oak Ridge was chosen as a major nuclear energy site, not only because it was isolated, but because of its proximity to TVA's electricity. It is a city built hurriedly in 1942, primarily to manufacture components for atomic bombs. It grew up almost overnight, like toadstools after a rain, in an area that had been farmland. It was a boom town of hastily erected frame buildings inside a chain-link fence guarded by soldiers who wouldn't admit anyone without a pass. Local people found jobs there in abundance, producing in urgent secrecy things whose functions were unknown to them. But many more workers were needed than could be provided locally, and they came from everywhere, especially from other parts of Appalachia. East Tennessee was inundated with change like the spring floods that came before TVA domesticated the rivers, and when the flood receded, there was the Atomic

City, cast up on the bank like old tires, clorox bottles and refrigerators.

The Atomic City. The name conjured images of progress, of vitality, of energy, and it advertised itself proudly. Today the frontier boom town is gone. You can drive into the city without having to show a sentry your pass. The sidewalks are concrete, not boards; the streets are asphalt instead of mud; and the buildings are of brick, glass and concrete. Oak Ridge is now pretty much like any city in America with its shoppping centers, pizza place, and Friday night football games. It represents physically the impact that the rest of the country can have on Appalachia. People came from outside to build the city and to live and work there, and the area and its people are dramatically different as a result.

Conversely, the world is dramatically different because of Oak Ridge, or at least because of nuclear energy, which Oak Ridge was and is so important in developing. Here, too, things have changed. The once bright dreams of cheap, abundant electric energy from nuclear fission are now tarnished. Slogans like "atoms for peace" have not been able to erase from the mind the overwhelming image, born in 1945, of a roiling mushroom cloud.

Like Oak Ridge, Green Bank, West Virginia was chosen as the site of a governmental installation because it was in an isolated area. But unlike Oak Ridge, secrecy was not the motive. Green Bank is in a region where man-made radio signals are relatively weak, making the detection of radio waves from space easier. It was therefore the perfect site for the National Radio Astronomy Observatory (NRAO).

Green Bank is a village of a few hundred people located in a wide, shallow fertile valley. The principal occupation is farming, and cattle graze matter-of-factly in fields adjacent to huge radio telescopes. When the observatory was first established, the site was felt to be too remote to attract permanent staff members, so the administrative headquarters was established in Charlottesville, Virginia, which has a more cosmopolitan atmosphere.

The principle activity at NRAO is listening. The radio telecsopes are giant earhorns used to eavesdrop on the whispering cosmos. It is an activity that cannot be rushed. One simply sits and listens, and the rotating earth sets the immutable schedule of what can be heard, and when. Because of this there is a measured quality to life at Green Bank. It moves in time to the ancient rhythms of the seasons, much like life on the land. The very nature of the activities at Green Bank encourages a contemplative atmosphere that is in step with the natural surroundings. Since there are no production facilities there is no need for a large labor force. The available jobs are filled by the local people, and in the cafeteria at the observatory (the only public place to eat in Green Bank) one can buy the quintessential Appalachian dish—brown beans and cornbread.

Instead of overwhelming the valley and its residents, the observatory has blended into the surroundings. A first time visitor is always startled by the sharp contrast between the radio telecsopes and the otherwise pastoral surroundings, but no one else notices. NRAO is an Appalachian place visited by astronomers from all over the world, and major discoveries have taken place there. The impact of NRAO on the rest of the world is large, but NRAO lies lightly on the landscape of West Virginia.

Oak Ridge and Green Bank present marked contrasts in style and temperament, mirroring the different impacts they and the world have on each other. At the same time, they mirror the contrast between science and technology. Oak Ridge was born in a whirlwind and leans forward eagerly toward the future. As a symbol of nuclear power, it embodies the parodox of modern technology, simultaneously offering hope and threatening disaster. Green Bank is a more contemplative place where esoteric knowledge is produced that is unlikely to result in any "practical" applications. What that knowledge is likely to do is to help us understand our place in the cosmos a little more clearly. For a region whose people have an especially strong sense of place, that would be an appropriate gift to the world.

BIBLIOGRAPHY

Anderson, Don N. "Megatrends and the Mountains (Reflections on Technology and Human Values)," *Consortium News*, Volume 9, Number 3, November 1984, pp.5-9.

Caudill, Harry M. *Night Comes to the Cumberlands*. Boston: Little, Brown and Company, 1962.

Groueff, Stephane. *Manhattan Project: The Untold Story of the Making of the Atomic Bomb.* Boston: Little, Brown and Company, 1967.

Groves, Leslie R. *Now It Can Be Told: The Story of the Manhattan Project.* New York: Harper, 1962.

Hathaway, J.W. "Response to Megatrends and the Mountains (Reflections on Technology and Human Values)," *Consortium News*, Volume 9, Number 3, November 1984, pp. 13-14.

Hauser, Alan. "Response to Megatrends and the Mountains (Reflections on Technology and Human Values)," *Consortium News*. Volume 9, Number 3, November 1984, pp. 11-13.

Hyatt, S. Aaron. "Response to Megatrends and the Mountains (Reflections on Technology and Human Values)," *Consortium News*. Volume 9, Number 3, November 1984, pp. 9-11.

Thompson, Marilou Bonham. *Abiding Appalachia: Where Mountains and Atom Meet.* Memphis, TN: St. Luke's Press, 1978.

Truit, Willis H. and Solomans, T.W. Graham. *Science, Technology and Freedom.* Boston: Houghton Mifflin Company, 1974.

CAPITALISM AND COAL: A REASSESSMENT
  Convenor: John Gaventa, Highlander Center
Capital Versus Labour in the Appalachian Coal Fields
  Vic Allen, University of Leeds
Capitalism, Patriarchy and "Men's Work":
The System of Control of Production in Coal Mining
  Mike Yarrow, Ithaca College

Capitalism, Patriarchy and "Men's Work": The System of Control of Production of Coal Mining

by
Mike Yarrow

I. Introduction

Harry Braverman's (1974) Marxian analysis of the developing labor process under capitalism has stimulated a burgeoning literature on the subject (see for example Nichols and Beynon 1977, Burawoy 1978 and 1979, Clawson 1980, Dix 1977, Edwards 1979, Elger 1979, Friedman 1977, Littler and Salaman 1982, Stark 1980, and Zimbalist 1979). Although there have been differences within this work, it has been based on the common assumption that the labor process, and more broadly the system of control or social relations of production under capitalism, is a product of the class antagonism between capital and labor (Edwards 1979). Feminist analyses of "women's work" have asserted that patriarchy as well as capitalism provides principles by which the work assigned to women is organized. They have added gender antagonisms to class antagonisms in their analyses of the social relations of production in clerical work (Davies 1974, Garson 1972, Howe 1977, Kanter 1977) and nursing (Ehrenreich and English 1973, Gamarnikow 1978). If this feminist intervention in the Marxist analysis of the system of control of labor is helpful in understanding "women's work," then it may also be applicable to "men's work." Here I wish to explore the extent to which coal mining, as "men's work," is organized by the logic of patriarchy as well as the logic of capitalism.

The logic of capitalism, according to Marx, derives from the condition of labor as a commodity and the goal of capital to make profits. Workers become commodities as they rent their capacity to work to a capitalist for a certain duration. As with other commodities, the owner has the right to use the workers as s/he wishes. In order to make a profit, the capitalist must get his workers to create a product worth more than s/he pays them in wages.

Since the amount of production can vary tremendously and the worker, who does not have the power to create and gain from the product as s/he wishes, is not very motivated to produce, capital must control labor to coerce maximum feasible production. Capital has used a number of strategies to increase its control over resistant workers, including Taylorist organization of the labor process (Braverman 1974, Clawson 1980), machine design (Braverman 1974, Noble 1979), domestication of labor unions (Aronowitz 1973, Burawoy 1981), controlling state regulation (Burawoy 1981), bureaucratic control of the work force (Clawson 1980, Edwards 1979), and the ceaseless quest for docile workers (Pollard 1963). Workers have struggled against these attempts at control with a variety of tactics which, when successful, have provoked new management strategies (Edwards 1979). Thus, the logic of capital with respect to organizing its labor centers on efficient, i.e., cheap and effective, control.

What then is the logic of patriarchal domination with respect to relations among men? As Stewart (1980) points out, one theme of patriarchal domination is the identity of interests of all men in the subordination of women. The brotherhood so created tends to be egalitarian, to stress similarities and promote bonding of the community of men as superiors to women. As Kanter (1977) found, in the sex-segregated milieux of the office, this patriarchal brotherhood is mobilized against women interlopers in managerial jobs. But what role might it play in an exclusively male work setting, as coal mining has been in this country until the 1970's?

It would seem to promote an egalitarianism diametrically opposed to capital's control project. There is also a hierarchal principle of relations between men under patriarchy. Under paternalism — rule of the father — some men are seen as "naturally" more powerful, wise, self-disciplined, fatherlike, than others. Thus, they should relate as fathers to the subordinate childlike men (Stewart 1980). The superordinate "father's" relationship to each "son" is personal and specific; he may have favorites among his "sons" and is able to exercise power in arbitrary ways on the authority of his presumed superior qualities and his interest in the welfare of all (Edwards 1979: 26-7). He dominates in the subordinate's best interest. Although there may be tensions, even fear and hatred of the powerful "father," there is assumed to be a harmony of interests. The "father" may be demanding, but he is personally committed to his subordinates and owes them reciprocal obligations for their loyal service. In analyzing the social relations of production of underground coal mining, I will explore the extent to which these contradictory principles of brotherhood and paternalism are operative.

In a study of how the struggle between capital and labor, and "fathers" and "sons", combine to shape the social relations of coal mining, it is important to look at the historical development of these relations. The current control system has developed out of an earlier system and cannot be understood without appreciating its origins. Remnants remain from that earlier system, especially in the miners' modes of coping with control attempts. At the turn of the century, as the demand for coal expanded, new coal fields were developed, often in sparsely populated rural areas where the coal operators had to build towns next to their mines to house their workers. The system of control which developed in these coal camps can be characterized as "piece-rate paternalism." In the following sections, I will analyze this control system and the changes it has undergone since 1930.

II. Coal Camp Paternalism

A. Social Relations of Production

During the early "hand loading" era, large mines were laid out with a central mainline entry tunnel connecting scores of "rooms," tunnels that branched off from it at right angles every 80 feet or so. These rooms were occupied on a long-term basis by coal loaders working individually or with partners. They used their own hand tools to pick, blast, and shovel the coal from the "face" at the end of their rooms into small rail cars, which they then pushed out to the mainline tunnel. The full cars were picked up and replaced with empties by mules and later small locomotives which pulled them out of the mine (Dix 1977: 8-14). In this individualized labor process, the only need for coordination was the delivery and retrieval of coal cars with the coal loaders production pace. This did not work very smoothly. One study in 1923 found that loaders spent 23% of an 8-hour day waiting for cars (Dix 1977).

The coal loaders were essentially treated by subcontractors and paid by the ton, after deductions had been made for any rock found in the coal. With this piece-rate system, the mine owner bought the miner's intention to mine coal in paying him by the product. Given this control built into the terms of the labor exchange, supervision could be minimal. Mines with more than a hundred coal loaders spread over miles of tunnels typically had one mine foreman who might make the rounds once a day or less frequently. Tonnage payment was an efficient means of control, not only because it required little supervision but because it forced the miners to absorb the inefficiencies of the system (e.g., loaders were not paid for work that did not produce coal, such as cleaning up the rock after a cave-in or for the time spent waiting for empty cars.)

Reliance on tonnage pay as the primary control mechanism fostered a self-concept among coal loaders of being independent craftsmen, and they guarded their prerogatives zealously. They claimed proprietary right to their rooms, even when absent, and walked out of the mine when they had earned enough for the day (Dix 1977). Miners exerted considerable craft control over their work, deciding how to do it and training apprentice miners to the craft, with or without a union to back up their claim for autonomy (Goodrich 1925). These conditions fostered an assertive autonomous stance, which Suffern (1926) called "a psychology of independence" and Goodrich

(1925) dubbed the "miner's freedom."

Tonnage pay also focused attention on the rate of exploitation — miners were aware of the discrepancy between the price the operator got for the coal and the price he paid them (Brophy 1964). To increase the rate of profit at stable prices, operators had to lower the rate of payment which tended to provoke resistance. The operators, therefore, often resorted to indirect means by docking a miner's pay excessively for rock in the coal, or by short-weighting his coal (Dix 1977). Miners' response to these widespread violations of the terms of the exchange was to organize and demand union checkweighmen. Thus, tonnage pay as a control mechanism had its limitations.

Operators augmented their control repertoire by mobilizing aspects of patriarchal domination, both inside the mines and in the camps. In the mines the foreman used his power to assign rooms and coal cars to reward productivity and loyalty: the good "sons" got preference. They also attempted to adapt the preexistent conception of manliness to meet their needs for a productive and tractable workforce. They appealed to valued male traits of physical prowess, mastery, competitiveness, and toughness to get production. The structure of the labor process with its stress on individual production lent itself to this appeal. Miners had to be ready for the next delivery of coal cars or it meant they could not keep up with "good miners" (Brophy 1964). One 70-year old Yugoslav I interviewed remembered a foreman-sponsored competition between himself and a black hand loader, to see who could load the most cars in a day. Also, miners who let their concern for personal safety interfere unduly with their ability to get out as much coal as possible from under a cracking roof before it caved in, were ridiculed (Brophy 1964).

Miners resisted these operator attempts to use patriarchal forms of domination. They took pride in their individual production, but when operators attempted to turn this pride to their own ends through divisive manipulation, the miners tried to resist. They demanded the "square turn," equal distribution of coal cars, and condemned miners who stole coal or otherwise tried to take unfair advantage of their workmates (Brophy 1964). The miners valued assertive independence from the boss and cooperation and concern for each other's safety. They realized that there was a necessary, though tension-charged, connection between the miner's ability to assert his independence at work and his ability to defend it by struggling collectively with his buddies (Goodrich 1925).

B. Social Relations Beyond the Mines

Unsuccessful in controlling the labor process, the early operators extended their control project to the miners' lives outside the mines. Coal camps were run as paternalistic fiefdoms in which the operator owned the housing, schools, stores, and churches, and hired doctors, storekeepers, school teachers, preachers, and guards. The miners were paid in scrip, redeemable at the company store. Often the frequent layoffs resulted in debt bondage to the operator. Attempts to challenge the system of control led to being fired, evicted, and blacklisted from mines in the region. If miners appealed to authorities beyond the coal camp, they typically confronted county officials beholden to the operators. For example, in Logan County, West Virginia, Sheriff Don Chafin was paid a royalty for every nonunion ton mined in the county (Nyden 1974: 34).

This paternalistic system of control, was one in which the lives of the miners' families were profoundly dependent on the "favors" of the operators who were viewed by themselves, the local press, politicians, and small dependent middle class, as architects of progress and benevolent guardians of their employees (Gaventa 1980, Tams 1963). Miners were viewed as irresponsible children whose carelessness caused accidents and who needed close supervision in the company towns to be protected from corrupting influences (Dix 1977, Gaventa 1980, Tams 1963).

The paternalism of the coal camps was reflected in a patriarchal family structure. Excluded from the one industry in the region, women could augment family income by gardening and taking in laundry and boarders, but they were economically dependent on their husbands. Operators reinforced the patriarchal family by giving preference to "family men" in hiring and layoffs (Corbin 1981). The economic responsibility of the patriarchal father role forced miners into dependent son roles versus the operators. Operators stressed family responsibility in claiming childlike loyalty. But there is evidence that miners felt the contradictions. In the early battles for union recognition, miners often articulated their fight as a struggle for their children (Corbin 1981). Their position as dependent worker-sons of the operators did not allow them to provide adequately for their families.

The most fundamental contradiction in the patriarchal aspect of the system of domination was between the miners' assertive individualism at work and their child role in the coal camp. The social relations of production encouraged, even required, assertive independence which was frustrated by the smothering paternalism of the camp. To the extent that the operator could keep his miners beholden to his largesse, both inside and outside the mine, this contradiction was suppressed. To the extent the miners were able collectively to assert their individual autonomy at work and found reason to question the benevolence of the operators' paternalism, the contradiction became oppressive.

The contradictions within coal camp paternalism were heightened by the contradictions between paternalism and the logic of capitalism. In this early period, the coal industry was very competitive and subject to periodic overproduction. Thus, survival was contingent on keeping costs down. This meant keeping wages low by fiat or deceit, providing few amenities in the coal camps and few safety precautions in the mine. When demand declined, the work force could not be carried. John Brophy depicts his family's existence in the central Pennsylvania coal fields at the turn of the century as involving frequent moves from one squalid camp, with a frequently unscrupulous operator, to another (1964). The authority of the patriarch is difficult to maintain under such conditions, where concern for the "sons" on which their loyalty is garnered seems to get lost in the scramble for economic viability and profits. Justus Collins, a prominent mine owner at the turn of the century, alludes to the contradiction in a letter of advice to his brother who had recently been appointed superintendent of one of his company's mines:

> Maintain good discipline at all times at your places, especially around the stores and offices, but it has always been my policy to pay small heed to those things which are purely a personal matter with my employees—it is very easy to draw the distinction—we are not running a Christian Endeavor Camp Meeting nor a Sunday School, yet a certain amount of decency and order must be required of our people. In this connection, never lose sight of the fact that the sole purpose of the organization is to make money for their stockholders (quoted in Dix 1977: 43).

Coal paternalism also contradicted the system of bourgeois democracy where workers as commodities were subject to their employers' control, but as citizens outside of work were entitled to freedom from control. The operators insisted that they were only exercising their property rights, while the miners raised strike demands for abolition of company guards, payment in scrip, and other operator control mechanisms. In the bloody Paint Creek-Cabin Creek strike of 1912-13, miners and their outside supporters called the coal camp system of control un-American, and compared it to Czarist Russia (Corbin 1981). In these early strikes, the women struggled along with the men. It was equally their fight — for a living wage and for emancipation from coal camp tyranny (Corbin 1981). This infringement by wives on the male preserve of protecting the family caused some friction, but was generally treated as an exceptional condition and traditional roles were reestablished after the strikes.

C. Conclusion

Capital's project of controlling labor in the early coal mines met with many difficulties due to the absence of machine control of the labor process and the inability, given the special conditions of the mines, of adequately overseeing the workforce. In these unfavorable conditions, operators used a piece-rate labor exchange as the most efficient control mechanism. But miners organized to collectively resist many of its control features. Capital, therefore, went outside of the mines and mobilized elements of patriarchal domination to achieve greater control. The resulting control system, coal camp paternalism, while effective for many years in many locales, contained serious contradictions. There was the contradiction between the miner's role as son of the paternalistic operator, patriarch of his own family, and brother to his workmates.

Although these three roles could be isolated to some degree, they were experienced as contradictory when they confronted each other under certain conditions. There was also often a contradiction between the capitalist logic of cost cutting in a competitive industry and the paternalist logic of caring for the loyal "sons."

Miners resisted this control system as workers, brothers, and citizens. As workers, they organized both informally in the mines and formally in unions, to fight for higher wages, an end to the abuses of the piece-rate system, and their employers' arbitrary power. As brothers, they developed a counter-definition of manliness to that of the operators. While the operators stressed responsibility to family and employer, hard work, competitiveness and loyalty, the miners stressed autonomy and independence versus the boss, cooperation and fair dealing with workmates and opposed treatment as children by the patriarch. As citizens, miners demanded the freedoms they were denied under coal camp paternalism.

Coal camp paternalism has been most successful in isolated regions of central Appalachia—southern West Virginia, eastern Kentucky and Tennessee—where cosmopolitan ideas of democracy and the rights of labor were remote, where other industries did not provide alternative employment and control systems, and where, due to control of county government, coal operators could back up their rule of their camps with state power. Coal camp paternalism has been weaker in cosmopolitan, multi-industry regions such as western Pennsylvania, northern West Virginia and Ohio (Nyden 1978). It has also been weakened when economic crises forced wage cuts and layoffs, thus bringing the benevolence of the patriarch into question. Both the bloody Paint Creek-Cabin Creek strike of 1912-13 and the great union drive of 1933 were preceded by wage cuts (Barkey 1971, Tams 1963).

III. Union Paternalism

Coal camp paternalism crumbled slowly as a result of a number of factors. As the coal companies expanded, the personal rule of the patriarch gave way to more bureaucratic procedures. The miners union, supported by the new deal administration, asserted miners' rights both in the mine and camp, thus blunting the absolute and arbitrary power of the operator. Better roads and automobiles allowed miners to escape the coal camps. The progressively mechanized and cooperative labor process of coal mining made the piece-rate system impractical. Coal operators are still searching for an effective new system of control, while miners are engaged in a variety of forms and levels of resistance.

In 1933, with Federal support for unionization, John L. Lewis, already president of the United Mine Workers since 1920, launched an energetic organizing drive with the paternalistic slogan "The President wants you to join the union." (Baratz 1955: 49). In two months over three-fourths of the country's coal miners joined. This firm establishment of a miners' union in most coal fields of the country doomed coal camp paternalism. It resulted in two decades of conflict between the union and operators, including eleven national strikes and many smaller ones. Out of these struggles, often mediated by the Federal Government, miners won significant gains in wages and benefits, and John L. Lewis won the miners' undying loyalty. Thus, coal camp paternalism was replaced by union paternalism. Lewis controlled the whole organization in a paternalistic style and insisted on making all major decisions. His success, as well as his bombastic authoritarian style, legitimated his claim to the mantle of the patriarch which the miners had just wrested from the operators. In grand paternalistic style, Lewis insisted that the miners were not yet ready for union democracy. Gaventa (1980) argues that faced with the awesome power of the operators, miners, particularly those in areas where coal camp paternalism was still intact such as eastern Kentucky and Tennessee, wanted to be championed by their own union strong man.

In 1950, as the coal industry started losing markets to oil, and mechanization resuced demand for mine labor even more, Lewis came to terms with the operators. The result was a period of twenty years with no major strikes and close cooperation between the union leadership and the unionized companies. Lewis and then Boyle ruled the union with a strong hand, appointing district officials and staff and using them to enforce labor peace in conjunction with the operators. Gradually, after two decades of decline, production and demand for labor started expanding in the late 1960's. The new young miners hired as a result were less awed by the paternalism they found in the mines and the union. They were more impressed with the neglect of health and safety and compensation benefits during the period of cooperation (Nyden 1974). Gradually a movement built which on its second try in 1972 was successful in ousting Boyle and electing a reform president.

With the election of Miller, the period of union paternalism came to an end, and the mid-1970's were a period of unprecedented power exercised by rank-and-file miners. This second crisis of management's system of control has led to renewed efforts to find a workable control system. In the following section we will explore the complicated dynamics of the developing system.

IV. The Current System: Union Brotherhood vs. Bureaucratic Control

A. The Social Relations of Production

During the golden age of Taylorism in the 1920's there were repeated calls for increasing the control of the coal mine labor process. Mine superintendent Thomas Stroup in 1923 thought that it would be necessary a la Taylor "to abolish the contract system, to mechanicalize (sic) the mines thoroughly," and "to standardize every operation down to the minutest detail so that no responsibility of any kind will fall on the worker" (quoted in Dix 1977: 62). The U.S. Coal Commission of 1923 called for the introduction of a loading machine which, by concentrating the workforce, would make closer supervision possible (Dix 1977: 64).* But the process of mechanizing and Taylorizing the production process in underground coal mining was fraught with problems.

The first wave of mechanization substituted machines for most of the hand tools used by the hand loaders; it is now known as the "conventional mining system." Many of these machines were large electric-powered, rubber-tired vehicles. The typical crew of twelve worked in five "rooms" and their connecting breakthrough tunnels. The machines rotated between the five coal faces, first undercutting, then drilling, blasting and loading the coal onto "shuttle cars," which are conveyer belts on wheels. Shuttle cars transported the coal to rail cars or the head of a stationary conveyer belt. After a room was cleared a team of two came to roof bolt the newly exposed section of roof. Roof bolting, laminating the immediate rock layers with long expansion bolts, had been substituted for timbering to allow room for the equipment to move round. Each of these twelve member crews had a foreman. The crew members had to cooperate closely to avoid endangering each other and to achieve high production with a minimum of breakdowns. No sooner was this "conventional" mining system established than it began to be replaced by the continuous miner system. The continuous miner is a huge machine which gouges the coal from the face and deposits it on the "shuttle cars" thus eliminating undercutting, drilling, blasting and loading. Continuous miner sections typically develop five tunnels but only work three at a time. Crew size is reduced to 6-8 miners and a foreman.

These changes in systems involved many of the "reforms" which the "scientific managers" had called for but the result was not the undisputed managerial control of the labor process they had anticipated. Mechanization resulted in higher productivity but, since the miner still controlled the speed and direction of the machine, it did not result in significant loss of power or skill. Specialization occurred as each miner's job was defined by the machine s/he operated but with frequent job rotation, the miner's skills were not fragmented. It was in mangement's interest to have a versatile, broadly trained workforce so that if a machine operator was absent the whole section would not be crippled. Mechanization and the increasingly cooperative nature of the labor process made attribution of production to individual miners impossible so payment by the ton was converted to hourly pay. With this change in the terms of the labor exchange, management lost a powerful work incentive but gained flexibility in introducing new technologies and speed-ups.

Although the production workforce was concentrated in a smaller area and the level of supervision was increased twelvefold from 1980 to 1969 (Seltzer 1977: 57), miners have been able to retain considerable control of the labor

---

*It is interesting to note that machine loading was rapidly introduced finally after reunionization. It was then, during the Depression, in spite of the industry's financial straights, that the need for a new control system was urgent.

process. First, an increasing proportion of the underground workforce (50% in 1969), works away from the coal face tending the miles of track, conveyer belts, cables, waterpipes, and air courses which are required in a mechanized coal mine (Dix 1977). Typically these support workers are only infrequently overseen by foremen with many miles to cover. Second, even at the production face where supervision is the most intense, miners still have many effective means for exerting some control of the labor process. A miner describes how a foreman can be disciplined by the miners he is supposed to control:

> You can stop production just like that. But you got to know what you are doing. I mean everybody knows what's going on usually. You can stop it legally. You can pull safety on them. You can stop and check your water sprays after every third buggy (shuttle car). 'There is not enough water on this miner (continuous miner)!' 'It's a Federal law.' You can stop and set all of your timbers just right, you know. If you work to rule you can really hurt them, and then you can deliberately sabotage the stuff. You can run over cable. You can just drive your buggy real slow. 'Can't you go any faster?' 'No sir!' Nothing in the contract that says how fast you have to work. (Interview June 23, 1978. Southern West Virginia)

Miners can use their control of the machines, and the protection of the union contract and the mine safety laws to slowdown. Even on a modern section the foreman cannot be everywhere at once. The hourly wage rate makes uniting a crew for a slowdown easier because their paychecks are not jeopardized while the foreman is vulnerable because he is evaluated by the production of his section. Mine management has not been able to turn miners into routine workers with simple stipulated tasks partly because of the unpredictability of the conditions which necessitates quick alterations in procedures but also because to get good production, miners must take shortcuts with safety. These violations of Federal and state laws cannot be stipulated by management.*

For miners to have a significant influence on the labor process through these and other power resources, they must achieve unity. Several aspects of the work seem to foster unity. First, it allows good communication between miners. The workforce at most mines is relatively small. Miners typically work on a shift with 20 to 100 "buddies." There is ample time to communicate with their fellows without being overheard by management. Miners spend forty minutes to an hour each day dressing for work and showering after work in the bathhouse. The ride to their work locations in the mine takes fifteen minute to an hour, and they take rest breaks and machine breakdown breathers throughout the day.

---

*For a more detailed analysis of the struggle for control in the current labor process see Yarrow, 1979.

Second, the work necessitates cooperation among miners. Production involves coordination which is not totally designed into the machinery and layout of the labor process. Instead, members of the crew must anticipate each other's actions so as to avoid bottlenecks and help out when a member runs into trouble. High production is a collective achievement, and so is safety. Operating huge machines in tight, dark, explosive surroundings requires watching out for your "buddies." Shoddy work is not shipped out as on an assembly line but creates the environment in which miners have to work for the next few weeks, Thus, there are typically strong collective efforts to socialize a new recruit to work safely and think about his "buddy." Their common struggles with the foreman protected by the union contract and the miner's willingness to strike locally to prevent disciplinary action against a mate, also reinforce solidarity.

B. Current Management Control Attempts

Faced with the effective unity of their workforce, coal operators have in the past decade tried various techniques to dissolve the miners' solidarity and nullify their power resources. Richard Edwards, in his book, *Contested Terrain* (1979), describes three type of management control systems which succeed each other in the historical development of capitalism but may all be used in varying degrees by one firm. "Simple control," the personal paternalistic control of the small entrepreneur, was followed by "technical control" which seeks to design control of the pace and movements of work into the physical organization of the production process through machine design and detailed division of labor. Due to the special conditions of mining and the collective resistance of miners, the attempt to establish technical control was relatively unsuccessful. Technical control, according to Edwards, is succeeded by bureaucratic control. Coal operators have recently turned to bureaucratic control measures in combination with simple and technical techniques in their desperate efforts to gain control of the labor process.

1. Technical Control

The primary focus in the area of technical control is to develop a new production technology. The system now slowly gaining a foothold in underground mining (still less than ten percent of production) is the mechanized long wall systems used in Europe. With this system, a coal face up to 800 feet long is developed. A machine travels across the face shearing the coal onto a conveyer pan which moves it to a belt at the end of the face from whence it is transported out of the mine. In this system the roof is held up by huge hydraulic jacks. As the face is sheared, these jacks are advanced, and the roof caves in behind them. This system is potentially very productive. With a crew the size of that on a continuous miner section, it can produce several times as much coal. It also turns many of the jobs into relatively unskilled reptetitive operations calling for little judgement. The workforce is more tightly coordinated by the machine and its pace dictated.

The long wall machinery, on the other hand, is very sensitive to geological and operational changes. It is not adaptable to many geological conditions of the relatively shallow American coal seams. It requires enormous capital to install, and it remains to be seen whether the long wall system will give management significantly more control or whether the miners will develop new effective strategies for exerting their control. All these difficulties with the long wall system have probably caused it to be adopted at a cautious pace.

With technical control providing questionable prospects for a significantly more effective control system, the coal companies have resorted chiefly to simple, patriarchal controls and increasing use of bureaucratic controls.

2. Patriarchal Control

Coal companies have attacked miners' unity with some "labors of division" which fit the logic of patriarchal control. Miners' unity was fostered by the increasingly social labor process, was protected by the union, and was strengthened in the mid-1970's by a strong demand for mine labor. It was formulated in terms of a brotherhood of male workers with common interests. To weaken the unity, coal companies used a variety of patriarchal control mechanisms to undermine the miners' brotherhood.

One is the old paternalistic tactic of favoritism. Miners have fought to have jobs, overtime, and layoffs awarded purely on the basis of seniority to prevent favoritism, but the contract includes the criteria of comptence along with seniority in job allocation. Miners complain that foremen use this to reward favorites. Job allocation is a powerful control mechanism. For an older, arthritic and black lung miner, assignment to a strenuous wet job could be life threatening (Arble 1976).

Miners have been concerned about the potential for increased paternalistic control provided by the replacement of the union-controlled health plan with private insurance carriers under contract with the coal companies. They fear the return to power of company doctors who have continued to be used in the coal fields to testify against miners' compensation claims. They also fear that the new system is divisive because miners who face difficulties with their health coverage may not share this problem with miners who work for other companies. Under the union-controlled plan, miners across the Eastern coal fields struck in 1977 when benefits were cut.

Subleasing mines and operating them non-union have also increased paternalistic control. Since the long 1977-78 strike and the subsequent decline of demand for metalurgical coal, many large companies have been content to sublease their coal properties to small operators. The union contract provides that these lease operators must recognize the union if the original company was unionized. But because of their precarious finances, these operators have been able to convince miners to give up some of their contract rights. I visited a sublease operation in 1982 where a militant union local had given up enforcing safety provisions because a previous sublease operator had gone bankrupt, owing each miner thousands of dollars in back wages. Under these conditions, the miners are persuaded that they share the operator's interest in the viability of the company. Other companies have reasserted paternalistic control by avoiding the union altogether. They have been willing to pay higher wages to operate non-union.

As in the past, foremen try to employ a capitalist patriarchal conception of manliness to divide and motivate miners. Foremen constantly encourage competition between sections and shifts in tons of coal mined. The 1978 contract allows production incentive bonuses, reinforcing the foremen's appeal to manly pride in production. Cautious miners may be ridiculed as unmanly. One told me of being assigned with two other men to lift heavy steel rails. The miner remarked that it looked like a four-man job. The foreman asked, "What's the matter? Aren't you man enough?" (Interview miner 143, July 1978. Southern West Virginia.)

The foremen's leadership style is usually a gruff authoritarian machismo characteristic of male groups such as sport teams, fraternal organizations and the military (Stewart 1980). But it is used on miners who, although they participate in the same dominant patriarchal culture, retain their traditional class-informed definition of manliness which includes autonomy versus the boss. Miners also retain considerable control. Foremen must therefore be careful not to overstep the bounds by unduly insulting the manly dignity of their subordinates who might retaliate. On sections with particularly militant miners, foremen are forced to give up the authoritarian style completely and ask politely for work to be done. More typically a rough give-and-take between foreman and miners allows for both the assertion of authority and the protection of dignity. The miners' brotherhood makes it problematic for coal mine management to mobilize the capitalist patriarchal system of dominance to gain more control of production.

Operators seeking to increase their patriarchal control might be expected to welcome women miners as a means of dissolving the brotherhood. Miners seem to fear the disruption of the brotherhood, as well as to fear the loss of pride in their claim to do work that is too arduous for women. Many have been socialized to the norm that gentlemen do not allow ladies to do such work. Working with women means they violate the norm with the resulting crisis of conscience and identity or doing the women's work as well as their own. Miners, as other male blue collar workers, have claimed high wages to support their patriarchal family roles. The low pay for "women's work" conversely has been legitimated as "pin money." Male miners may at some level fear the loss of the status "men's work."

Operators have not generally welcomed women miners. Their opposition is stated in terms of their firm believe that women are not strong enough or sufficiently skilled with machinery to make good miners. Another product of foremen's participation in the dominant patriarchal culture is their ideological investment in having mining remain "men's work." Their opposition may also be based on a realization that their control system will be challenged if mining is no longer "men's work." Foremen will lose their appeal to machismo, and the underground work environment and labor process may have to be changed to take more account of miners' health, safety and comfort. Women have not been socialized to consider danger and discomfort, reaffirmations of their womanhood.

Ironically, operators have gained a measure of control through the relatively high wages for blue collar workers that coal miners have attained through their years of struggle. Far from giving miners independence, these wages have financed their participation in consumerist mainstream culture. They have been able to obtain mortgages for homes in suburban developments removed from the coal camp. They must work to keep up the payments and, since mining is the only high wage blue collar work in many coal fields, they must work in the mines. This produces a new high wage dependency on the operator which fosters a fear of strikes and any actions which might put them in management's disfavor.

Far from being a control system discarded as anachronistic by coal company management, simple paternalistic control is an important part of the control repertoire. The recent assault on union-administered health and pension funds and the union itself indicate a renewed determination by operators to return to this control system.

3. Bureaucratic Control

In the period since the overthrow of union paternalism the coal companies have pushed for increasing bureaucratic control. Since the union president can no longer guarantee "labor stability" in return for wages and benefits increases, the companies have sought to negotiate control into contracts, to arbitrate it into the body of contract interpretation, and to litigate it into judicial decisions. In this effort, the Federal government and various other organs of the state have been most cooperative. They have tried to bring the coal industry in line with the industrial relations arrangements worked out since the New Deal.

Bureaucratic control seeks to dissolve rank-and-file unity by dividing workers into many minute hierarchically arranged categories, and to prevent collective action on disputes by instituting formal, quasilegal procedures which isolate the worker from his workmates. Attempts to establish bureaucratic hierarchies among miners have not been very successful. The union-based seniority system does lead to a group of older workers with a larger choice of jobs and more stake in their pensions. But pay differentials are based on danger as well as skill, and young miners often take a stint at high paying dangerous jobs such as roof bolting to gain experience on a machine and then bid off to less dangerous lower paying work. This circulation between the pay grades defeats the establishment of a divisive meritocratic hierarchy. A few jobs such as electrician-mechanic require formal training and state certifications which acts as a barrier to easy access and establishes a certain distinction. Miners have fought divisions by insisting that all miners be part of the brotherhood. They use harsh initiation rituals for neophytes and practical joke sanctions against anyone seeming to set himself apart (Vaught and Smith 1980). During the period of rank-and-file mobilization, miners fought against great disparities in pay. In the last three contracts the pay differential between the highest and lowest paid union miner decreased to under ten percent.

The operators have been more successful in establishing bureaucratic procedures for controlling conflict. In reform in President Miller's first contract in 1974, a fullblown grievance procedure culminating in an Arbitration Review Board was established. Miners found the grievance procedure long and drawn out and biased in favor of the operators. They did not accept it lying down. During the three years of the 1974 contract one of the biggest waves of wildcat strikes in American labor history occurred (Yarrow 1982: 168-169). Miners joined this battle in spite of a 1970 Supreme Court decision which allowed companies to sue for damages and get injunctions against wildcat strikes (Seltzer 1977: 529). Massive wildcat strikes were conducted in the summers of 1975 and 1976 against the injunctions. The 1976 strike was successful in forcing a judge in Charleston, West Virginia, to revoke an injunction and enormous fines (Nyden 1978a). This confrontation, between the operators' attempts to institute bureaucratic control and the fiesty brotherhood of miners' resistance to it, was a standoff. The operators went into negotiations for the next contract determined to restore "stability and improve productivity in coal" (Bituminous Coal Operators Association Opening Statement October 6, 1977). The contract finally adopted tacitly included an Arbitration Review Board decision which allowed operators to summarily fire wildcat strike instigators. The level of wildcats has been low ever since.

The operators have also been successful in instituting bureaucratic procedures for dealing with absenteeism and weakening union organizing. As stated above, miners have used safety provisions as a power resource. Operators have sought to bring these provisions under more bureaucratic control so that individual miners or union safety committees may be penalized for "unreasonable" use of their right to refuse work or to stop production if they believe they are in "immanent danger." Recent court decisions and the 1981 contract have weakened miners' ability to maintain union representation and to organize non-union mines. The union organizing efforts are increasingly constrained by legal regulation.

Although a personnel officer from an industry with more fully developed bureaucratic control would be dismayed by the coal industry, bureaucratic procedures are gradually being established. The resistance is not only from the miners. As described above, management is still wedded to patriarchal controls such as favoritism which contradicts bureaucratic procedures. Some of the bureaucratic procedures negotiated in national contracts have been honored in the breech especially by the smaller independents who tend to be more committed to simple control. But at least for the time being, with a protracted slump in the demand for coal labor, the operators seem to have won a crucial round in the institution of bureaucratic control by establishing bureaucratic regulation of conflicts.

V. Conclusion

The control system in coal mining has gone through a dramatic evolution in this century. Throughout that evolution, coal operators have relied heavily on patriarchal forms of domination in the struggle to gain control of the labor process and the miners. Under coal camp paternalism and then union paternalism, the patriarchal form of hierarchy among men was used in the face of ineffective technical control systems. Currently, technical control is still ineffective and remnants of paternalistic control are still employed along with an increasing use of bureaucratic procedures.

Miners have responded to these control systems by also employing claims to elements of patriarchal culture. They have aggressively asserted their rights as craftsmen and men to autonomy from demeaning supervision. Thus, the control of coal mine labor is a contested terrain both in terms of concrete decision-making power and in terms of ideology with both capital and labor struggling over the definitions of the rights and obligations of labor and the rights and obligations of men. Out of the fray has come a conception of coal mining as men's work which entitles miners to certain prerogatives but also allows management to ignore certain amenities.

Goldberg (1980) has suggestd in her analysis of "women's work" in the office that application of elements in Edwards' three control systems produces contradictions which can foster a militant feminist job consciousness. This may also be the case for "men's work" in coal mines. Certainly there is a contradiction between paternalistic favoritism and bureaucratic principles of fairness, and between formal safety rights recognized by the bureaucratic system and safety as a matter of trusting in and obeying the "Father" under paternalism. But the three systems also are congruent in their denial of decision-making power to workers, and they reinforce each other. It may therefore be the relative weakness of technical control which causes problems for the composite system. To explore how this may work in the current control system I will describe briefly how that system seems to be experienced by miners.

My tentative conclusion is that the failure of technical control in underground coal mining in conjunction with the compensatory use of paternalistic and bureaucratic control mechanisms creates a characteristic montage of experiences promoting a militant male working-class consciousness. What are the salient features of the control system, and why does it foster a male specific class consciousness? Because of the failure of technical control, the labor process provides miners with the experience of relative strength vis-a-vis capital and promotes unity. Compare the miner to the typical assembly-line worker. The assembly-line worker's job pace, movements and coordination with other workers are determined by the line. The line is, as the architype of technical control, capital's ideological apparatus par excellence because it convinces the worker of his or her powerlessness while mystifying the exact locus of power in the mediating machine.* Because of the effectiveness of technical control of the labor process in this case, foremen are freed from the driving function and chiefly perform bureaucratic control functions to keep the line supplied with workers. The coal miner controls his or her own machine. Production is the result of a skilled, cooperative effort by a section crew. The exercise of management power is unambiguously communicated by the foreman's orders. Moreover, miners become aware over time that the foreman's goal of production and their goal of survival conflict; the veneer of paternalistic concern is peeled off by exposure to unavoidable class conflict. The assembly-line worker's job experience tends to lead to a feeling of powerlessness and insignificance, which is congruent with the feeling of being a child under paternalistic control and being a number under bureaucratic control. S/he is likely to respond by leaving the job (the turnover rate has been thirty percent a year in car assembly plants) or by resignation punctuated by brief episodes of frustrated rebellion. The coal miner's work, in spite of the horrible working conditions, involves satisfying experiences of intense comraderie with "buddies," of the exercise of skill, and of the collective exercise of power vis-a-vis capital. Attempts to control the powerful miners' brotherhood whether by paternalistic or bureaucratic means, are viewed as an assault on miners' manhood and brotherhood. They contradict a position of power and community already won.

This mix of collective power with subordination seems to be fertile ground for the development of rebelliousness because the subjects of the imposition of control face it with confidence, and a heightened sense of loss of entitlements. It is this mix which the current control system has in common with the fundamentally different coal camp paternalism. Under that system miners experienced power and autonomy in the mine and subordination in the camp. Under the current system power and subordination are experienced in direct confrontation at work.

---

*Autoworkers from the Linden GM Plant in New Jersey suggested that older workers who have been on the line for a number of years tend to "get beaten down by the line" and do not oppose GM's power. Another indication of the affect of the line is that these Linden respondents and autoworkers from the Lordstown plant interviewed for the film "Loose Bolts" observe that line workers are usually not active in local union politics.

Literature Cited

Arble, Meade. *The Long Tunnel: A Coal Miner's Journal.* New York: Atheneum Publishers, 1976.

Aronowitz, Stanley. *False Promises: The Shaping of American Working Class Consciousness.* New York: McGraw-Hill Book Co., 1973.

Baratz, Morton S. *The Union and the Coal Industry.* New Haven: Yale University Press, 1955.

Barkey, Frederick A. *The Socialist Party in West Virginia from 1898 to 1920: A Study in Working Class Racialism.* PhD. Dissertation. University of Pittsburgh, 1971.

Braverman, Harry. *Labor and Monopoly Capital.* New York: Monthly Review, 1974.

Brophy, John. *A Miner's Life.* Edited and supplemented by John D. P. Hall. Madison: University of Wisconsin Press, 1964.

Burawoy, Michael. "Toward a Marxist Theory of the Labor Process: Braverman and Beyong." *Politics and Society* 8:3-4, 1978.

———.*Manufacturing Consent: Changes in the Labor Process under Monopoly Capitalism.* Chicago: University of Chicago Press, 1979.

Clawson, Dan. *Bureaucracy and the Labor Process: The Transformation of U.S. Industry, 1860-1920.* New York: Monthly Review Press, 1980.

Corbin, David Alan. *Life, Work and Rebellion in the Coal Fields: The Southern West Virginia Miners, 1880-1922.* Chicago: University of Illinois Press, 1981.

Davies, Marjorie. "Women's Place is at the Typewriter: The Feminization of the Clerical Labor Force." *Radical America* 8:1-37, 1974.

Dix, Keith. *Work Relations in the Coal Industry: The Hand-Loading Era, 1880-1930.* Morgantown, W.V.: Institute for Labor Studies, West Virginia University, 1977.

Edwards, Richard C. *Contested Terrain: The Transformation of the Workplace in the Twentieth Century.* New York: Basic Books, 1979.

Ehrenreich, Barbara and Deidre English. *Witches, Midwives, and Nurses: A History of Women Healers.* Oyster Bay, N.Y.: Glass Mountain Pamphlets, 1973.

Elger, T. "Valorisation and De-Skilling: A Critique of Braverman." *Capital and Class* 7, 1979.

Friedman, A. *Industry and Labour: Class Struggle and Work and Monopoly Capitalism.* New York: Mac-Millan, 1977.

Garson, Barbara. *All the Livelong Day.* New York: Penguin Books, 1972.

Gaventa, John. *Power and Powerlessness: Quiescence and Rebellion in an Appalachian Valley.* Urbana, Ill.: University of Illinois Press, 1980.

Goldberg, Roberta. *Dissatisfaction and Consciousness among Office Workers: A Case Study of a Working Women's Organization.* PhD. dissertation. American University, 1981.

Goodrich, Carter. *The Miners' Freedom: A Study of the Working Life in a Changing Industry.* Boston: Marshall Jones, 1925.

Howe, Louise K. *Pink Collar Workers: Inside the World of Women's Work.* New York: Putnam, 1977.

Kanter, Rosabeth. *Men and Women of the Corporation.* New York: Basic Books, 1977.

Littler, C. and G. Salaman. "Bravermania and Beyond: Recent Theories of the Labor Process." *Sociology* 16:2, 1982.

Noble, David. "Social Choice in Machine Design: the Case of Automatically Controlled Machine Tools, and a Challenge for Labor." *Politics and Society* 8:3-4, 1978.

Nyden, Paul. *Miners for Democracy: Struggle in the Coal Fields.* Ph.D. dissertation, Columbia University, 1974.

_____. "Rank-and-File Organizations and the United Mine Workers of America. *The Insurgent Sociologist* 3, 1978.

_____, and Linda Nyden. *Showdown in Coal: The Struggle for Rank-and-File Unionism.* Pittsburgh: Miner's Report Pamphlet, 1978 a.

Pollard, Sidney. "Factory Discipline in the Industrial Revolution." *Work and Society.* Mary M. Robisehon et al. (eds.). Detroit, Mich.: Wayne State University, 1977.

Seltzer, Curtis. *The United Mine Workers of America and the Coal Operators: The Political Economy of Coal in Appalachia, 1950-1973.* Ph.D. dissertation, Columbia University, 1977.

Simon, Rick. *The Development of Underdevelopment: The Coal Industry and It's Effects on the West Virginia Economy, 1880-1930.* Ph.D. dissertation, University of Pittsburgh, 1978.

Stark, David. "Class Struggle and the Transformation of the Labor Process: A Relational View." *Theory and Society* 9:1, 1980.

Stewart, Katie. "The Marriage of Capitalist and Patriarchal Ideologies: Meanings of Male Bonding and Male Ranking in U.S. Culture." *Women and Revolution.* Lydia Sargent (ed.). Boston: South End Press, 1981.

Suffern, Arthur E. *Coal Miners' Struggle for Industrial Status.* New York: MacMillan, 1926.

Tams, W.P. *The Smokeless Coal Fields of West Virginia.* Morgantown, W.Va.: West Virginia University Library, 1963.

Vaught, Charles and David Smith. "Incorporation and Mechanical Solidarity in an Underground Coal Mine." *Sociology of Work and Occupations* 7:2, 1980.

Yarrow, Michael. "The Labor Process in Coal Mining: Struggle for Control" *Case Studies on the Labor Process.* Andrew Zimablist (ed.) New York: Monthly Review, 1979.

_____.*How Good Strong Union Men Line It Out: Explorations of the Structure and Dynamics of Coal Miners' Class Consciousness.* Ph.D. dissertation, Rutgers University. 1982.

Zimbalist, Andrew. *Case Studies on the Labor Process.* New York: Monthly Review, 1979.

WORDS AND PHOTOGRAPHS:
ENDURING IMAGES OF APPALACHIA
 Convenor: Jim Lloyd, Western Carolina University
Mary Prescott Montague: Last of the Appalachian Local Colorists
 Dexter Collett, Asher, Kentucky
The Schoolmarm Motif in Appalachian Fiction
 Heidi Koring, Lincoln Memorial University
Early Regional Photographers: Margaret Morley and William Barnhill in Western North Carolina
 Richard Straw, Radford University

Early Regional Photographers: Margaret Morley and William Barnhill in Western North Carolina

by
Richard A. Straw

Southern Appalachia has been extremely fruitful ground in which hundreds of photographers in this century have found a rich source of inspiration for their art. Among the earliest regional photographers were Margaret Morley and William Barnhill. Morley's book, *The Carolina Mountains*, appeared in 1913 and though it contained only twenty-four photographs, her images chronicle the everyday lives of mountain people all over western North Carolina in an engaging and sensitive manner. Her best works show women doing the tasks that filled their days and defined their place in pre-industrial mountain society. Her photos are an open and deliberate attempt to capture what she believed to be the honesty and straightforwardness of life in the Southern Highlands.

William Barnhill arrived in western North Carolina from Philadelphia in 1914 and immediately set out to record on film all aspects of mountain life in Madison and Buncombe counties. He was probably the first photographer to make pictures of mountain culture for his own enjoyment. He was independent and worked for no newspaper, no editor, nor did he have a studio of his own.[1] He was something of the vagabond and set out to photograph the region to satisfy his own curiosity and inner drive. For this he is certainly unique in the history of early Appalachian photography. His works are significant historical documents of Appalachian life in the early 20th century (although he did not mean for them to be) and are remarkable for their artistry and lack of bias or romanticism. What is especially amazing about his photos is that they were kept in private hands for over

The author would like to thank Richard Dillingham of Mars Hill College for all his kind help and support.

a half century until published in *American Heritage* and *Life* magazines in 1969 and 1970 respectively. The half century dormancy of Barnhill's photos removed them from the mainstream Appalachian image makers who gained national recognition during the 1930s and who determined much of the country's perception of the region.

Margaret Warner Morley was born February 17, 1858 and lived for a decade after the publication of *The Carolina Mountains*.[2] She is not well known and in fact, information on her life is scarce. She is best remembered for a long string of children's books on the lives of birds, insects, and small animals. *The Carolina Mountains* was her only major work for adults. Morley was born in Iowa, but her family moved to Brooklyn, New York while she was young, and it was in the East that she received her formal education. She was drawn to teaching and graduated from New York City Normal College in 1878. Her main interest was biology, and she pursued that subject at several different schools in Chicago and Massachusetts. It was in connection with data she prepared for her classes that Morley began to gather material for her books (17 in all). Coming at a time when nature study was being established as a definite part of grade school courses, her books had some pioneering importance. In addition to the specific information in them, her books offered important moral lessons to children about being kind to animals and conservation. It is unknown exactly why she initially chose to go to western North Carolina, but once she was there, she was enthralled by the scenery and the environment, so much so that she spent part of each year for twelve years at the resort community of Tryon, south of Asheville.

From her base at Tryon she explored the surrounding mountains and described them in lavish and loving detail. She also took pictures. Her photographs show us a personal image of the mountain environment with little of the influences that premeated her writing. Because she grew up and she was educated in the 1870s and 1880s, it is most likely that Morley came into contact and read the works of local colorists who published stories about Appalachia in the popular magazines of the day. Perhaps this was the impetus which drove her to go to western Carolina. It was the local colorists who created the notion that Appalachia was a strange land inhabited by a distinct and peculiar people who were unchanged from an earlier period of American history. The static image, as Ronald Eller calls it, had become accepted as fact by the 1890s when Morley first began to travel to Tryon.[3] She created in her writing and especially in her photos a dichotomy between herself and her readers on the one hand and the natives on the other. This hinders her prose but improves her photography because her images stand alone and neither she nor her audience are a part of the scene. That is why her photographs lack sentimentality and an attachment to what was thought to be quaint. The images unfold before us without our interference or justification.

By the time Morley published her photos, railroads, economic development, and an influx of northern missionaries and teachers had brought vast changes to the mountains. Obviously the image of mountain life that she presented was that of a passing and vanishing age. This provides a key to why she sought out scenes which depicted everyday life and the material aspect of the highlanders' world. She was comfortable writing about and photographing nature and, therefore, she sought in her photography to highlight the relationship that existed in pre-industrial Appalachia between nature, home, and work. That fiber which held the fabric of this world together, the connection between land, home, and family is the dominant theme of her photos and suggests that she was at least suspicious of the changes that she could not help but witness around her. The old life of the high country was passing away, and she worked hardest with her photos to preserve that image. Her photos do not strike a condescending chord, rather they stand as documents and reflect the positive side of her perceptions. She did not have the painter's license to leave anything out of her photos, and thus they appear as clear evidence of pre-industrial reality. Morley was an outsider and she was in the mountains to observe. She described in detailed photos the mountain peaks, the coves, the streams, the animals, and of course, the people. She liked the mountain people with whom she visited on her nature treks, and they emerge from her work as neither pathetic nor heroic. Perhaps her awareness of change stimulated her to document a lifestyle as it had been during a time when land, family, and work intertwined in a stable, workable, and balanced society.

A contemporary of Morley's, although there is no evidence at present that they ever met, was William Augustus Barnhill. He was a free spirited and adventurous individual who began vacationing in the South during the first decade of this century. In 1910 he decided he would like to move to western North Carolina, and he began to correspond with the Secretary of the Asheville Board of Trade about the possibility of locating in that resort city. In 1913 Barnhill read Horace Kephart's book, *Our Southern Highlanders*, and was convinced that western Carolina was the place for him. He moved there in 1914 and spent the next three summers photographing the land and people within a twenty-five mile radius of Asheville. In 1917 he went off to World War I, returned to Asheville in 1918, and worked as a commercial photographer until 1922 when he moved to Cleveland.[4]

Barnhill was quite taken by Kephart's descriptions and photos of mountain life and when he moved to North Carolina he went to Bryson City to meet Kephart and to show him some of his photos. Kephart was impressed and told him he would use some of them in a future book on the mountains. Kephart died, however, before the book was written. Like Kephart, Barnhill was a dedicated hiker who backpacked with his camera into remote mountain areas. Barnhill's photos are striking representations of the texture of mountain life. They are sensible and believable and like Morley's, are free of much bias and romanticism. His images are also primarily of people working: women churning butter, knitting, spinning, weaving, drying foods, men splitting shakes, plowing or hoeing corn. His photos are a record of agricultural self-sufficiency in a time when one's ability to work the land defined the quality of life.

Many of Barnhill's photos are set on or around Mt. Mitchell. He made the first of many trips there in the summer of 1914 accompanying a party which included a motion picture photographer who was making publicity photos in the area.[5] In the summer of 1915 a party of newspaper editors who were attending a conference in Asheville were taken on a courtesy trip to Mt. Mitchell and again Barnhill went along. During this trip he took pictures of what he saw on the way and solicited orders from a sample album he had made previously along the railroad.[6] Barnhill had an entrepeneurial bent and did not pass up an opportunity to sell his photographs. It is curious that he has stated in an interview that he was not aware of the historical value of his photographs until the 1950s but had he been, he probably would have sold them earlier.[7] When the Perley and Crockett Company of Black Mountain, North Carolina started an excursion trip over the logging railroad to Mt. Mitchell, Barnhill had a photographic concession, and he later shared a photographic and souvenir business with the owner of Camp Alice at the foot of the mountain.[8]

Barnhll spent days at a time hiking into the mountains around Asheville, and his enormous curiosity drove him to record as much of what he saw as he could. His motivation was simple. As he has said, "I wanted to have a record of where I'd been to have something to talk about."[9] He won the confidence and friendship of the people with whom he came in contact and lived with them for short periods of time. He moved freely and obtained intimate photographic studies of their way of life. He photographed the people he met because, "I was as interesting to them as they were to me."[10] There is no evidence that Barnhill consciously attempted to alter the culture of the region or to present a specific image of it to the public. He did not select those images that fit with outside expectations of what "mountain people" were like. Instead he sought to record what he saw around him because he was aware of its existence and he was somehow stimulated by its presence. "What I've seen there is just what I've seen with my own eyes."[11] His photos are so important in this context because we are able to look at them without wondering about his intentions or for whom he worked. He did not even think of himself as a documentary photographer and has claimed that, "Documenting is the last thing I consider."[12]

Barnhill had no special interpretive message to convey through his images, although from the distance of time, we are grateful for his meticulous attention to detail in people's lives. He stimulated others to document the region, but he did not discuss his photography with them. He claims, "I wouldn't talk much that way, not that I had intentions of covering up, but I was just making pictures. That's what I wanted to do and that was my answer. My story was there."[13] The rare comment he has made about his work concerns his interest in process and design and how they operated in an orderly fashion in mountain society. He photographed the pottery works in the Beech Community of Madison County, for example, and he made a series of photos that show the process by which wool is worked into cloth. He sought in his images a natural composition which would illustrate the essence of a moment suspended in time but not outside or removed from the system of which it was a part. His images are, an artist's expression not those of a cultural politician. His photos are, "what came out of me...what I saw."[14]

Like Morley, Barnhill photographed people engaged in all facets of work, and he was particularly interested in what we now refer to as mountain crafts. He was, however, unaware of the intentional revival of certian crafts in Appalachia at that time, and he has said his only interest was his curiosity about how people "made every simple thing."[15] Neither did Barnhill attempt to make a statement about the changes that had altered tradition in the mountains nor did he use his photos to illustrate how people were losing the self-sufficiency that he so admired. He was, in his own words, "just photographing people."[16]

Barnhill's images can be classified into three styles: record photos, character photos, and process photos. The first type is simply the image of what happened before the eye of the photographer, and he recorded it to capture a moment in time; the character study was the product of his interest in the different people he met, and these photos resulted from his attraction to a particular face, the look in an eye, the turn of a head, or a certain nuance of appearance; the process photo captured what he saw as the organic design of life, and he recorded the process because he admired its orderliness and function, not to document its existence. What Barnhill vigorously pursued was an accurate image of the people he met. He sought to portray their individuality, to know each one's different story, but not to lose sight of their place within the larger group. He is sensitive to the pitfalls of image making but believes that his early work was neither influenced by an awareness of nor an avoidance of Appalachian stereotypes.[17]

The result of this approach is that Barnhill's photos stand above later works by photographers such as Doris Ullman because his photos have a candid, genuine look to them. Barnhill developed a relationship with his subjects that was based on mutual curiosity tempered with a straightforwardness that each could respect of the other. Barnhill did not have to ask people to pose for him because he was so comfortable around them, and they accepted him completely. He cannot remember anyone talking to him or asking him anything about what he was doing. No one questioned why he was taking their photos. He did not have to beg people to sit for him and in fact, he is adamant about how unposed his photos were. Most of his photos have a spontaneity to them that suggests that he just happened to be someplace at the right time. For example, one of his photos is of a man salting sheep on Craggie Mountain. When he took that shot the man did not look at Barnhill or even bother to ask what he was doing.[18] To describe another of his photos Barnhill states, "I started setting up the camera and I don't remember saying anything. And she didn't ask me anything. Just like that one...with the woman with the wagon out of Weaverville with the strange costume and all. She just stopped along the road and I set up my camera and she just looked at me like the oxen, without much expression. They were just curious, I think. I don't remember talking at all. Tell them how to pose? I never asked them..."[19]

In order to fully understand the importance of historical photography it is necessary to ask certain questions. For example, what are our perceptions as viewers, and what were the motives and goals of the photographer? Photos clearly guide and fashion our most basic sense of reality and many of our most cherished images of the past have come from frozen pictorial descriptions more so than from the written word. "Photos are magical illusions, matchless pieces of information, descriptions of things, scenes, and persons infinitely more vivid than words...They seem miniature worlds, not copies but the things themselves."[20] Photos are certainly historical documents, but they are also experiences in their own right because they give us the opportunity to witness the past as if it were, momentarily, at least, present. The historian Michael Lesy pioneered the study of photos not simply as illustrations of history but also as revealing documents and expressions that are a source of insight as well as information.[21] What makes this true is our ability to read the picture, to reconstruct some small drama before the taking of the photo that evokes more than meets the eye. The viewer defines to some extent what is depicted as reality in a photo through his own imagination and relates this to other images he has seen and then he determines if the image is representative or fanciful. To the historian the most difficult task is to decide if a given photo is a fairly reliable image of what did exist. Would the photographed scene have taken place even if the camera had not been present? Documentary photographers have a great deal of power to manipulate a scene, but they are limited by their desire to show us what is there. It is because of this that the photographic image is the closest we can come to an objective representation of past reality.

Equally important is to know by what criteria the photographs were originally made. Both Morley and Barnhill photographed a place and time which was passing into history before them. They were both alien to their subject matter but were drawn to it either out of curiosity or to document it for other outsiders. What Barnhill has said about his motives does not lead one to conclude that he consciously helped to shape the image of what was defined as Appalachia. The fact that over fifty years later his photos influence our image of what the region was like during the early 20th century is not equivalent to saying that he went there to intentionally reveal a particular image of the mountain people through his photography. He did of course do this through his choice of subjects and settings, but what is crucial is whether he did this with the intent to change or present the culture according to his selective view. The evidence does not support the argument that he did.

Margaret Morley was in the mountains to study nature and to write a book about the region and its people, and she took her photos to supplement her prose. Morley clearly tried to present an image of the mountains to the outside world, and her view was so popular that a copy of her book was for many years in each guest room of the Grove Park Inn of Asheville. What is fascinating about her choices is that she photographed images and scenes that are remarkably similar to Barnhill's. This suggests two possibilities. Either Morley and Barnhill shared a vision of the region which was already well-established in the national mind, or they both were drawn quite naturally to those aspects of the region which appealed to their artists' imagination and sensitivity. Unfortunately, we know very little about Morley, and it is therefore difficult to speculate on her motives. She was a naturalist and had a driving curiosity to discover the relationship between various aspects of the natural world so she pictured the people in her photos close to nature, outdoors, walking, and working. She caught them as they were, and there is little visible evidence of posing in her work. Morley's photos are lasting historical documents and are not overly endowed with romantic or sentimental visions of Appalachia's past. One possible explanation for this is that her subjects appear to be in control of her photos and she was, therefore, in a position to depict them very nearly like they appeared to her.

Taken individually and as a group, what do the photos of Barnhill and Morley reveal to us about Appalachia? Barnhill did not consciously attempt to rearrange aspects of the culture for public consumption. Certainly his work has an impact upon our perception of what Appalachia was like during the pre-industrial era, but the photographer was not motivated by a desire to create or alter the image of the region that is laid before our eyes when we look at his photos. Morley, however, is much more difficult to understand. Her photos certainly depicted what she wanted her readers to see but was she photographing selectively to present a preconceived image of the region that would support the assumptions popularized by the local colorists of her youth? If this is true, do her photos present an accurate image of the mountain people at the turn of the century? Since they so closely parallel Barnhill's we can assume they do.

Most of their photos are middle distance and distant views which suggest that there was a unity to this life, that every event had its place in the overall scheme of things. This approach to photography gives a detached feeling as if one is viewing a drama unfolding. There is no suggestion that the people in any of their photos are posing for an audience. Most are off alone, apparently unconcerned with the photographer, without the sense that the intrusion of the camrea has in any way altered their ordinary patterns of behavior.

In the end, photographs, like any other historical document, exist in two worlds, that in which they were made and that in which they currently exist. But they cannot tell us everything regardless of how carefully the photographer sought to capture reality. They retain, as works of art, a precious amount of mystery that fires our imaginations, and as historical documents they stimulate us to learn more about the region so we can compare the visual image with the literary image. Fortunately Morley and Barnhill are two sympathetic and sensitive photographers whose lives and work are vital in understanding what Appalachia has been and continues to be.

FOOTNOTES

1 Sam Gray, "Mountains and Valleys and People in 'The Back of Beyond,' " *The Arts Journal* (Asheville, N.C.), February 1982, p. 3

2 For general biographical data see, New York *Times*, February 15, 1923.

3 For a complete discussion of the static image and its impact on Appalachian history see, Ronald D. Eller, *Miners, Millhands, and Mountaineers: Industrialization of the Appalachian South, 1880-1930.* (University of Tennesse Press, 1982), pp xv-xxvii.

4 Asheville (N.C.) *Citizen-Times*, August 19, 1979.

5 Interview, William A. Barnhill by Polly Cheek, Richard Dillingham, Linda March, and Rob Amberg, Mars Hill, N.C. November 17, 1982, p. 41. Appalachian Room, Mars Hill College.

6 *Ibid.*, p. 42.

7 Conversation by the author with Richard Dillingham, Mars Hill, N.C., January 25, 1985.

8 Asheville (N.C.) *Citizen-Times*, August 19, 1979.

9 Interview, William A. Barnhill by Polly Cheek, et al., p. 28.

10 *Ibid.*, p. 33.

11 *Ibid.*, p. 60.

12 *Ibid.*, p. 60.

13 *Ibid.*, p. 50.

14 *Ibid.*, p. 51.

15 *Ibid.*, p. 68

16 *Ibid.*, p. 70.

17 *Ibid.*, p. 60.

18 Interview, William A. Barnhill by Richard Dillingham, Mars Hill, N.C. August 24, 1983, p. 38. Mars Hill College Oral History Program, Mars Hill College Archives.

19 Interview, Barnhill by Polly Cheek, et. al., pp. 36-37

20 Exhibitions Staff, The American Image: Photographs From the National Archives, 1860-1960. (National Archives and Records Service, 1979), p. ix.

21 One of several books which illustrates this concept is, Michael Lesy, *Bearing Witness: A Photograhic Image of American Life.* (Pantheon, 1982.)

JOCKS AND JUNKETS: COME PLAY AND STAY
    Convenor: Russell Dachert, Western Carolina University
Sports and Play in Southern Appalachia: A Tentative Appraisal
    Robert J. Higgs, East Tennessee State University
Appalachian Documentaries: Hyping the Myth
    Sharyn McCrumb, Virginia Polytechnic Institute
Appalachia: A Tourist Attraction?
    Melinda Bollar Wagner, Lynn Batley, Kai Jackson,
    Bill O'Brien and Liz THrockmorton, Radford University

Sports and Play in Southern Appalachia: A Tentative Appraisal

by
Robert J. Higgs

Wright Morris in *The Territory Ahead* says that no matter where we go in America today we will find what we just left. As far as sports and play are concerned, I would not want to argue with that assertion in the least. Once, not really so very long ago, sports and play in Appalachia were quite different from those forms found elsewhere, but not any more. Athletics and recreation are essentially the same across the American landscape as are the problems, which, it seems, are forever increasing. In fact writers from this region have been among the first to decry the now familiar dehumanizing trends in sports, and they have continued to speak out on issues as a few examples will make clear.

Sherwood Anderson who made Southwest Virginia his permanent home was one of the first Amerian writers to regard the athlete as a cultural symbol and to suggest that sports are art forms providing the possibility of relief from the world of commerce. He also saw, like Johan Huizinga and others, the reverse occurring, the world of business encroaching upon the domain of sports and the athlete becoming a specialist and a celebrity.

Thomas Wolfe was witness to the same complex and shifting scene in American sports. In Nebraska Crane of *The Web and the Rock* and *You Can't Go Home Again* he created an enduring hero of natural strength and virtue who could do what Wolfe himself could not, "remain detached from the fever of the times" and go home again. In Jim Randolph in the *The Web and the Rock* he shows an opposite type of hero, one who is victimized by all the flattery that his athletic success has fostered, and he succinctly paints a devastating picture of alumni and fans who are all too ready to bestow praise, providing there is a victory of course:

> They fill great towns at night before the big game. They go to night clubs and to bars. They dance, they get drunk, they carouse. They take their girls to games, they wear fur coats, they wear expensive clothing. They are drunk by half time. They do not really see the game and they do not care. They hope their machine runs better than the other machine, scores more points, wins a victory. They hope their own hired men come out ahead, but they really do not care. They don't know what it is to care. They have become too smart, too wise, too knowing, too absurd to care. They are not youthful and backwoodsy and naive enough to care. They are too slick to care. It's hard to feel a passion from just looking at machinery. It's hard to get excited at the efforts of the hired men.[1]

Indeed Arthur Miller was only echoing Wolfe a quarter of a century later when he said, "There doesn't seem to be any humanity left in big-time sports...people go to watch a machine operate. That wipes out the connection between spectator and team. The human side is out."[2]

Wilma Dykeman also suggests that the human side is out or perhaps going out. In a few pages in *Return the Innocent Earth* describing the big game between Jackson (read the University of Tennessee) Dykeman identifies every reprehensible facet of the do-or-die game: the bromidic mentality of the Alumni, the post-season bowl lust, the swelling arrogance sure to come with victory, and most of all "the dark malevolent growl" that "moves through the multitude." Is this, Dykeman seems to ask, sublimation of violence or the incipient weening of an awakening monster? Deborah Einemann (Dykeman's character), a Jew and citizen of the world, had "heard this crowd before"—in Germany of course. So too had Nobel Prize winner Elias Canetti heard crowds before, as he makes clear in his unsettling book, *Crowds and Power*.

What type of men make up the machines that characters in Dykeman's novel witness? Dan Jenkins gives us his version in his novel *Semi-Tough* in his picture of T.J. (Torn Jock) Lambert:

> They say that when T.J. was in college at Tennessee, he kept a mad dog chained up in his room in the dorm and used to feed it live cats. They say that instead of going down the hall to the toilet, T.J. had a habit of taking a dump in his closet. And when it got smelling so bad in his room that even T.J. would notice it, they say he would throw a bunch of newspapers on the closet and set fire to the whole thing.[3]

Some would say that Jenkins surely jests and I suppose he does, yet in another sense he is right on the money in description of T.J. in college in the athletic dorms for he has found the spot—second only to the frontier cat house—where anecdote and macho lore blur into fables of studliness. If one were to look for a character reminiscent of the world beater and ring-tailed roarer out of the literature of the old Southwest, there is only one place to turn, the athletic dorm at what Mark Harris called SSU (Southern State University). The picture in Gary Shaw's *Meat on the Hoof* of the athletic dorm at the University of Texas would tend to confirm this observation.

No doubt Lisa Alther is jesting too to a degree in a chapter entitled "Walking on the Knife's Edge or Blue Balls in Bible Land" in her novel *Kinflicks*, but she has also zeroed in on the very real problem of muscular Christianity in our culture which seems sometimes to be headquartered in the very heart of Appalachia. Note the following prayer of Brother Buck during the city-wide Preaching Mission in the cavernous gymnasium of the Civic Auditorium in Hullsport as Ginny and Joe Bob obediently hold hands, "sweating and trembling."

> "Let us pray," Brother Buck instructed. "Father, our Coach, hep us, Father, to run Thy plays as Thou wouldst have them run. Knowing, Lord that Christ Jesus Thy quarterback is there beside us with ever yard we gain, callin those plays and runnin that interference. Hep us, Lord, to understand that winnin ball games depends on followin trainin. Hep us not to abuse our minds and bodies with those worldly temptations that are off-limits to the teammates of Christ....
>
> ....and hep us, Celestial Coach, to understand that the water boys of life are ever bit as precious in Thy sight as the All-American guards. And when that final gun goes off, Lord, mayst Thou welcome us to the locker room of the home team with a slap on the back and a hearty, 'Well done, my good and faithful tailback.'"
>
> "A-man," Brother Buck added as an afterthought.
>
> "A-man," echoed the rest of us.[4]

This type of satire of muscular Christianity has become commonplace in the last few years but it is timely and needed as long as evangelists insist upon the heretical notion that sports are the bridesmaid of religion and slant their proselytism accordingly. Jerry Falwell, Oral Roberts, and Billy Graham all acknowledge the power of sports in attracting converts, and Falwell has said that he wants to build "Champions for Christ." "Presumably," says Sheryl Hoffman about the techniques of Falwell and Roberts, "the Lord likes to see his favorite team win, and trouncing the heathens from the state college up the road proves, in its own inexplicable way, that the institution's theology was right all along."[5]

What does all this mean for us in Appalacia today? It means, I think that sports and play in Appalachia and elsewhere have become either ends in themselves or means of serving the goals of religion, patriotism, or commercialism. If we look at the last Super bowl game, watched by 115 million, and the half-time program put on by the Air Force as a recruiting effort and remind ourselves of all the links between sports and religion, we must admit, I think, the distinct possibility that we have become a leisure-class society characterized by the four occupations of sports, government, warfare, and religion, as identified by Veblen in *Theory of the Leisure Class*. The rise of competitive sports and the decline of imaginative and unregulated play provide an index of the extent that a society has moved toward a leisure class of what Veblen would call a barbaric culture.

Basically, the difference between sports and play is the difference between *paidia* and *Ludus*. These terms, coined by Roger Caillois in *Man, Play, and Games* represent principles which permeate all types of play. *Paidia is a type of "uncontrolled fantasy, frolicsome, impulsive, or capricious"; ludus* is the tendency toward "effort, patience, skill, ingenuity."[6] *Ludus* lends itself to rigid competition, complexity, organization, and to easy alliance with the state; *paidia* by contrast, is unstructured, simple, and highly individualistic in the sense that the player is not so tightly bound by rules, and even secretive in that the nature of the play depends to a large extent upon the imagination of a limited number of participants. In *ludus,* the player displays ingenuity in the method or technique by which he attempts to win highly competitive contests already well established within a particular culture. In *paidia* ingenuity is displayed in the inventiveness of the player in creating new games, on adopting variations, as his ability, as it were, to entertain himself. The principles of *ludus* and *piadia* are always bound together, but, as Caillois points out, they always move in any game, and I would add in any culture, in opposite directions. Again, what is true elsewhere is true of Appalachia, and the big switch seems to have begun in the 1920's, though much research is needed to document this tentative assertion.

The one thing we do know for sure is that things have not always been this way, if we trust observations of earlier observers. The children, says Horace Kephart in 1913, "play few games, but rather frisk about like young colts without aim or method."[7] "The young people of the mountains," wrote John C. Campbell in 1921, "as a whole do not know how to play." Even when they do play, he says, they wish passionately to win and are inclined to take whatever means necessary to reach a goal. What is missing says Campbell, in addition to sportmanship, is organization, which organizations would provide:

> The Young Men's and the Young Women's Christian Associations might also find a special field for service in supplying and stimulating recreation. The young people of the mountains as

a whole do not know how to play. They need to be directed into lines of wholesome vigorous activity. No definite program can be suggested. Here, as elsewhere, it will not be enough to supply the means. There must be definite fostering and supervision, and in places a traditional and religious opposition must be overcome, sympathetically and tactfully. The greater use of music—of community singing in particular—would be helpful, as well as the encouragement of games in which all may take part, folk dancing, and sports of various kinds.[8]

It may have been true that "as a whole" the mountain children in 1921 did not know how to play, but as Pamela Henson showed in her unpublished paper "A Study of Children's Play in Appalachia," based on a survey of numerous texts, it is certainly not altogether true. Mountain children did know how to play to a significant degree. In her survey of games in Kentucky, Tennessee, and West Virginia, Henson "found 277 games with distinctive titles, all collected since 1930. After classifying these games....Henson discovered that of those that could be identified, 136 used words, while 28 were non-verbal. Eighty were exclusively played outdoors, thirty-five indoors, and forty-nine could be played either place. Perhaps the most interesting discovery is that thirty-four of the games required only one player, forty-two could be played with a minimum of two players, thirty with three, seventeen with four, fifteen with five, fifteen with ten players and one required twenty-two."[9] Henson's study is valuble since all of her conclusions on various games are telling. In the case of jump rope, which is essentially a West Virginia game, Henson found that "none of the 63 jump rope games...entailed competition between jumpers." Among her conclusions Henson cites a "rarity" of competitive and team games, and games which entail assumption of roles."[10] The games Henson surveyed reflect a clear divergence from the dominant American culture. (p.36)

In appendix 1 it is evident that children's games of all sort, relatively simple and unorganized, are, according to Caillois' classification, forms of *paidia*. They are also, especially some of them such as counting-out rhymes, quite familiar to anyone raised in Appalachia and, say, over fifty years of age. They are also disappearing though I have no data to support that claim. Also disappearing are the almost pure examples of *paidia* that Caillois calls "tumult", "agitation", and "immoderate laughter," which also helped to define traditional Appalachian culture in the form of tall tales and practical jokes. That tumult and agitation existed on a wide scale throughout the region, we have on authority of one in whose honor this conference was established, and in his discussion of George Washington Harris's Sut Lovingood, in whom tumult abounded most gloriously:

> Sut's pranks, which belong to that low type of humor that derives its relish from the sight of gore and the infliction of pain

APPENDIX I
Classification of Games
by Roger Caillois

	AGON (Competition)	ALEA (Chance)	MIMCRY (Simulation)	ILINX (Vertigo)
PAIDIA Tumult Agitation Immoderate laughter Kite-flying Solitaire Patience Crossword puzzles LUDUS	Racing Wrestling Etc. Athletics } not regulated Boxing, Billiards Fencing, Checkers Football, Chess Contests, Sports in general	Counting out rhymes Heads or tails Betting Roulette Simple, complex, and countinuing lotteries	Children's initiations Games of illusion Tag, Arms Masks, Disguises Theater Spectacles in general	Children "whirling" Horseback riding Swinging Waltzing Volador Traveling carnivals Skiing Mountain climbing Tightrope walking

NB. In each verticle column games are classified in such an order that the *paidia* element is constantly decreasing while the *ludus* element is ever increasing.

upon others, are in the mainstream of mountaineer humor, which is preserved intact from the wild and boisterous frontier. That Sut's counterparts have not appeared in the fiction of the mountains to any marked degree merely indicates that polite taste excluded them. The pranks that Sut rigged on his enemies have been the stock in trade of his counterparts in the mountain country down to recent times. Such pranks as turning snakes and lizards loose in church, throwing nests of hornets among praying congregations, howling their sins at the mourner's bench, tying cans of lighted kerosene to dog's tails, multilating cats, dogs and horses, luring preachers, sheriffs, candidates for office, and school teachers into compromising situations with women, and frustrating weddings have their local adaptations in the oral traditions of most mountain communities.[11]

Praise God, it might be said, that such forms of play and humor are no longer prevalent in the region if existent at all, and enough has been said in derogatory vein about such sadistic practices that it is not necessary for me to add another note of outrage. Edmund Wilson, remember, called Sut "not a pioneer contending against the wilderness but a peasant squatting in his own filth." He also acknowledged that the *Yarns* is "by far the most repellant book of any real literary merit in American literature." Sut's hatred, Wilson contends, "is directed against anybody who shows any signs of gentility, idealism of education."[12] "Hatred," I believe, is much too strong a word, reflecting a fundamental misunderstanding of the nature of play, or the ranges of play, on Wilson's part, and he also fails to see, as others of Sut's detractors have, that Sut's pranks are directed for the most part against institutions or representatives of institutions, preachers, politicians, and teachers and pretense in general. Indeed one could easily imagine Sut letting loose a bag of lizards during the height of Brother Buck's sermon in the Hullsport auditorium in Alther's novel or for that matter, recalling the scene in *Return the Innocent Earth,* in a section of Neyland Stadium either during the pre-game prayer or during a heroic goal-line stand on which some commercial bowl bid depends. Can we not say, in fact, without being charged with absolute sadism, "Sut, where are you now that we need you?"

The point I wish to emphasize to a degree and defend is not infliction of pain upon man and beast but a sense of independene in forms of play and a rejection of blind acceptance of organized games that lend themselves so easily, especially with promotion techniques of the modern world, to perverse relationships with commerce, religion, and the nation state. There is a case to be sure for rules and structure, but how far do we go from the spontaneity of *paidia* that has always been a distinguishing feature of sports and play in Southern Appalachia? Note that unregulated athletics, racing, wrestling, etc., is a feature of *paidia* and it is such forms of competition, indeed usually violent, that were a distinctive feature of the people who formed a very large part of the population of the region. I speak of the Scotch-Irish whose contests are described by Reverend Edward L. Parker in *The History of Londonderry:*

> Their diversions and scenes of social intercourse were of a character not the most refined and cultured; displaying physical rather than intellectual and moral powers, such as boxing matches, wrestling, foot races, and other athletic exercise. At all public gatherings, the "ring" would be usually formed; and the combatants, in the presence of neighbors, brothers, and even fathers, would encounter each other in close fight, or at arms length, as the prescribed form might be; thus giving and receiving the well directed blow, until the face, limbs and body of each bore the marks of almost savage brutality. All this was done, not in anger, or from unkind feeling toward each other, but simply to test the superiority of strength and agility.[13]

Note that in these contests there are no material prizes, and, apparently, little or no animosity between competitors or combatants; and though the body pain in boxing matches can easily be imagined, the injuries would appear to be minor compared to those in any ordinary football game in Southern Appalachia where I have seen as many as eight people carried off the field in a single game. Still the contests of the Scotch-Irish seemed brutal to observers and no doubt contributed to the image they acquired of a "pernicious and pugnacious" people in the mind of easterners in the United States.

Franklin, for example, regarded them as "violent, narrow-minded drunkards—white savages," as pointed out in *Vengeance and Justice: Crime and Punishment in the Nineteenth Century American South* by Edward T. Ayers who goes on to present this composite picture:

> A Particularly virulent strain of violence entered the South in the culture of the Scotch-Irish, the majority of whom chose the South for their home in the eighteenth century. In Carl Bridenbaugh's language, the Scotch-Irish were "undisciplined, emotional, courageous, aggressive, pugnacious, fiercely intolerant, and hard-drinking." All observers agreed that the Scotch-Irish had little patience for legal forms and found quick recourse in their guns, knives, or fists. "It appears to be more difficult for a North-of-Irelander than for other men to allow an honest difference of opinion in an opponent," a contemporary and sympathetic biographer of Andrew Jackson argued, "so that he is apt to regard the terms opponent and enemy as synonymous." Southern mountain culture, indelibly dyed by the Scotch-Irish origins of so many early settlers, became famous for its sensitivity, as Horace Kephart observed, "to any disparaging remark or imagined affront.[14]

This is also a point of Campbell in his call in 1921 for reform of play in the mountains without specific reference to the Scotch-Irish but mountain youth in general:

> The Highland boy has, however, little knowledge of play as play. When he plays he plays to win. In contests of any kind he wishes passionately to be the victor, and if he finds defeat threatens him he is too inclined to give up or take what means he can to reach his end. He is, more-over, very sensitive and swift to take offense. Ridicule, or the suspicion that someone is "throwing off on" him, he cannot bear, and he is quicker with the knife, or, when he is older, with the pistol, than with the fists. Thus he incurs the reproach of being, in popular parlance, a "poor sport," one who does not know the art of "playing the game to a finish," regardless of what it costs. It must not be inferred from this statement that he is a coward, although from a true sportsman's standpoint there is an element of cowardice in his failure to meet defeat squarely and honestly. In feats of daring the mountain youth is brave to recklessness, and as has been indicated in a previous chapter, no man in the country makes a more valiant soldier. He needs, however, to learn the code of honest sportsmanship—the

code of the "good loser"—which can best be taught through games which bring him into touch with his fellows in team-play and healthful competition.[15]

Without approving of quick recourse to gun or knife any more than the cruel pranks on man or animals, can one not ask where the American revolution itself would have been had the Scotch-Irish played the game of the British? Was not that spirited independence and suspicion of organizations, in whatever form, the very quality that made them, in the words of British historian Leeky, go "almost to a man on the side of the insurgents. they supplied some of the best soldiers of Washington."[16] Though I cannot prove it at this point, I believe the Scotch-Irish are the key to the understanding of the history of sports and play in the region. Even the celebrated Grandfather Mountain Highland Games, "America's Braemer" appears to be almost an imported event when viewed in terms of the traditional play of the mountains,[17] shaped so much, I suspect, by the proud and independent Scotch-Irish. Their descendents, however, have, like most of the rest of us, embraced with open arms all the mass forms of sports and play that now surround us.

Are there not corporate dangers in the present forms of sports and entertainment far outweighing those spontaneous, unregulated, and often violent forms of the older generations? Are there not dangers in crowds and hero-worship, the two requirements for spectator sports that now surround us? Ring Lardner apparently thought so and in 1921, the same year that Campbell said the mountain children did not know how to play, voiced exactly the same complaint about the dominant culture. We do not know how to play in America, said Lardner:

> because (1) we lack imagination, and (2) we are a nation of hero-worshipers....
> But hero-worship is the national disease that does most to keep the grandstands full and the playgrounds empty. To hell with those four extra years of life, if they are going to cut in on our afternoon at the Polo Grounds, where, in blissful asinity, we may feast our eyes on the swarthy Champion of Swat, shouting now and then in an excess of anile idolatry, "come on, you Babe. Come on, you Baby Doll!"[18]

Over a decade later Lardner is still disenchanted with the anile idolatry of crowds as seen in his novel *Lose With a Smile*. The narrator, Danny Warner, is a busher from Booneville, Missouri, and in his letters home he tells his girl friend what life is like in the big leagues:

> Some of the boys has got nick names like wear they come from like 1 of the pitchers Clyde Day but they call him Pea ridge

Day because he comes from a town name Pea ridge and he was the champion hog caller of Arkansaw and when he use to pitch in Brooklyn last yr he use to give a hog call after every ball he throwed but the club made him cut it out because the fans come down on the field every time he give a call and the club had to hire the champion of iowa to set up in the sand and call them back.[19]

In such satire the heritage of frontier humor is alive and well, and the object of attack, sports fans, seems today as deserving of such treatment as ever.

Here, then, is the familiar situation again. As in so many other aspects of Appaclahian life, the effort in sports has been not to learn from the mountain culture but to transform it in imitation of mid-America. No doubt in the 1920's many mountain kids profited from new teachers and coaches bringing to them new knowledge of new sports, but could not America then (and now) have learned just as much from the habit of mountain kids "who frisked about like young colts without aim or method"? A whole new series of books proposing alternative forms of play and non-competitive games[20] were in effect anticipated by children of Appalachia for over the past one hundred years. There is, in fact, or has been, an Appalachian physical education if we care to look back and see. It is a way of play quite at odds with the modern sports industry which reflects the same traits as the rest of modern society. The old ways were not perfect by any means, but their virtues were hidden, not proclaimed and boosted as are the supposed ones of modern sports. To the degree that contemporary sports and play are reformed, they will in fact move back toward the old order, toward fun, simplicity, spontaneity, and naturalness, toward *paidia,* the spirit of childhood.

ENDNOTES

1. Thomas Wolfe, *The Web and the Rock* (New York: Harper, 1939), p. 122.
2. "Human Side is Out of Sports—Miller," Knoxville News Sentinel, February 13, 1986.
3. Dan Jenkins, *Semi-Tough* (New York: New American Library, 1972), p. 6.
4. Lisa Alther, *Kinflicks* (New York: Alfred A. Knopf, 1975), p. 42.
5. Sheryl J. Hoffman, "Evangelism and the Revitalization of Religious Ritual in Sport", unpublished article scheduled for publication in summer issue of *Arete: The Journal of Sport Literature.*
6. Roger Caillois, *Man, Play, and Games.* trans. Meyer Bararh (New York: Free Press, 1961), p. 13.
7. Horace Kephart, *Our Southern Highlanders* (New York: Outing Publishing Co., 1913), p. 259.
8. John C. Campbell, *The Southern Highlander and His Home* (Russell Sage Foundation: New York, 1921), pp. 319-20.
9. Quoted in Bernard Mergen: *Play and Playthings: A Reference Guide* (Westport, Conn.: Greenwood Press, 1982), p. 208.
10. Pamela Henson, "A Study of Children's Play in Appalachia," unpublished paper, Georgetown University, 1973), p. 36.
11. Cratis Williams, "Sut Lovingood as a Southern Mountaineer," Appalachian State Teachers College. *Faculty Bulletin*, 1966, p. 3-4.
12. Edmund Wilson, "Poisoned," *Voices from the Hills,* eds. Robert J. Higgs and Ambrose N. Manning (New York: Frederick Ungar Co., 1974), p. 414.
13. Quoted in Henry Jones Ford, *The Scotch-Irish in America* (Princeton, N.J.: Princeton University Press, 1915), p. 243.
14. Edward L. Ayers, *Vengeance and Justice: Punishment in the Nineteenth Century American South* (New York: Oxford University Press, 1984), p. 22.
15. Campbell, p. 126.
16. Quoted in Ford, p. 208.
17. For a history of the Scottish games in North America, see Gerald Redmond's masterful study, *The Sporting Scots of Nineteenth Century Canada* (Rutherford, N.J.: Fairleigh Dickinson University Press, 1982).
18. Ring Lardner, "Sport and Play," *Civilization in the United States: An Inquiry by Thirty Americans,* ed. Harold E. Stearnes (New York, 1922), p. 461.
19. Ring Lardner, *Lose with a Smile* (New York: Scribner's, 1933), p. 2.
20. In addition to the Bibliography in *Play and Playthings* see *Recreation Alternatives: Ways to Play,* 1978; Jeffrey Sobel, *Everybody Wins, 393 Non-competitive games for young children* (Walker and Co., 1983); and Nora Gallagher, *Simple Pleasures, Wonderful and Wild Things to do at Home* (Addison-Wesley Publishing Co., 1981).

Applachian Documentaries Hyping the Myth

by
Sharyn McCrumb

The "hill-billy" stereotyping of the Appalachian region by Hollywood feature filmmakers is a well-known phenomenon, easily recognizable by those familiar with the region. More subtle is the distortion of Appalachia by documentary filmmakers who have perpetuated old stereotypes and generated a few new ones in an effort to sell tourism or local products.

Advertising has been an institution in Appalachia for most of this century—from barns plastered with "See Rock City" signs to the souvenir salesmen at the Floyd Collins mine incident. In the past fifty years, the selling of Appalachia as a region of "Disneyland" has progressed from "hillbilly" motels and Hatfield and McCoy outdoor dramas to include the film medium. In a chronological sampling of documentaries made over the last half century, it is interesting to note the shifts of emphasis from one decade to the next as filmmakers try to inform the outside world about Appalachia. After viewing a score of films made between 1930 and 1983, I found it difficult to believe that all these places described were actually the same region: 19th century throwbacks carding wool, unspoiled wilderness, industrial centers, and the costumed inhabitants of the Land of Oz were all offered by one film or another as "Appalachia". Over the years, filmmaking techniques became more sophisticated, and the films became more commercially oriented, but they seemed to come no nearer to presenting any kind of worthwhile introduction to the region; recent documentaries have changed Appalachia into another roadside attraction, designed to see that a tourist and his money are soon parted. This paper will examine the various media stances presented as "Appalachia" leading up to the most recent and atrocious incarnation, which is designed to convince the world that the "normal" Appalachian town is Gatlinburg, Tennessee.

The oldest available documentary film on Appalachia was made in 1932 by a now-defunct company known only as "Educational Productions". The title, "Primitive America", is the perfect representation of the attitudes of the filmmakers, who contend that Appalachia is the last stronghold of the "true pioneers" on the North American continent. The film shows mountain people making their own candles, spoons, chairs, etc., with no indication that they may also own cars, listen to radios, and live down the road from the Oak Ridge nuclear research center. *Children Must Learn*, a 1940 film made by New York University, contends that children in rural Appalachia are hampered by ignorance and a tradition which resists change. The filmmakers claim that the children cannot relate to stories in standard textbooks, and that they should be given reading matter containing vocational information, such as the techniques of contour plowing and raising goats, so that they can be taught something "useful" besides literacy skills. These documentaries represent the "Deliverance" view of Appalachia, often reflected in feature films: that the region is a land that time forgot, bypassed by progress and education. Such films were made by outside groups of filmmakers, who used isolated incidents—and often *staged events*—to create the impression that this was the way of life for the entire region. For example, a woman who bought her household linens at J.C. Penny's in Knoxville, but who knew how to spin, might be asked to haul down the spinning wheel from the attic and give a demonstration for the filmmakers. The camera presents an image of a woman spinning cloth, and the audience is invited to believe that this is the norm in the southern highlands.

One of the worst examples of the "primitive Appalachia" documentaries is a 1957 film distributed by the Virginia Department of Education, "Southern Highlanders". The narrator is the community's schoolteacher, who explains that the mountains are "shrouded in mists, like an old man's memory". She speaks indulgently of the people — sounding rather like a missionary: "People who still live by simple, honest values while the world grows complicated around them." In the film, the schoolteacher navigates the back roads in her new Ford Fairlane to observe her neighbors making sugar on a sorghum press and generally maintaining a nineteenth century lifestyle. What these people need, she concludes, is a good dose of progress: "They need no longer be slaves to the mountains, if they listen to the music of the future." The film's message seems to be that Appalachia is a backward place, but that there is hope for civilization there, eventually.

By the mid-sixties the prevailing attitude toward Appalachia was that it was America's backyard — a nice place to visit if one went properly prepared. *Happy Holiday—Camping in the Smokies*, a 1966 American Oil Company production, urges suburban families to pile into their Winnebagos and head for the 'unspoiled wilderness' of the Smoky Mountains. The only indication of human habitation in the region — other than the camping tourists—is Gatlinburg, Tennessee, pictured as a strip of flashy gift shops. The film gives the impression that Appalachia is a land without schools, churches, factories, or ordinary people — since all the non-tourists appear in pioneer garb.

Unfortunately this distorted image of the region — a wilderness punctuated by gift shops — became the accepted myth employed to lure tourists into the mountains. Subsequent films followed this format, sinking deeper and deeper into the trap of hyping the region as one vast 'Disneyland' existing for the amusement of 'normal' America. A strong motive for making this sort of film was the fact that the various commercial tourist attractions in the region could be sponsors of the film by paying part of the production costs in exchange for a feature spot in the film.

North Carolina offered prospective tourists *Variety Vacationland*, a mid-seventies film by Doubles Film Productions, written and edited by Hugh Morton, the owner of Grandfather Mountain. Since this film was meant to interest visitors in the entire state of North Carolina, eastern attractions such as Kitty Hawk and the Lost Colony Outdoor drama were included; the western North Carolina region was represented by Grandfather Mountain, Tweetsie Railroad, Linville Caverns, and the Oconoluftee Indian village at Cherokee — all attractions charging an admission fee of several dollars.

The 1976 film *Holiday in the Sky*, by Walter J. Klein Films of Charlotte, N.C., offers the same paid-sponsor format in an even more unattractive package. The film is narrated as a series of "postcard" texts addressed to the folks back home from a vacationing family. "I saw the Bible come alive at Christus Gardens," lisps the eight-year old. While scenes of the Three Mountaineers Craft Shop near Asheville occupy the screen, the audience hears 'Dad' telling the folks: "This is the kind of place you'd like to be lost in for ten or twelve years." Other paid-attractions visited by the family include: Ruby Falls, Dinosaur Land, and the Kingport-Johnson City Econotravel Motor Lodge. There is no hint in the film that between all these costly attractions there are free national parks where nature can be enjoyed, and that towns and farms full of ordinary people (as opposed to tin men and talking scarecrows) also populate the mountains.

Probably the most widely-circulated tourist film advertising the southern Appalachian region is a 1980 movie made for Kodak by Hugh Morton. *The Southern Highlands*, available on free loan to any group who wishes to borrow it, is a detailed collection of tourist-trap vignettes covering North Carolina, Tennessee, and western Virginia. The audience is urged to pack its camera for a wonderful series of photo opportunities as they visit Rock City, Ruby Falls, Lost Sea, Christus Gardens, Gatlinburg, Frontier Village, Biltmore House, Grandfather Mountain, Blowing Rock, Ghost Town in the Sky, Luray Caverns—and most revolting of all—The Land of Oz, where Dorothy and her magical friends will pose with visiting tourists for heartwarming vacation pictures. It is no wonder that people believe the Dukes of Hazard after seeing documentary films depicting the region as an endless stream of commercial fluff. Ruby Falls and Luray Caverns are over-hyped commercializations of authentic natural phenomena, but there is no excuse for some of the man-made contrivances which are featured to represent the region: Ghost Town in the Sky is a western town, complete with shoot-outs and saloon girls; Christus Gardens is an imitation Holy Land on the wrong continent; and The Land of Oz is nowhere near Kansas and certainly 'no place like home' as far as Appalachia is concerned. The film was sponsored by the entrepreneurs who profit from the tourist's visits, at the expense of the region's national image.

The state governments of the Appalachian states have entered the competition for the tourist dollar, using state production teams to film public relations movies inviting visitors to vacation there. The approaches vary greatly: all are better than the paid-attraction films, but most leave something to be desired in the search for a balanced presentation of the region. The Tennessee Department of Tourism offers *Follow Me To Tennesee*, featuring a plethora of nature shots, and more emphasis on history than on artificial theme parks, but the dignified tone of the film is marred by the on-screen narrator, a "pioneer" in a deerskin outfit and coonskin cap. He makes an incongruous presence, chatting to the audience about water-skiing on the Mississippi.

Kentucky did not respond to requests for the loan of a state film on tourism. Their ads say that such films must be requested one year in advance; apparently, a vacation in Kentucky is not a thing to be undertaken lightly. North Carolina lists a number of tourist films most of which are no longer available. *Variety Vacationland,* one of the sponsored films, served as the North Carolina film for this study. West Virginia seems to be trying hard to live down the standard media image of Appalachia. One of its films, *The Hills Are Alive,* a 1982 production, features a breathy, Tinkerbell-voiced narrator reciting the poetry of West Virginia poet laureate Louise MacNeil (sing-song rhymed couplets) to a panorama of wildlife and forest shots of West Virginia. White-water rafting and outdoor recreation is emphasized; regional accents are not present in the film.

The second West Virginia publicity film, *Wild, Wonderful West Virginia,* is a 1982 Ellis Dungan production for the West Virginia Chamber of Commerce. Its target audience seems to be the executives of national corporations, and perhaps middle management people who have just been transferred to the region. After a few wildlife shots, the visuals and narration emphasize progress and potential in science and industry. There are shots of steel mills, hospital operating rooms, open-classroom elementary schools, and buildings on various college campuses within the state. The second half of the film shows golf courses, suburban brick homes, an art gallery, and a symphony orchestra. This approach makes one think that West Virginia doth protest too much. In producing such a scrupulously ordinary, non-regional picture of their state, they have sacrificed any individuality the state possesses. The symphony, hospitals, college campuses, and factories are all twentieth-century bland, and they could have represented South Dakota, Vermont, New Jersey, or Arizona without changing any aspect of the film. This could have been an all-purpose, interchangeable state promotional movie, for any state you chose. The result is a film which lacks in interest and character what it gains in dignity.

There is a delicate balance between pioneer-garbed narrators and characterless hospital-and-art-gallery films, but the state of Georgia has managed to find the happy medium. *Georgia,* a 1982 production by the Georgia Department of Natural Resources, is a beautifully filmed pictoral tribute to the state. The musical background is *Georgia On My Mind,* a nice touch to individualize the film. Instead of bombarding the viewer with statistics as the West Virginia film did ("sixth state in mineral production"), the Georgia film paints an impressionistic portrait of the state, as described by residents of the various regions. In characteristic regional accents, off-screen voices describe Atlanta, the Georgia mountains, the Savannah coastal region, and the southern marshes, with affectionate pride. The Appalachian segment features an articulate man with a mountain accent, who describes the region: "These mountains have been through the fire and the ice, and now they're just resting." Excellent cinematography is exhibited in shots of a school bus on a mountain road, a small town's main street, a farmer beginning his morning chores, and nature shots of white-water rapids and panoramic mountain vistas. "If you get used to walking on unlevel ground," the narrator says, "You won't ever want to live anywhere else." The film features no tourist attractions, no costumed natives, not even any breath-taking natural wonders — just a few native Georgians talking affectionately about their regions. The film leaves the viewer with a warm, positive feeling about the state which was missing in every other tourist film in this study. Georgia, one feels, doesn't want to trick you out of your money, or put on an act, or try to impress you with their industry — but if you want to drop in for a visit, they'll be nice to you. The film maintains the dignity of the state without sacrificing its individual flavor.

Film-making and avertising have become considerably more sophisticated in the past decade. *Georgia* reflects this new low-key approach to tourism, but it also indicates a healthy change from the apologetic "primitive America" films of the thirties and forties, and from the "carnival barker" approach of the past two decades. The message in Appalachian tourism of the eighties seems to be: "We are proud of our regional character, but we're not backward or strange. Come and visit, but don't expect it to be Disneyland." It is a message the rest of America has needed to hear for a long time.

Appalachia: A Tourist Attraction?
by
Melinda Bollar Wagner, Donna Lynn Batley, Kai Jackson,
Bill O'Brien, Liz Throckmorton

Hypothesis: Commercialization of Cultural Difference
We want to make clear that we are neither advocating nor decrying tourism per se. We are not, in fact, studying tourism. Our study is not on the numbers of people coming to the region, nor is it on the attractions that Appalachia actually offers or does not offer. Rather, we are examining the literature of the tourist industry to study the image of Appalachia which it projects.

Our study of the image of Appalachia as it is portrayed in tourist literature was born as a child of Wagner's (1981, 1982) theory that the image of Appalachia serves as an "alter ego" for urban American or middle American culture. Wagner's hypothesis is that America looks toward the image of Appalachia as its opposite, perhaps what it once was and might be again. This hypothesis is borrowed from anthropologist Victor Turner's (1969) delineation of "community" and "communitas" which he says every society must have. "Community" is Turner's label for a society's social structure. It is a norm-governed, institutionalized and abstract structure which delineates how people behave toward one another according to the roles they play. "Communitas," on the other hand, represents spontaneous, immediate, and concrete relationships among human beings as human beings, rather than as role bearers. Communitas suggest what "could be;" it is the crucible which holds human potentialities and universal human values. Turner (1969:203) sets forth the idea that society "needs" both:

> Society seems to be a process rather than a thing—a dialectical process with successive phases of structure and communitas. There would seem to be—if one can use such a controversial term—a human"need" to participate in both modalities.

Thus the image "non-Appalachian America" has of Appalachia may serve as a "communitas." This image of Appalachia represents middle America's opposite — a less complex, community-oriented, rugged society. Like the American Indian, Appalachia is viewed in sentimental retrospect by an urban population which longs to free itself of its mechanized, computerized bonds and live in simplicity, at least for awhile. By looking toward its opposites, middle America may thus identify and appreciate itself through contrast. For example, if middle America is individualistic, then Appalachia is seen as collective. If middle America is task-oriented, then Appalachia is seen as person-oriented. If middle America's music is classical and rock and electrified, then Appalachia's music is "folk," "traditional," and acoustical. If urban America is concrete and pavement, Appalachia is mountains and trees.

We hypothesized that this desire to find "cultural difference" in Appalachia would be reflected in the literature of the tourist industry. By embarking on an analysis of the travel literature of each state, we set out to see if there is indeed an image of "cultural difference" displayed in this medium.

It is not surprising that we should look to *tourist* literature to see if the image we expected to find was "played out" there, for tourism *itself* may indeed serve a "communitas" function. Modern tourism along with "much expressive culture such as ceremonials, the arts, sports, and folklore" serve "as diversions from the ordinary, which make life worth living." Tourism is "functionally and symbolically equivalent to other institutions that humans use to embellish and add meaning to their lives" (Graburn 1977).

The most obvious example of this might be the pilgrimage, and we should note that Batteau has identified the "pilgrimages" of outsiders into Appalachia during the troubled time of the 1930s and 1960s as one of the "forms that have figured prominently in the image-making of Appalachia" (along with myth, journalism, and to a lesser extent commodity) (Wagoner, Batteau, Green 1983).

As pilgrimage, as well as in its less serious forms, tourism is supposed to offer us "re-creation," a difference from the workaday world, a getting away from it all. "Tourism provides a... counterpoint to ordinary life." (Graburn 1977:24)

Tourism, then, is an "alternative state" (Graburn 1981:470) wherein one may seek the opposite of his everyday "social structural" world. Tourism thus is akin to rituals which embody communitas by carrying their participants through a "liminal" state (a state of transition, or marginality, or being on the "threshold") (Turner 1969). For a tourist, just as a participant in ritual, is "out of the normal, everyday social-structural and cultural environment and beyond its social and moral constraints." The tourist is outside his normal space and outside his normal time (Akeroyd 1981:468).

The history of tourism within Western civilization gives further fuel to our thought that an image of Appalachian otherness would be perpetuated in the tourist literature of today. In medieval Europe, travel was for religious purposes, as in pilgrimages or crusades. People of that day (who could afford to) travelled to religious retreats on spiritual quests for truth. This truth was to be obtained by reflection.

The Renaissance brought with it the view that "truth lay outside the mind and spirit" (Graburn 1977:24). Travel then turned way from seeking for truth as religiously understood toward exploration of facts as scientifically understood, and to an appreciation of the "high culture" of Europe.

The Industrial Revolution brought with it, among other things, safer and cheaper travel for the bourgeoisie. It also spawned "the romanticism that glorified nature and the countryside" (Graburn 1977:25). The aftermath of World War I had the effect of further loosening the hold of the aristocracy on tourism as a recreational activity.

During the 1920s the aristocracy and its pleasures were further relegated to the realm of the "stuffy," and there was heightened interest in the lifestyles of common people. Ethnic or cultural tourism became popular; folk music and jazz were sought after (Graburn 1977:26). Tourism as a product of industrial societies became a "search for the natural and the simple" (Pi-Sunyer 1981:475).

This brief history of Western tourism shows that the motivations for tourism have evolved from the religious, cultural, historical, and educational to, more recently, a seeking after the themes of nature, recreation and ethnicity. Thus we were expecting to see a commercialization of a longing for cultural difference in the tourist literature of the Appalachian area.

Another reason for choosing tourist literature as our medium is that tourism is a major activity in the area. It has been hypothesized that tourism "is quite likely to become the world's largest business by the end of the 20th century" (Sutton 1967), and the Appalachian region is no slouch in this regard. Since the 1950s, the Southern Appalachians have been considered one of the principal tourist areas of the country. Among national parks, the Great Smoky Mountains and Shenandoah are annually ranked among the leaders in numbers of visitors. Related attractions such as the Skyline Drive and the Blue Ridge Parkway have a high volume of usage (Morris 1967).

In monetary terms, Virginia has a two billion dollar a year tourist industry, which is "as big an industry as agriculture and is more than equal to the combined dollar value of the industries of forestry, mining, and fishing" (MacCord 1981). West Virginia sees 1.4 billion dollars a year in "direct travel industry expenditures,"; a figure which is "exceeded only by manufacturing" in that state. (*Appalachia* 1984).

IMAGES WE EXPECTED TO FIND/TYPES OF TOURISM

To summarize what we expected to find, let us clarify what the tourist/seeker seeks. A common task in socieities the world over seems to be an attribution of meaning through a process of defining "Culture" in opposition to "Nature." (This is the same process we go through when we seek to discover the meaning of any concept; we find out what it is *not*.) For the same reason, "communities" seek "communitias," in rituals, or by imagining it or seeking after it. Thus the highly "Cultured" city dweller seeks after Nature in two forms: One is to seek nature in the purest form, to get out "into" Nature, and the fewer people (bearers of Culture) around the better. But you can also get close to nature through Nature's "children" — the peasants of the world. "Interaction with them is possible and their naturalness and simplicity exemplifies all that is good in Nature herself" (Graburn 1977:27; See also Batteau 1979 on Culture seeking after Nature).

The seeking after Nature in its purest form has been labelled *"natural tourism"* by those who study tourism, and of course, we expected to find this in the tourist brochures from the Appalachian region.

"Natural tourism" includes driving and hiking through mountains and countryside, sight-seeing things like natural land formations. This kind of tourism is represented in the tourist literature by pictures of landscapes that look as though they were taken from cars on scenic highways, and by pictures of natural "oddities" like the Natural Bridge in Virginia.

As an example, we offer this ear-jangling put together of downhome and media hype: "we've set aside some of the prettiest country you'll ever see... We call 'em State Parks... and all in the middle of some of the prettiest country the good Lord ever made."

The kind of "cultural difference" image we expected to find has been labelled by those who study tourism as *"ethnic" or "cultural" tourism*. This is communing with Nature through her children or their artifacts. It includes the "picturesque, vestiges of a vanishing life-style... with old-style dwellings, horse-drawn carts and plows, and handmade rather than machine-made crafts." Activities may include meals in rustic inns and folklore performances (Smith 1977:2). This kind of tourism includes the seeking after crafts, music, and dance.

To further explain what sort of cultural tourism we thought we would find, it is necessary to clarify that there are at least two constellations of images of Appalachia, which sometimes overlap. These "types" correspond to the distinction made by Batteau and Green between "stereotype" (a popularized cartoon-like image) and "archetype" which relies on "some basic ideas within our cultural understandings," is akin to myth and legend, and harbors dichotomies like those included in the social structure/communitias model discussed earlier. (Wagner, Batteau, Green 1983). The first might be called a "hard" image; these are the stereotypes which have been played out in cartoons, jokes, television series, and advertisements. This stereotype relies on the slouch hat, the moonshine jug, the rifle, and Snuffy Smith's junked-up cabin. The "softer" image emphasizes values that have been repeatedly attributed to Appalachia: a sense of beauty, modesty, self-reliance and pride, fatalism, collectivism (a person-orientation, as opposed to a task orientation), love of land, religiosity, family loyalty, and a slower, laid back pace of life (e.g. Jones 1972). Added to this should be artifacts and activities such as stringed instruments, folk and bluegrass music, clogging, quilts and quilting, and handmade wooden furniture, toys, etc.

We did expect to find Appalachian "cultural difference" to be heavily commercialized by the tourist industry. We expected this commercialization to be of a "soft" type — i.e. using the more subtle images such as bluegrass musicians, quilt makers, etc. as opposed to "hard" stereotyped images of lazy, moonshine-drinking hillbillies. Let us reiterate that we did *not* expect to find a "hard" exploitation of Appalachia through stereotypes such as the L'il Abner character. At least, we did not expect to find this in the official literature of the state travel bureaus. We did not expect to find this, and we did not find it.

Before we tell you about our method and our findings let us clarify the remaining types of tourism which students of tourism have identified. (The types of tourism discussed here have been adapted from Smith 1977 and MacCord 1981).

"*Recreational tourism*" is often the beach and the package of coastline activities, and "sexy pictures and images" that attract tourists who want to "relax or commune with nature," but in a comfortable way with the conveniences that a resort-type place can offer. This type of tourism also includes ski resorts and large, glamorous cities with a night life, like the "Big-A" (Atlanta) as shown in the Georgia travel literature (Smith 1977).

"*Historical tourism*" stresses the past, with tours of historical structures (like the "covered bridges" we found in abundance in the West Virginia literature) and reconstructions of past environments (like Williamsburg, Virginia).

"*Industrial tourism*" would include tours of factories, mines, mills, and the like. An example would be the Museum of Atomic Energy at Oak Ridge, Tennessee.

Thus, we thought we had good reason for looking for a commercialization, some might say an exploitation, of cultural difference in the travel literature, and we set out to see if it was indeed there. Keep in mind that our research is not aimed at determining whether the Appalachian region is *actually* culturally different from the rest of the United States. It has been "imaged" as if it were, and we wanted to see whether this image prevailed in the tourist literature. Whether these cultural differences are actually to be found in the area is beside our current point. We simply wished to see if they were used as part of the "come on" in the tourist literature of the Appalachian states.

The method we used to test this hypothesis was to request travel literature from each of the 13 states recognized as part of Appalachia by the Appalachian Regional Commission. We did this by writing to the Tourist Division of each state government. In fact, we wrote two letters, using two different addresses, to each state office. In one letter, we requested literature on "travel and recreation" in that state, and in the other we specifically stated an interest "in the Appalachian area of the state." Our point here was to compare the separate sets to see whether the information would be different in the general state brochures and in the specifically "Appalachian" ones.

Most of the states sent the exact same package in reply to both requests. Georgia and South Carolina sent no reply to the "Appalachian" request. North Carolina sent one extra item — a list of hotels — in answer to the "Appalachian" request. Tennessee was the only state that sent different materials to the two different requests. In Kentucky, the general literature came from the Office of Tourist Development, while the literature for the "Appalachian" request was sent from the governor with a special letter. Otherwise, it was the same packet of information.

Originally all 13 states were analyzed (Anthropology 411 1984), but for purposes of this paper, we have narrowed our focus to these seven states: West Virginia, Virginia, Kentucky, Tennessee, North Carolina, South Carolina, and Georgia, and will discuss only these in the remainder of the paper.

Analysis was done on the content of text, pictures, and on the feelings one got when looking at the literature. We gradually worked our way from broad, overall images of the material, to more detailed and specific things which included more concrete data such as the number of times certain images appeared or certain phrases that were used. We then looked for patterns which our analysis had shown were common in the literature.

FINDINGS

In general we found that commercialization of a soft "Appalachia as different" image was little in evidence.

"Variety" is the Spice of Tourist Life

Each state's literature has a particular theme. In no state was Appalachia — either its cultural or its natural attractions — the main emphasis in the tourist literature. For most of the states, the main emphasis was "VARIETY" — something for everyone. This was true even of West Virginia, which, of all the states, we expected to lean most heavily on its Appalachian heritage. Out of the seven states, four had variety or something for everybody as their theme (West Virginia, South Carolina, Georgia, and North Carolina.) Tennessee had the theme of "recreation or outdoors." Virginia stressed "history."

Kentucky's theme was "bluegrass."

The literature of the four "variety" states used all four types of tourism discussed earlier. All of the coastal states took advantage of their beaches as the major tourist attraction, while the land-locked states, Tennessee, Kentucky, and West Virginia, promoted outdoor recreation, including hiking, sight-seeing and a variety of other activities. Appalachian seems to become lost in the innumerable pages of golf, tennis, rafting, skiing, swimming and other recreation activities as well as the history and heritage of other sections in the states. Appalachian culture may be a tourist attraction, but to the states in which it lies, it is just one among a variety of choices for the potential vacationer.

All of the states except Tennessee and Kentucky sent us a main book (a "big beautiful book" as they advertised it), and many of them accompanied this with smaller brochures about particular places. These books were all divided into sections (ranging from three to eleven sections), each section emphasizing a different thing to see, thus underscoring the VARIETY available within the state. Each travel section was given a name under which the activities, events, attractions, and accommodations in that area's vacation spots were listed, described and illustrated.

In five of the states, these sections were geographically determined and labelled. For example, Virginia's book was divided into Northern Virginia, Tidewater, Eastern Shore, Central-Southside, Shenandoah, and finally, the Highlands. In North Carolina and Georgia, however, the books were divided and the sections titled by relating them to history or the type of people who live there or once lived there. For example, in North Carolina's literature, one of the sections was called "The Birthplace of English America" and another was called "The Land of the Sky," an area where many Indians lived.

Within these books, the placement of the section which would be considered Appalachian differed. In four states it was the last thing in the book (Virginia, Kentucky, South Carolina and West Virginia); in two states it was at the front (North Carolina and Georgia).

Appalachia as "Historyless"

In most of the literature, Appalachia appeared "historyless." There was little to indicate that any history had ever taken place here, other than a few references to Daniel Boone. In some of the states, history was a major part of the discussion of several of its areas, but not mentioned at all in the Appalachian section of the state. One student noted that it seemed as though Appalachia had no people and no culture, just land and natural beauty.

"Appalachia" Rarely Used

We found that the word "Appalachia" was not much in evidence. No state used the word "Appalachia" to label the Appalachian region of its state, instead they used labels like "High Country," "Mountaineer Country," or "Highlands." (See the following chart which lists these labels for each state, along with the predominant theme of each state's literature and the kinds of tourism found in each state.)

When the word Appalachia was found, it was used to refer to geological phenomena, or it was used as part of a proper name, such as the Appalachian Mountains, the Appalachian Plateau or the Appalachian Trail. That is, it was very rarely used to refer to culture or to cultural traits. South Carolina did not use the word at all in its literature. Virginia used the word only once, to refer to the "Appalachian Plateau." In Georgia, the word Appalachia wsa used only when referring to the Appalachian Trail.

Appalachia as (Nearly) "Cultureless:"
Cultural Images Found: Arts and Crafts

With the exception of South Carolina, all of the states portrayed some part of the traditional images of Appalachia in their travel literature. Thus we found *some* emphasis on Appalachian culture in nearly all of the states, but not nearly as much as we had expected to find. The cultural aspects which we did find were quilting, traditional music, dancing, and festivals which featured all of these. Arts and crafts were the predominant form of "cultural" tourism.

The most popular Appalachian images included: mountain or Appalachian arts and crafts in general, quilts, and stringed instruments like the fiddle and the dulcimer (all found in 5 of the 7 states); square dance, folk dance, flatfoot or clogging, and hillbilly or mountain costume (in 3 of the 7 states), moonshine and stills, love of land, folk music, and a relaxed, rural atmosphere (in 2 of the 7 states). (See the chart which delineates the items of cultural tourism found in the various states.)

As an example, Virginia's literature, which made very little mention of Appalachian culture, did say "And there's the Southwest Virginia Museum at Big Stone Gap, for a close-up look at mountain culture and customs. There you'll find... century old quilts, b'ar guns and a homemade still." Likewise, the Northeast Georgia Mountain region sports a "down home atmosphere" with "rustic accommodations available from friendly people who are as widely known for their cleverly fashioned handicrafts as they are for their delicious country food."

Listings of things to do included many arts and crafts festivals and fiddlers' conventions such as Tennessee's "Old Time Fiddler's Championship" with "flatfoot dance... and non-electric instruments."

The pictures also showed these particular facets of the image of Appalachian culture. In Tennessee, pictures depicted men with long white beards, men playing fiddles, old women quilting, and log cbins. One picture depicts

SUMMARY OF PREDOMINANT THEMES AND TYPES OF TOURISM FOUND IN THE TOURIST LITERATURE

STATE	PREDOMINANT THEME OF THE LITERATURE	TYPES OF TOURISM IN THE LITERATURE / TYPES OF TOURISM IN THE APPALACHIAN SECTION	LABEL FOR THE APPALACHIAN SECTION
West Virginia	Variety	N,H,R,C,I/N,R,C	"Mountaineer Country"
Virginia	History	H,R,N,C/N,R,C	"Shenandoah," "Highlands"
Kentucky	Bluegrass	R,N,H/N,R,C	"Eastern Kentucky"
North Carolina	Variety	R,N,C/N,C,	"High Country"
Tennessee	Recreation Outdoors	N,R,H,C/N,R,C	"East Tennessee
Georgia	Variety	H,R,N,C/N,R,H	"Pioneer Territory," "Northeast Georgia Territory"
South Carolina	Variety; Beaches	R N,R,	"Up Country Carolina"

Key:
Types of tourism:
C—Cultural (includes Indian as well as Appalachian)
H—Historical
I—Industrial
N—Natural
R—Recreational

The types of tourism for each state are listed in the order which indicates which form was most prevalent in the literature of that state.

a man in overalls with a mule; another is of a woman in traditional garb who is sewing on a quilt. Another shows some men sitting in front of a log house in flannel shirts and overalls playing music on banjo, guitar and fiddle while a couple of other men watch and carve on pieces of wood. Virginia's "Highlands" section pictured a mill, a rocking chair and a spinning wheel, a man making a dulcimer, a barn on a hill, a banjo player, a guitar player, and people on a porch. Kentucky's literature included a man playing fiddle, a picture of a chair in the woods with a shawl and some pottery sitting on it, and pictures of bluegrass musicians, log cabins and a mill.

The travel literature of Tennesse, West Virginia, and Kentucky gave the strongest of these images of the Appalachian region(s) of their states, by including more pictures, phrases, and events that convey an "Appalachia as culturally different" image. But this still represented a small portion of all the images to be gleaned from the literature of the state. For example, in Kentucky's literature, the pictures described above were drowned in the overriding emphasis on "bluegrass." There were twenty-two pictures of horses

Items of Cultural Tourism Found in Tourist Literature

Mountains (Natural Tourism)	Mountain or Appalachian Arts & Crafts	Quilts & Quilting	Stringed Instruments/Dulcimers, Fiddles	Folk, Square, and Flatfoot Dance & Clogging	Hillbilly & Mountain Costume	Moonshine/Stills	Love of Land	Relaxed/Rural Atmosphere	Mountain Life	Pioneer Legends	Mountain Heritage	Hatfields & McCoys	State	Totals
x	x	x		x	x		x	x			x	x	West Virginia	(9)
x	x	x	x	x	x	x	x						Kentucky	(8)
x	x	x	x			x			x	x			Virginia	(7)
x	x	x	x	x	x								Tennessee	(6)
x		x	x					x					North Carolina	(4)
x	x		x										Georgia	(3)
x													South Carolina	(1)
7	5	5	5	3	3	2	2	2	1	1	1	1	**Totals**	**38**

x indicates that this item is *present* in the state's literature

in the literature, greatly outnumbering those with an "Appalachian" emphasis. "Bluegrass" was the most often used word in this literature, appearing sixteen times.

Appalachia as "Nature"

Much more in evidence were representations of natural attractions such as mountains, water, trees and other scenery. Mountains and scenery seem to be the universal symbols used to represent Appalachia. Our research showed a preponderance of beautiful pictures of the sun setting over rows of mountain ridges.

Morris' (1967) article on "The Potential of Tourism" in the Ford study emphasizes the "diverse natural features" of the area, including mountains, ridges, gorges, valleys, rivers, caves, and forests. The only thing the area lacks is natural lakes, and the dams have taken care of that. All this is joined with mostly moderate temperatures and a comfortable relative humidity to make it nice for the tourist. A listing of the attractions Virginia has to offer says "Virginia is hard to beat for variety" when it comes to natural attractions. There are "waterfalls, natural tunnels and bridges, caves, cliffs, peaks, scenic overlooks, dunes, virgin forests, areas and streams for hunting and fishing, streams for canoeing, open water for boating and water-skiing, mineral and fossil deposits" (MacCord 1981).

SUMMARY AND THOUGHTS ON WHY THERE IS LITTLE COMMERCIALIZATION OF CULTURAL DIFFERENCE

Thus, we thought we would find commercialization of cultural difference, and found instead largely an ignoring of cultural differences. We found a nuance of cultural tourism, drowned in other forms of tourism.

While our purpose was not to theorize why we found what we did, but rather to simply look to see what was there, we have given this some thought.

First, we have to consider what tourism is. It is, after all, an industry — "an organized industry, catering to a clientele who have time and money and want to spend them, pleasurably, in leisured mobility" (Smith 1977:15). Areas thought to be the most profitable and best liked by vacationers may predominate in the literature of the state. Some of us have suggested that the tourist industry may not view communion with culture as lucrative, compared to communion with beaches, golf courses, restaurants, and motels. In other words, cultural tourism itself may not be considered profitable. (Although others of us have argued that it certainly is made much of in other areas; for example, Pennsylvania "sells" its Amish population to the point of genuine exploitation, and the literature we looked at used its Indian population as a "selling point" whenever possible.)

Secondly, we need to remember who produced the literature we used as our sample. This literature came from the Tourist Division of each state government. The few examples we had of a stereotyped negative image came from privately produced and distributed advertising of privately owned tourist traps. We may not find a commercialization of cultural difference in the state-produced literature for the same reason that Virginia has mandated that its plantations now be labelled "grand manor houses." (The state NAACP objected to this, saying it was a not so subtle way to rewrite Virginia history, and that a plantation should be called a plantation.) We call this a "blandifying" of the literature, a sanitizing of it to make it bland enough so as not to offend any particular group.

Some of the students to whom we have presented our findings have suggested that perhaps the makers of tourist literature themselves have only a negative stereotype of the Appalachian region, and do not want to project this in the literature, and so project no image at all.

Third, since the Appalachian region is just one part of most of these states, it is logical that they would not give it more than its "quota" of notice in their travel literature.

Fourth, *perhaps*, after all, Appalachia is *not* actually different, and the tourist industry knows that better than we academics do. (This is not to be construed as a fact, merely a perhaps.)

A more theoretical argument, and one which might lay the foundations for our next paper, is that if the cultured person is truly seeking Nature, any view of a culture to be found in that Natural setting (albeit a culture that is thought to be "different" from the tourist's own) only interferes with the Nature-seeking. If you want cultural tourism you can go to "Amish Country" or you can hobnob with the natives in New Guinea. But Appalachia is portrayed as one of America's last bastions of uncultured *Wilderness* (which you can see from a car).

APPENDIX

The following are examples of attractions and activities, taken from the travel literature, that each state claimed to offer. All of the states, except two, are divided on the basis of Appalachian and non-Appalachian sections. Tennessee and West Virginia could not be divided this way because one did not have a major book that divided the state into specific sections and one was entirely Appalachia. The examples from the Appalachian section of each state are more detailed and specific to give a clear idea of the images of Appalachia presented in the literature. The non-Appalachian sections are more generalized to give an overall picture of what that state offered.

WEST VIRGINIA

"mountain heritage"
"Appalachian arts and crafts"
quilts
"mountaineer"
"mountain arts and crafts"
"Appalachian craftsmen"
Appalachian Wildwater, Inc.
13 out of 81 pictures of mountains
4 out of 81 pictures of covered bridges
"racing rapids"
country inns
mills
Mountaineer Dinner Theater

glassmaking companies
coal mine tours
Hatfields and McCoys
museums
horse racing
fishing
Coal Festival
Country Festival
"shimmering lakes"
"luxurious resorts"
barns
Civil War battle grounds

VIRGINIA

Appalachian Section
mill
Sugar Maple Farm Festival
Natural Chimneys
Natural Tunnel
"pioneer legends"
rocking chair
guitarist
barn on a hill
stringed instrument concerts
deer
Southwest Virginia museum at Big Stone Gap
Old Fiddler's Convention

Natural Bridge
Winchester Apple Blossom Festival
"handmade quilts"
"homemade stills"
sunsets
banjo player
people on porch
man making a dulcimer
Barter Theater
caverns
"century old quilts"
Cumberland Gap

Non-Appalachian Section
Williamsburg
people visiting historical houses
skiing
hiking
beaches
mountains
"unspoiled natural beauty"
Old Church Tower
Woodrow Wilson Birthplace
battle re-enactments
canoeing
rafting
amusement parks
trees
Old Capital City of Richmond

KENTUCKY

Appalachian Section
mountains
lakes
"bluegrass music"
The Appalachian Celebration
Kentucky Logging Show
Sorghum Festival
Annual Hillbilly Days Festival
dancing
Black Gold Festival
clogging
"bean soup dinner"
"moonshine demonstration"
Berea College

boating
fishing
Morehead State University Appalachian Collection
Harvest Festival
Appalachian Development Center
Jesse Stuart Nature Preserve
crafts
square dancing
folkdancing
folk music
Great American Dulcimer Convention

Non-Appalachian Section
fishing
tubing
old houses
historic documents
mountains
chair with a shawl on it
mill

horse racing
historical monuments
mills
sunsets
old cabins
log houses

NORTH CAROLINA

Appalachian Section
Hollerin' Festival
New River
Appalachian Trail
7 out of 9 pictures in this section are of mountains

Collard Festival
Grandfather Mountain Scottish Festival
"authentic mountain life exhibits"
quilting

Non-Appalachian Section
mountains
restaurants

beaches
pine trees

TENNESSEE

hiking
"flatfoot dancing and non-electric instruments"
Seventh Annual Dulcimer Conventions
Squaredancing
"pioneer crafts"
"folk festival"
women quilting
log cabins
mountains
31 arts and crafts festivals listed
fishing
hunting
Andrew Jackson Home
Jonesborough — oldest town in the state
fiddle playing
woodcraving

Old time Fiddler's Championship
Appalachian Music
Frontier Days
"hammer and mountain dulcimers"
"fiddle contest"
men playing fiddles
men with long white beards
men in suspenders, dirty work clothes, and hats
state parks
men in overalls with mule pulling cart
sailing
men in flannel shirts playing banjos and guitars
quilting
men carving sticks

GEORGIA

Appalachian Section
Lookout Mountain
Appalachian Wagon Train
"rustic accomodations"
cat on a fencepost
"Indian lore"
Craftsmen's Fair
"friendly people"
"delicious country foods"
Mountain Arts and Crafts Festival

Birthplace of Sequoia
Old Time Fiddlin' Convention
"cleverly fashioned handicrafts"
waterfalls
southern plantations
Sorghum Festival
"a down home atmosphere"
farmlands
The Gold Rush Days

Non-Appalachian Section
colonial houses
seafood
Indian culture and heritage
amusement parks
golfing
fishing

water
plantations
Sioux Indians
trees
tennis

SOUTH CAROLINA

Appalachian Section
mountains
waterfalls
camping
crafts

lakes
Rock Bluff
hiking
rafting

Non-Appalachian Section
beaches
sailboats
seafood
golfing
The Grand Strand
Pee Dee Country

sun bathers
women
water
restaurants
Historic Charleston
Thoroughbred Country

REFERENCES CITED

Anthropology 411 Appalachian Cultures Class. 1984. *Appalachia: A Tourist Attraction.* Radford, VA: Radford University Appalachian Studies Program. The authors and their chapters are: Marcia Cooper — ARC; Daphne Carr — New York; Barry Sites—Pennsylvania; Susan Finley — Maryland; Ben Steinberg — Ohio; Carl Rhodes — West Virginia; Liz Throckmorton — Virginia; Lorna Smith — Kentucky; Tami Stark — North Carolina; Bill O'Brien — Tennessee; Jeff Jarvis — South Carolina; Kai Jackson — Georgia; Lynn Batley — Alabama; Kelly Morris — Mississippi; Ana Sutphin — Blue Ridge Parkway. Their work has been used throughout this paper.

Akeroyd, Anne V. 1981. Comments on anthropology of tourism, *Current Anthropology,* October.

Appalachia. 1984. Recreation and Tourism. *Appalachia,* May-August.

Batteau, Allen. 1979. The American Culture of Appalachia. Paper presented at the annual meeting of the American Anthropological Association, Cincinnati, Ohio.

Graburn, Nelson H.H. 1977. Tourism: The Sacred Journey. IN Smith, Valene, Ed., *Hosts and Guests.* University of Pennsylvania Press.

_____. 1981. Comments on Anthropology of Tourism. *Current Anthropology,* October.

Jones, Loyal. 1972. Appalachian Values. *Twig Magazine.*

MacCord, Howard. 1981. Your Locality and the Travel Industry. Virginia Travel Council

Morris, John W., 1967. The Potential of Tourism. IN Ford, Thomas R., Ed., *The Southern Appalachian Region: A Survey.* Lexington: University of Kentucky Press.

Pi-Sunyer, Oriol. 1981. Comments on Anthropology of Tourism. *Current Anthropology,* October.

Smith, Valene. 1977. Introduction. IN Smith, Valene, Ed., *Hosts and Guests.* University of Pennsylvania Press.

Sutton, W.A. 1967. Travel and understanding: Notes on the social structure of touring. *International Journal of Comparative Sociology 8:218-23.*

Turner, Victor. 1969. *The Ritual Process: Structure and Anti-Structure.* Chicago. Aldine.

Wagner, Melinda Bollar. 1981. America's Alter Ego. *Radford Magazine.* Fall.

_____. 1982. Appalachia in America's Future: Alternative Cultural Forms. IN Simon, Rick, Ed., *Critical Essays in Appalachian Life and Culture.* Boone, NC: Appalachian Consortium Press.

Wagner, Melinda Bollar, Allen Batteau, and Archie Green. 1983. Images of Appalachia: A Critical Discussion. IN Buxton, Barry, Ed., *The Appalachian Experience: Proceedings of the 6th Annual Appalachian Studies Conference.* Boone, NC: Appalachian Consortium Press.

BEFORE THE YELLOW BUSES: THE QUEST FOR EDUCATION
   Convenor: Gerald Roberts, Berea College
Toward a Definition of Folk Schools
   Pauline Cheek, Mars Hill, North Carolina
Settlement School Goes to the People:
Pine Mountain School's Community Centers
at Big Laurel and Line Fork, 1919-1940
   Nancy Forderhase, Eastern Kentucky University
Northern Presbyterians in Southern Appalachia: Mountain Mission Schools
   Barbara Hempleman and Joan Moser, Warren Wilson College

Settlement School goes to the People: Pine Mounain School's Community Centers at Big Laurel and Line Fork, 1919-1940

by
Nancy Forderhase

"Located high above the road in a woodland in one of the wedge shaped valleys peculiar to this region of the Southern Appalachians is the little log cabin settlement. Pine Mountain towers above—a formidable barrier between it and the big outside world. Nevertheless, here lives a bit of 'the outside': two 'fotched-on' teachers, an industrial worker and a nurse supplement in many ways the meager educational opportunities through classes in cooking, preaching in the little log cabin house and in their own lives, the *gospel of health*."[1] This picturesque introduction to Line Fork, an extension center of Pine Mountain School, was a capsule description of mountain community work sponsored by the settlement school by the mid-1920's.

   Pine Mountain Settlement School, founded in 1913, was a complex and multifaceted institution. Building on the experience of the Hindman School which had begun in 1902, Katherine Pettit and Ethel deLong launched a project to establish a similar school in a more remote region of Kentucky on the 'far side' of Pine Mountain. These two energetic and enthusiastic women hired Mary Rockwell, an architect from Kansas City, to draw up a master plan for the school grounds and future buildings which would be built as money was raised. They embarked upon a fund raising campaign and began to construct the first buildings at the beautiful site near Greasy Creek.[2]

Those first four years from 1914 to 1918 were busy ones as Pettit and deLong struggled under primitive conditions to get the school operating efficiently. Several major buildings, including Big Log House, Laurel House, Open House, Far House and the Mary Sinclair Burkham School were constructed.[3] After the completion of the first structure, Big Log House, deLong, in an enthsusiastic publicity letter to friends, discussed the blend of the old and the new found in Big Log House: "Typical of its aims, too, is the juxtaposition of loom and dictionary, spinning wheel and globe, home-made baskets and victrola!"[4]

The women also coped with farm problems. During the first year, Katherine Pettit, who particularly enjoyed farming, supervised adequate ditching of the farm, the planting of grape vines, fruit trees and berry bushes, as well as a garden. In subsequent years, Pine Mountain workers, with advice from expert agriculturists, planned for future farm operations and constructed a barn and corn crib.[5] An equally important project was a reservoir designed to insure an adequate and pure water supply for the little community.[6] Getting supplies to Pine Mountain was a constant problem as well as a major expense for the school, and by 1916 Ethel deLong and another Pine Mountain worker, Celia Catheart, initiated a major fund raising drive with a goal of $50,000 for constructing a road over the mountain.[7]

The physical plant was one of enormous number of obligations borne by the Pine Mountain administrators. Organizing the school, supervising teachers and other personnel, and overseeing the children's physical welfare as well as their academic needs absorbed considerable time and effort on the part of deLong and Pettit as the capacity of the school expanded from thirty-three pupils in 1914 to seventy children in 1918.[8] In that year Ethel de Long's personal responsibilities increased as well when she married Luigi Zande, an Italian stone mason who had been working at Pine Mountain.[9]

Despite the backbreaking responsibilities shouldered by the two leaders of Pine Mountain Settlement School in those early years, they continued to plan for future directions of work for the school. Like their counterparts in the urban settlement houses, Pettit and deLong Zande believed their obligations extended beyond the school grounds to the community at large. From her earliest days in the mountains, Pettit had enjoyed visiting mountain families. Those friendships she cultivated in the community helped to create a positive image for Pine Mountain School and made its community work easier.[10]

Lack of health care was a pressing problem in the mountains. The women of Pine Mountain hired a nurse the first year of the school's existence to help cope with the medical necessities, and in 1917, the school sponsored a tonsils clinic.[11] In subsequent years, Pettit and deLong Zande invited dentists and doctors to participate in other clinics — dental, trachoma, hookworm, and the like.[12] While these medical services provided for the community were beneficial, Pine Mountain School workers were equally interested in preventive health care. In 1914, in an article written to garner support for the school in the *Smith Alumnae Quarterly*, deLong Zande deplored the lack of medical knowledge. "They are utterly ignorant of the germ theory of disease. Knowledge of sanitation is as foreign to them as it has long been to the rural population of the north..."[13] Pine Mountain workers continually taught preventive health lessons to the children of the school, and as time passed, carried these health lessons to children and families in the surrounding rural schools and communities.[14]

Pettit and Zande were concerned about other problems in the mountains beyond the boundaries of the school property. Although they frequently extolled the virtues of the individualistic mountain people in their publicity letters and fund raising efforts, they realized that excessive individualism, a well known mountain characteristic, could be a handicap in community development, especially as the mountain regions were experiencing dramatic changes. The railroad had wound its way into the remote parts of the hills, and this enhanced transportation mode was opening up the coal regions to exploitation. Like many workers from outside the region, Pine Mountain women, perhaps reflecting a widespread anxiety in American culture about the onrush of modernity, viewed these changes with ambivalence.[15] In an article written for *Survey* magazine, deLong Zande presented an idealized view of the mountain people, using such adjectives, as 'virile' and 'vigorous' to describe them. "Poverty you find; lack of knowledge you find; conditions needing to be corrected; still, here are a people to bring hope to America."[16] In another article in 1914, she warned of the problems related to the rapidly developing region:

> A new problem has come to the hills from the encroachments of the world outside. Every year the railroads push farther and farther into the hills for coal and timber, and the cheapest ideals come in with them first... (Young people believe) nice people outside do not work with their hands and they want to escape the contempt of the outside world. Store clothes, chewing gum, cigarettes, and superficial scorn of farm or housework, are its first gifts to the primitive folk in the heart of the hills.[17]

These negative aspects of modern society, at least in the eyes of the Pine Mountain women, became a special cause for concern with the outbreak of World War I. The war produced a great demand for coal, and this demand contributed to a tremendous boom in the coal fields of eastern Kentucky. Coal camps and new coal towns sprang up almost over night; indeed, the mountains were changing. In the summer of 1918, Zande visited Evarts, a rapidly growing coal town, and was most distressed at what she saw. She had visited the area three years before," ...when it was beautiful beyond my power to tell you, and where if people's homes weren't clean, they had at least privacy and beauty about them and a dignified independence, and no vulgar surroundings."[18] By 1918, the scene had changed. "... I felt that the worth-while things had been taken away; they cannot raise their food, they have no smoke house, no privacy, the houses being set so close together with no yards, the toilets were indecent, much worse than the old mountain method of no closets at all..."[19] Zande insisted that the inhabitants of the camp had learned only "...the veneer of modern life," and lamented that "...the future of the mountain people look(ed) very dark... unless the condition of mining camps can be elevated someway (sic)."[20]

In 1918 and 1919, Zande worked hard to find solutions to the problems of the mining camps. As a product of the fact-finding generation of the Progressive Era, she believed that the coal towns needed to be studied in order to identify the problems and to seek solutions to those problems. To that end, she searched for some organization which would sponsor a survey of the mining camps of Eastern Kentucky. Unable to persuade the Women's Board of Home Missions of the Presbyterian Church to take up the survey, Zande contacted persons connected with the Kentucky Child Labor Committee, and managed to get the National Child Labor Committee to conduct a survey of conditions in Harlan County.[21] Pine Mountain lent its financial support to the study in which results were published in *The American Child*.[22]

This increasing concern with changing conditions in the mountains led the women of Pine Mountain to seek support for neighborhood extension centers. Pettit and Zande were influenced by the ideas of John C. Campbell whom they had known during their years of mountain work. Early in 1918, Pettit wrote Campbell, asking him if Pine Mountain should undertake community work in its neighborhood.[23] Campbell strongly approved of the extension idea. He maintained that workers would receive more community support if they lived among the people and provided positive examples of a better way of life. Certainly Pine Mountain School was an outstanding example of an excellent educational institution, but he insisted that the school could be even more influential if some of its workers lived in the neighborhood.[24]

Campbell's endorsement of the extension centers seems to have been a positive source of support for projects they were already contemplating. Both Zande and Pettit had been in contact with Harriet Butler, formerly a worker at Hindman Settlement School. Butler and a friend, Dr. Grace Huse from St. Louis, were anxious to come to the mountains to begin an extension center. After a lengthy correspondence, the two women agreed to come to Kentucky to begin their work at Big Laurel in the spring of 1919. Pettit and Zande were especially anxious for this project, aptly labeled Medical Settlement, to get underway because they recognized the great health needs of the area and believed Huse and Butler would fill a void.[25]

Plans for Medical Settlement almost went awry early in 1919, when the newly constructed Mary Sinclair Burkham School House burned to the ground. Although the staff was saddened by the death of a worker and four students, Pettit and Zande insisted the work of the School should continue and they looked forward to the opening of Medical Settlement in the summer of 1919. Work began on the doctor's house that summer; by the fall, Dr. Huse and Miss Butler, her assistant, were firmly installed at the Medical Settlement and their medical work began.[26]

At the same time that Huse and Butler were establishing the beginnings of a working relationship in the community of Big Laurel, Pettit and Zande were going ahead with plans for a second extension center. In 1918, the county school superintendent, A.C. Jones, had asked Ethel Zande to supervise eleven district schools in the area near Pine Mountain School.[27] Anxious to improve the quality of the public schools, Zande enthusiastically took up the challenge. To aid her in this work, the Pine Mountain administrator chose Marguerite Butler, a young woman who had been associated with Pine Mountain School since 1914. Butler made frequent trips into remote parts of the county, and as a consequence, became intensely interested in extension centers. Her work provided the foundation for the newest community center, Line Fork.[28]

In the summer of 1920, the two young women, Isabella McClannan from Louisville, and Martha Van Meter of Lexington, spent the summer at Line Fork teaching school. They had gone to Line Fork at the urging of Mrs. Field, a school trustee. Members of the local community met and agreed to provide the logs and labor for a permanent extension center. The women at Pine Mountain School were especially encouraged by the project because the local citizens were providing the initiative and support for the center. They quickly recruited a nurse, teacher and industrial worker, and Line Fork became the second extension center to be established in the vicinity.[29]

The first five years of work at Big Laurel and Line Fork were a time of enthusiasm and perhaps unwarranted optimism. Pine Mountain's *Notes* contained frequent references to the work of the extension centers, and Zande's and Pettit's constant correspondence and appeals for funds from their long list of potential donors made financial support for the centers one of their highest priorities.[30] Brochures describing the work of Medical Settlement and Line Fork were prepared to send out to friends of Pine Mountain.[31] As Pettit and Zande looked forward to the future, those two outposts were just the beginning of work in the region. In a letter written to a potential donor in Lexington in 1919 Pettit stated: "As we see our extension work in about ten years from now, there will be a chain of such settlements through the country, all related to the Pine Mountain School and financed by it...I wish I could give you a picture of the various little communities where we want to start work,—Incline, the Line Fork, Little Laurel, Abner's Branch and Cutshin."[32]

Both Big Laurel and Line fork workers believed they should provide, by example, community development. Because the Medical Settlement at Big Laurel had the services of Dr. Huse, its primary role was to provide adequate medical attention to the people in the area. Although the local residents may have been a bit skeptical about the services of a woman doctor, they were quickly won over by the quiet ways of Dr. Huse who was called upon to perform innumerable medical tasks, from attention to 'risins', cuts and bruises to infections caused by hookworm and trachoma. The settlement school was especially proud of her work with delivering babies and caring for young children. "The only 'diplomy doctor' in a circle of twenty five miles, she rides her horse Billy by day and night, wet, hungry, muddy, frozen, exhausted, to take care of the sick and introduce little newcomers to a world incredibly happier and more wholesome because of her." Those newborn babies would be healthier toddlers because of the Medical Settlement's preventive health care programs and classes for young mothers. "As we remember the sore-mouthed, sore-eyed, sore-headed, fly-covered babies of three years ago, suffering too from sick stomachs or locked bowels, we rub our eyes at the rosy, fresh babies of today.[33]

Line Fork's activities were directed by a public health nurse, teacher and industrial worker, and much of the work was carried out through school activities. In a December, 1924 issue of *Child Health Magazine*, Anne Ruth Medcalf, the public health nurse at the community extension center, described some of the community projects that she had used to teach better health habits. In 1921, she began a health program for the schools. Through stories and games, she demonstrated simple health practices such as washing one's hands and hair and keeping the head free of lice. She weighed the children monthly and instituted toothbrush drills with shaved dogwood sticks which were used for toothbrushes. At the community center she began babies' clinics, and the center sponsored a dental clinic as well as a tonsils, adenoid and trachoma clinic.[34]

One community project sponsored through the school was a hot lunch program. The school bought the original equipment, and children brought from home, 'pokes' from which they made napkins, dish clothes and towels, and a curtain partition for the 'kitchen.' The children planned the meals, and cooked and served them. Initially, some opposition existed, as the boys in the school objected to doing 'woman's' work, and the students were reluctant to try new foods; however, the teacher and industrial workers, with moral support from the nurse, won the children over. Workers at Line Fork believed that valuable lessons in cooperation, nutrition and health standards were being taught by the hot lunch program. As they saw it:

> The development of cooperation is the keynote of community work. With this group of individualists, for such are the people in these creeks and hollows, it is seen that this spirit of cooperation must be developed from its very beginnings. The people will

come to 'meetings' simply because they are meetings. To graft upon these meetings the spirit of self-service and self-training, a feeling of comradeship, a desire to live and to feel the better things of life, is the problem of the industrial worker. It is felt that the work so far carried out has made some steps in this direction: the school lunches, the Sunday meeting for the adults for general discussion and interchange of ideas, and the recreational activities for the young people.[36]

From 1924 to the early 1930's, medical and community work continued at both centers. Dr. Huse and Harriet Butler left Big Laurel in 1924, and the Pine Mountain administrators found another woman doctor, Alfreda Withington, a former surgeon who had worked with the Red Cross in France.[37] Withington, like many other women who had come to the region in the past, fell in love with the mountains. In 1932, she published an account of her mountain experiences, printed over a three months' period in *The Atlantic Monthly*. Along with her descriptions of midnight trips into remote hollows to minister to the sick, she also included her impressions of the mountain people.[38] During Withington's tenure at Big Laurel, a series of teachers and industrial workers attempted to continue the community work begun by Huse and Butler. From the irregular reports sent to Pine Mountain, the impression was one of an uphill struggle to keep the community center going. Although workers attempted to maintain a garden and provide a variety of programs for the young people, attendance lagged. In 1929, a typical report to the Pine Mountain authorities, described the Big Laurel situation as "...one long struggle against the results of illiteracy, lack of employment, moonshine, guns, and a quick temper.[39]

> Here, where a large percentage of the older people, and even some of the younger ones, cannot read or write, there is little in the way of mental recreation that they could enjoy. Added to this is the fact that, due to the isolation of the settlement, there is little work to do outside of work in the mines and lumber camps, and one can see how many an hour that might profitably have been spent for reading or constructive work is turned over to mischief and unlawful practices. Where fathers and grandfathers for years past have been in the moonshine trade, and sons observe the free use of it every day, these same sons can hardly be expected not to follow in their fathers' footsteps. And breaking of the law brings fear of the law, hence the need for guns. And the carrying of guns, in turn, brings fear of each other, and a lowering of the value of life.[40]

Workers at Line Fork were experiencing some of the same frustrations as those being felt at Big Laurel. After the departure of Anne Ruth Medcalf in the mid-1920's, the two district schools in the Line Fork area returned to local control, and the workers lost an important source of contact with the community.[41] Recruitment of workers for the extension center was a constant problem, and it was difficult for the Pine Mountain staff to supervise the activities. In the fall of 1926, a middle-aged couple, Robert and Ida Stapleton, assumed duties at Line Fork. They had served as missionaries in Armenia, and Mrs. Stapleton, a doctor, provided medical attention for the neighborhood. The couple remained at Line Fork until 1937. While their presence at the extension center provided a continuity in leadership at Line Fork, their interminably detailed reports from the settlement, indicated that they were more interested in saving souls than in fostering community development.[42]

By the 1930's, the first generation of leadership at Pine Mountain was ending. Ethel deLong Zande had died of cancer in 1928, and Katherine Pettit was in retirement. The new director, Glyn Morris, reluctant to give up the Big Laurel settlement, searched for new directions and financing for the centers. One such plan suggested a cooperative farming project for the community, a grade school taught by teachers from Pine Mountain to prepare students for entry into the Settlement School, and continued medical work emphasizing a preventive health program and sanitation and clean up campaigns. Morris also cast about for financing for the centers and corresponded with New Deal agencies to see if federal funds could be found for the centers. None of these efforts were successful, and as the 1930's ended, Pine Mountain's work with extension centers was coming to an end.[43]

Pettit's and Zande's dreams of a chain of community extension centers in the shadow of Pine Mountain did not come to fruition. Nevertheless, their vision and efforts represented the idealism, energy and enthusiasm of a remarkable generation of women dedicated to the improvement of the quality of mountain life. Initial efforts for fund raising and staffing the two centers were successful. Interested donors gave their support to the project, and the women who staffed the centers at Big Laurel and Line Fork possessed the necessary idealism and self-sacrifice needed to work in the remote, mountainous regions of eastern Kentucky. Most of them were well acquainted with mountain life and understood the obstacles that would have to be overcome if the area were to develop.

By the mid-1920's, however, that initial enthusiasm waned. Although Ethel Zande showed a continual devotion to Pine Mountain, her time and attention were divided between her young children and her losing battle with the cancer that claimed her life in 1928.[44] Katherine Pettit was no longer a young woman by the middle of the decade, and she spent increasing periods of time away from Pine Mountain on extended trips.[45] As time passed, staffing became a problem. The self-sacrificing generation of Women Progressives no longer stood ready to take up the challenge of mountain work, and it became more and more difficult to recruit and supervise individuals who would work in those remote centers. Only a dedicated missionary couple like the Stapletons would choose to remain in the region, and their approach to community development was limited.

In his thorough and excellent study of Pine Mountain Settlement School, James S. Greene suggests that moonshining was a major problem in the area and inhibited community development. Although workers made major efforts to provide alternatives to the production and consumption of alcohol, they did not substantially alter the local mores.[46]

An even more fundamental problem recognized by mountain workers was the lack of community spirit and cooperation. Workers, not only at Pine Mountain, but elsewherre in eastern Kentucky, were continually frustrated by this problem and never seemed to overcome it. This frustration could be seen in the letters of Alice Cobb, the Pine Mountain secretary in the 1930's who wrote to friends familiar with the extension centers and asked their advice. Cobb explained that the extension centers were a financial burden on Pine Mountain School because it did not have the monetary resources necessary to support a good staff and effective program there. Yet Cobb was reluctant to give up the centers. "That means admitting that we've failed, and that the hopes, and unselfish labor, and thousands and thousands of solicited dollars spent there for these many years, have been sunk in a hole."[47] At the same time, however, she was pessimistic about the potential of the centers to effect fundamental changes in attitudes. She held out some hope for the children, but little for their parents whose habits and patterns of living were already set by the time they reached adulthood.[48]

Ruth Campbell, a friend who responded to Cobb's request for advice, was equally pessimistic about the future role of the centers. She pointed out that the people "...have been exposed to medical training, parties, preaching, at times to cooking and sewing classes and home nursing; and the children have been exposed to Pine Mountain for years on end; and yet Greasy has not changed its spots." She recognized, however, that the mountain communities were changing, and perhaps the extension centers in their present form were no longer needed "...with the increasing ease in getting about in that remote section. The families will ever more easily be able to go to Pine Mountain, with the shrinkage of mileage and the trucks and autos that are pervading even Greasy and its tributaries."[49] The visionary plans of Pettit and Zande had not been fully realized, but many of their ideas about community development would be revived in the 1960's by another generation of reformers who, with federal support, would 'rediscover' Appalachia.

FOOTNOTE

1. Anne Ruth Medcalf, handwritten manuscript, Line Fork File, 1920-41, Microfilm edition of the Pine Mountain Settlement School Collection, Berea College Archives, (hereafter cited as PMSS).
2. Articles of incorporation of the Pine Mountain Settlement School, PMSS; for a good description of the work of Mary Rockwell, see: Buildings of Mary Rockwell Hook, 1916-40 file; Publicity file, letters, 1914-1921, PMSS; the best description of all the school's activities during the Pettit-deLong Zande years can be found in James S. Greene, III, "Progressives in the Kentucky Mountains: The Formative Years of Pine Mountain Settlement School, 1913-1930," (Ph.D dissertation, Ohio State University, (1982).
3. For a brief, chronological account of Pine Mountain building activities, see Evelyn K. Wells, "A Record of the Pine Mountain Settlement School, 1913-1927," typescript, pp. 6-10, PMSS. (hereafter cited as Wells, History).
4. Ethel deLong to friends, Nov. 14, 1914, Publicity file, PMSS.
5. Wells, History, pp. 6-9, 31.
6. *Ibid.*, pp. 8-9
7. An extensive correspondence about the road fund can be found in the Pine Mountain records. See Celia Catheart letters in General Correspondence, 1916-18, PMSS. Catheart conducted a surprisingly sophisticated fund raising campaign in several cities. For a detailed account of the road campaign and subsequent problems connected with building the road, see James Greene, "Progressives in the Kentucky Mountains," pp. 335-48.
8. Wells, History, pp. 6-8.
9. *Ibid.*, p. 26.
10. Greene, "Progressives in the Kentucky Mountains," pp. 268-72; Katherine Pettit to Frances P. Tanner, Jan. 4, 1929, Katherine Pettit letter file, PMSS. Pettit's letter is typical of many examples in the Pine Mountain collection describing her friendship with the mountain people. She took frequent trips into the remote mountain areas and visited with the families.
11. Wells, History, p. 9
12. *Ibid.*, pp. 9, 11, 14-16, 37-40.
13. Ethel deLong, "The Appeal of the Kentucky Mountains," *Smith Alumnae Quarterly*, 3 (April, 1914), 164.
14. Wells, History, pp. 37-40.
15. From my research and reading on outsiders' views of Appalachia, I have come increasingly to believe that at least part of the interest in the region came from anxieties present in American culture caused by confusion and concern about the rapidly changing society of late nineteenth and early twentieth century America. Those who romanticized the simple, primitive nature of Appalachia seemed to be searching for traditional values which they might find in the isolated region—hence the fascination with the ballads and crafts of the region. I have been influenced by the account of antimodernism found in T.J. Jackson Lears, *No Place of Grace* (New York, 1981). See pages 60-96 for his discussion of the arts and crafts movement.
16. Ethel deLong, "The Far Side of Pine Mountain," *Survey*, 38 (March 3, 1917), 627-9.

17. Ethel deLong, "The Appeal of the Kentucky Mountains," *Smith Alumnae Quarterly*, 3 (April, 1914), 165.

18. Ethel Zande to Elisa Kendrick, July 15, 1918, Gen. Corr., 1916-18, PMSS.

19. *Ibid.*

20.. *Ibid.*

21. Ethel Zande to Mrs. F.S. Bennett, Aug. 27, 1918, Oct. 15, 1918, Jan. 9, 1919, March 17, 1919, April 22, 1919; Ethel Zande to Mary Carter, May 12, 1919, Ethel Zande to Mr. W.W. Swift, May 5, 1919; Ethel Zande to Calvin Kendall, Jan. 29, 1919, Gen. Corr., 1919, PMSS.

22. Mable Brown Ellis to Ethel Zande, June 26, 1919; Ethel Zande to Marguerite Butler, Aug. 20, 1919; Ethel Zande to Mabel Brown Ellis, c. late 1919, Ethel Zande to Owen Lovejoy, Feb. 16, 1920, Gen. Corr., 1919, PMSS; Mabel Brown Ellis, "Children of the Kentucky Coal Fields," *The American Child,* 1; (Feb., 1920), 285-405.

23. Katherine Pettit to John C. Campbell, Jan. 4, 1918, Gen. Corr, 1916-18, PMSS.

24. See brochure describing work at Big Laurel and Line Fork in Big Laurel file and Line Fork History file, PMSS. Although Campbell had died by the time these brochures were printed, he was still considered to be the leading authority on mountain work, and obviously the Pine Mountain administrators believed it important to receive an endorsement from Campbell's writings on the subject.

25. Ethel deLong to Harriet Butler, Jan. 17, 1917, Feb. 7, 1918; Katherine Pettit to Harriet Butler, May 7, 1918, July 15, 1918, Sept. 13, 1918, Feb. 26, 1919, Big Laurel file, PMSS.

26. Details of the fire are found in the Gen. Corr. file 1919. For a vivid account of the fire, see Marguerite Butler letters and Evelyn Wells letters, PMSS. The Gen. Corr. file of 1919 also contains many examples of appeals for money for Big Laurel. Typical letters include: Katherine Pettit to Mrs. B.F. Achison, May 22, 1919, Katherine Pettit to Dr. Norman Bridge, Sept. 6, 1919; Ethel Zande to Mary Carter, May 12, 1919, Ethel Zande to Mrs. Fitz, July 10, 1919, Gen. Corr. file 1919, PMSS.

27. Wells, History, pp. 11, 42; Abner C. Jones to Ethel Zande, July 8, 1919, July 14, 1919, Extension centers file, PMSS.

28. Marguerite Butler to Mother, c. June, 1919; Marguerite Butler to Jeannette, c. Summer, 1919; Marguerite Butler to Mother, c. Fall, 1919; Green, "Progressives in the Kentucky Mountains," pp. 296-303.

29. Wells, History, pp. 44-5; Isabella McLennan McMeeking, "The Beginning of Line Fork," typescript; Martha Van Meter, "Memories of Line Fork," typescript, Line Fork history file, PMSS.

30. *Notes from the Pine Mountain Settlement School,* Feb., 1919, Oct., 1919, Nov., 1920, Nov., 1921, March 1922, Nov., 1923, May 1924, April, 1926; (hereafter cited as *Pine Mountain Notes*); Angela Melville to Mrs. Haggin, March 13, 1920, Katherine Pettit to Mrs. F. Beachamp, Sept. 15, 1920, (Katherine Pettit) to Mr. Gray, Peabody Coal Company, Nov. 3, 1920; Ethel Zande to Mrs. Kate W. Baker, July 12, 1921, Ethel Zande to Gertrude Gladwin, Aug. 21, 1921, Ethel Zande to Anna Bogue, Oct. 25, 1921. Ethel Zande to Harriet Clarke, Aug. 21, 1922, Katherine Pettit to Ruth Dennis, June 20, 1922, Ethel Zande to Edna Fawcett, Oct. 25, 1922, Ethel Zande to Mary E. Abercrombie, Dec. 14, 1923, Ethel Zande to Darwin Martin, July 2, 1923, Ethel Zande to Elizabeth Bolinger, June 9, 1924, Katherine Pettit to Major D.J. Burchette, July 5, 1924, Ethel Zande to Luella Latta, Mar. 21, 1924, Gen. Corr. file, 1920, 1921, 1922, 1923, 1924, PMSS.

31. Brochures, Line Fork history file, Big Laurel file, PMSS.

32. Katherine Pettit to Miss Watson, Oct. 23, 1919, Extensions centers file, PMSS.

33. Brochure, c. 1923, Big Laurel file, PMSS. While the rhetoric in these brochures may have been somewhat exaggerated, the records indicate that the people in the neighborhood gratefully accepted medical assistance and did not object to a woman doctor.

34. Anne Ruth Medcalf, "In the Line Fork Country," *Child Health Magazine*, 5 (Dec., 1924), 503-511.

35. *Ibid.*

36. Elizabeth Smith, report, 1923-4, Line Fork file, PMSS.

37. Wells, History, pp. 43-4.

38. Alfreda Withington, "The Mountain Doctor," *The Atlantic Monthly*, 130 (Sept., Oct., Dec., 1932), 257-67, 469-77, 768-774.

39. Report of community work at Big Laurel, March 30, 1929, Big Laurel file, 1927-37, PMSS.

40. *Ibid.*

41. Wells, History, p. 45.

42. The Stapletons wrote long reports with minute, irrelevant details included in them. See those reports in Line Fork file, PMSS. For information about recruiting efforts, both for Pine Mountain school and the extension centers, see corr. file throughout the 1920's and 1930's.

43. Glyn Morris to Presbyterian Board of Foreign Missions, July 12, 1932, July 13, 1932, Tentative Outline for Social and Economic Survey of Big Laurel Community, n.d., Glyn Morris to Leonard Doyle, March 14, 1934, Glyn Morris to Earl Mahew, KERA, March 11, 1936, Glyn Morris to Rexford Tugwell, Sept. 26, 1936, Glyn Morris to C.R. Conley, Dec. 10, 1936, Big Laurel file, 1927-37, PMSS.

44. *Pine Mountain Notes,* Sept., 1928. PMSS. This issue contains a number of tributes to Ethel Zande.

45. Katherine Pettit to Miss Bartells, Aug. 13, 1925, Gen. Corr., 1925; Katherine Pettit to Miss Browne, Dec. 6, 1926, Gen. Corr., 1926, PMSS. Katherine Pettit was a very active woman and loved to travel. In addition to her frequent treks throughout the mountains, she traveled elsewhere. In 1926 she took a trip around the world, and in the early 1930's she went to Latin America. A small collection of her letters in the Pine Mountain papers includes her short diary of her trip to Latin America. It was quite an adventure.

46. Greene, "Progressives in the Kentucky Mountains," pp. 323-35.

47. Alice Cobb to Miss Campbell, Jan. 22, 1937, Big Laurel file, 1927-37.

48. *Ibid.*

49. Ruth Campbell to Miss Cobb, Feb. 2, 1937, Big Laurel file, 1927-37, PMSS.

ISSUES OF THEORY AND METHOD IN REGIONAL RESEARCH
    Convenor: Herb Reid, University of Kentucky
Class and Gender: New Theoretical Priorities in Appalachian Studies
    Sally Ward Maggard, University of Kentucky
Beyond the "Traditional Mountain Subculture":
A New Look at Pre-Industrial Appalachia
    Mary Beth Pudup, University of California, Berkeley

Class and Gender: New Theoretical Priorities in Appalachian Studies

by
Sally Ward Maggard

ABSTRACT

    Scholarship in Appalachian Studies has failed to address the contemporary and historical particularities of women's relationship to the region's social institutions and its history of social change. Treatment of Appalachian women includes: a romantic view of pre-industrial 'womenfolk' tilling soil and raising babies; a romantic view of post-industrial 'womenfolk' still raising babies while making quilts and apple butter; a ridiculing attack on Appalachian mothers which posits faulty child-rearing as the cause of a perpetuating culture of poverty; a slippery focus on 'the family' which assumes all household members have identical experiences and interests; and the 'Mother Jones syndrome' which attempts to recover Appalachian women as historical actors but which misrepresents their history as a collection of biographies of a few-great-women-of-courage.

    Recent efforts to document and analyze the everyday worlds of the region's working-class and ordinary people has made little improvement. Women are either missing in these works, or are treated as appendages of men. In the new social history of the region, women appear as flag-wavers who manage soup lines during industrial strikes, or as loyal family members who stand-by-their-men on a day to day basis. This otherwise promising work in Appalachian Studies too often turns out to be the history of the common *man* in a *man-made* world.

But what difference does it make to study women? Doesn't this just add a small overlooked piece of the pie — an addition which may add to the flavor of the pie but does not alter its basic structure? Recent research on the relationship between class-based and gender-based structures of power suggests othewise. Analysis informed by a sustained attention to gender challenges essential theoretical and methodological tenets of class analysis.

This paper examines the manner in which gender shapes the way women and men experience class, argues that the intersection of class and gender should be a theoretical priority in Appalachian Studies, explores new analytic tools for class/gender analysis, and re-examines recent social history of the region.

Introduction

During the decade since the Appalachian Studies Association was formed in 1977, the academic field of Appalachian Studies has come of age. Hundreds of courses are taught each year in college and high school classrooms. Research has been published in prestigious journals in each of the disciplines the Association incorporates. Books treating Appalachian topics have received national and international acclaim. Scholars from the United States and a number of other countries have established a solid international connection, as comparative research flourishes on many Appalachian-related issues.

Given the overall health of the field and the variety of scholars attracted by its interdisciplinary nature, it is surprising that so little Appalachian scholarship touches on the experiences of women and their place in the region's history. On the one hand, disturbing stereotypes of mountain women plague much Appalachian scholarship. On the other hand, many scholars deny that any new understanding of the region's history or social organization would emerge from a systematic examination of women's lives.

This paper offers some reflections on the treatment of women in Appalachian research and suggests that Appalachian scholars could do well by paying attention to recent developments in feminist and marxist scholarship. In particular, the argument is made that sustained attention to gender relations is essential to understanding such popular Appalachian Studies topics as work, community, class divisions, social change, and collective protest. The importance of gender relations in shaping the central features of a social system is equated with the importance of class relations. The interaction of gender and class is identified as a theoretical and empirical priority, and new analytic tools are discussed.

The many myths of the mountain woman

The 'Daisy Mae' image of mountain women as ignorant, barefoot, and pregnant has been slow to die. A variation of this image informs a ridiculing attack on Appalachian mothers by those social scientists who posit faulty child-rearing practices as the root cause of the region's persistent poverty (Loof, 1977, 1971; Weller, 1965).

Equally troublesome is the 'womenfolk' image of mountain women. 'Womenfolk' are said to be stalwart individuals who hold families together in times of trouble. Pre-industrial 'womenfolk' are described s industrious tillers-of-the-soil who have babies and stand by their men (Eller, 1982). Post-industrial 'womenfolk' are described as just as industrious — only now they are being industrious in coal camps or mill towns. They, too, have babies and stand by their men (Eller, 1982; Corbin, 1981). In other words, 'womenfolk' are thought to help things along somewhat, and they do bear the next generation. Other than that, they don't seem to have much to do with the course of history. Above all, 'womenfolk' are marginal people.

In a related theme, mountain women are 'family'. In a near reflex action, scholars in Appalachian Studies, and many other fields as well, tend to equate women with the family. The assumption is that the family is somehow the essence of women's existence. Or, as Catherine MacKinnon writes:

> ...women become 'the family', as if this single form of women's confinement (then divided on class lines, then on racial lines) can be *presumed* to be the crucible of women's determination (1982: 525).

'The family' here is a slippery concept with little explanatory value. It serves as a dumping—or lumping—ground for all of women's lived experiences.

Another treatment of mountain women could be called the 'Mother Jones syndrome'. Some scholars have begun to recognize Appalachian women as historical actors in their own right. Biographies and oral histories of women who were leaders in community organizations, work-place struggles, or social services do add information about women's behavior and their perceptions. But the danger in this approach is that it can misrepresent women's history as the collection of biographies of a few-great-women-of-courage.

The 'Mother Jones syndrome' in Appalachian Studies parallels what historian Gerda Lerner (1976) termed 'women's contribution history'. As feminist scholars began to search for women's historical record, their early focus on biography resulted in an 'add-on' approach which did not challenge traditional male-defined interpretations of history. The result in labor history provides a good example of the problems which resulted. Women were portrayed as supporting male leaders—an assumption which implies united women in a united movement and ignores conflict within social classes as well as the particular experiences of women (Lewis, 1981).

Recent scholarship in Appalachian Studies covering an exciting range of topics has dramatically improved our understanding of the region's history and social order. A growing number of scholars are at work unfolding the mechanics and consequences of the industrialization of the region, probing the causes of rebellion and containment of protest, detailing the nature of community life, scrutinizing the political economy of development strategies, and exploring sources of cultural and social psychological conflict (Eller, 1982; Corbin, 1981; Gaventa, 1980; Whisnant, 1980; Banks, 1983-84).

While this new scholarship represents fresh insights and approaches, as a whole it is seriously inadequate in its treatment of women (Maggard, 1984). Women are either missing in these works, or are treated as appendages of men. They appear as flag-wavers who manage soup lines during industrial strikes, or as loyal family members (usually as 'wives') backing up husbands, sons, fathers on a day-to-day basis. In short, we still know very little about the everyday lives, pressures, motivations, and histories of Appalachian women. Above all, we lack any sense of them as active human beings shaping the course of the region's history.

Introducing gender

But what difference does it make to study women? Doesn't this just add a small overlooked piece of pie — an addition which may add to the flavor of the pie but which does not alter its basic structure? Recent research on the relationship between class-based and gender-based structures of power suggests otherwise.

As a way to lead into this discussion, I will first touch briefly on some of the issues identified as feminist scholars began to attempt a coherent theory of women's oppression under contemporary capitalism. I will then point to some promising new direction in research on class and gender. Finally, I will speculate about the implications of these issues for Appalachian Studies.

Feminist theory has called attention to the ways in which reproduction and family roles operate to construct women's lives in general. These roles are said to result from a gender-based division of labor which creates a fundamental inequality between women and men felt throughout the social structure. *Gender* is identified as a social category as fundamental as social *class* in shaping the central features of the social system.

Marxist analysis locates individuals in the class structure by their relation to the prevailing means of production, a method heavily focused on economic relations and frequently on an individual's relationship to the wage economy. Any set of people with a common relationship to the economic order are said to form a class. It is assumed that these people share certain objective situations which shape the interests they will pursue ordinarily or in the long run, as well as their consciousness of the way their worlds operate.

Feminist scholars have been uncomfortable with the tendency among marxist practitioners to gloss over sharp differences in the objective conditions of the lives of women and men who occupy the same social class position. In addition, there is a tendency in class analysis to overlook forces which may divide women themselves who are grouped in the same class. Women's class position has traditionally been located simply by connections to men or to family.

Recent feminist scholarship challenges this oversimplification and attempts to identify the central importance of gender-based inequality to the class structure. The relationship between class and gender is one of the most pressing concerns on the agenda of these scholars today (Petchesky, 1983; Bene´ria and Sen, 1983; Goldberg, 1983; Kessler-Harris, 1982; Rapp, 1982; Hartmann, 1979; Tilly and Scott, 1978). It is increasingly recognized as a priority by marxist scholars as well (Burris, 1982; Benenson, 1980; Seccombe, 1980).

Efforts to link gender and class include arguments that women constitute a reserve labor force; that women's lower wages provide extra surplus value to employers; that women as managers of household consumption shore up capitalist consumerism; that housework and the reproduction of workers is central to capitalism; and that women as mothers reproduce not only laborers and capitalists, but also the psychodynamic of sexuality which underpins capitalism (Hartmann, 1979; MacKinnon, 1982; Rapp, 1979; Kaplan, 1982; Chodorow, 1978; Dalla Costa and James, 1979).

The overall result of these efforts is a general agreement that *production* and *reproduction* cannot be treated as separate spheres. The precise nature of their interaction, however, remains problematic. If production and reproduction are not separate, what is the specific relationship which binds them? To what degree are they autonomous? How does their interaction affect women's and men's interests and needs? When do class-based and gender-based interests lead women and/or men to act together collectively?

Debates about connections between gender and class are frequently at a high level of abstraction. They are complicated by competing and contradictory uses of such key concepts as patriarchy, reproduction and ideology, (Barrett, 1980; Burris, 1982). Attempts by radical feminists to treat patriarchal social relations as autonomous from (pre-dating and/or logically distinct from) capitalist economic relations are frought with problems. At the same time, efforts by socialist feminists to treat gender relations as simply 'functional' to (i.e. created by and/or subsumed under) the capitalist economic order are equally unsatisfactory.

Space does not permit a recounting of these arguments or an analysis of the conceptual snares which have developed. The central problem which remains, however, is the identification and interpretation of specific relationships at any given point in time between gender, modes of production, and modes of reproduction. Concrete, empirical, historical research is required to move analysis of the class/gender connection further.

Empirical research and new theoretical directions

Examples of this kind of research are available and help to illustrate the issues raised in this paper. Two very useful recent studies are (1) Ann Game's and Rosemary Pringle's analysis of gender, the labor process, and technological change and (2) Harold Benenson's dissertation on the structure of the American working-class since World War II.

The Game and Pringle study examines the reorganization of work and the allocation of jobs during periods when new technology is being introduced. The authors' intention was to build on research on the intentional use of technology by management as a tool to control the labor process and the work force (Edwards, 1979; Burawoy, 1979; Braverman, 1974). By considering the gender context of the implementation of technology, Game and Pringle expected to elaborate on the idea that the sexual division of labor is 'functional' to capitalism. They expected to find examples of manipulation of the sexual division of labor by management to obscure its own interests in technological innovation (such as the displacement of or deskilling of labor to increase productivity and surplus value).

Defining the sexual division of labor primarily as functional to capitalism suggests that gender inequality is merely a side effect of economic relations under class society. Or to put it another way, that gender inequality is a product of class exploitation.

Game and Pringle found, however, that they had to treat gender in a more fundamental manner in order to make sense of the reorganization of the work process and the division of jobs which accompanied technological change. Case studies of manufacturing, banking, retailing, computing, nursing, and housework, revealed a much more complex pattern of relations in the struggle over technology than was expected. Beyond the predicted, class-defined struggle between workers and management over machines, a second set of relations shaped the conflict — a struggle between males and females over work reorganization. Two sets of relations were operating, mediating, overlapping, and contradicting each other.

The logic of the reorganization of work that emerged was related to more than the dynamics of class conflict. It was also related to the dynamics of the construction of gender identity. Notions of 'masculinity' and 'femininity' are continually produced and reproduced through a myriad of daily rituals and processes — including relationships at work. Game and Pringle found that the reorganization of work and introduction of technology disrupts and threatens these processes. In such times, gender relations and the power relations they embody become highly visible. In each of the cases studied, the process of renegotiating disrupted gender relations was just as important as, and was frequently in conflict with, the imposition of capitalist rationalization of the labor process.

Game and Pringle concluded that gender inequality cannot be treated as a reflex or appendage of class relations. Instead, it must be considered as a central defining feature of contemporary capitalism. As they suggest:

> ...there is nothing inherent in a job that makes it male or female. The gender definition of jobs, and sexual division of labor, are socially and historically constructed (1983:23).

Study of the labor process, they concluded, requires that the economic real is examined in relation to the sexual and symbolic.

Harold Benenson (1980) also argues that our understanding of class society has suffered from an artificial isolation of the economic sphere from broader social dimensions. The result has been a failure to recognize deep divisions within social classes and profound differences between class modes of life.

Benenson argues first that the meaning and determinants of membership in a class are not the same for all members of that class. Second, he argues that this is because members' lives are structured by fundamental relations outside production. Third, he targets patriarchal relations of authority, the sexual division of labor, and family relations under capitalism as central aspects of social structure. These forces create sharp differences between men and women in determining class position and in modes of participation in class activity.

According to Benenson, traditional assumptions of class theory underlie our failure to understand class dynamics. His research on post-war occupational and family change in America challenges those assumptions. For instance, Benenson rejects the dominant orientation in class analysis which treats the unit of analysis as the individual worker. This orientation treats the worker as divorced from social relationships outside work, and the analysis occurs solely within the bounds of the economic structure of employment. This framework, he argues, marginalizes the significance of change in the social composition of the workforce, or in the family relationships and sexual bases of employment patterns.

Benenson also rejects conceptions of a uniform, generalized impact of narrowly economic processes (crisis, unemployment, labor intensification) upon an undifferentiated 'class as a whole'. He rejects the focus on the single employed family member (usually the male wage earner) as the simple connection of family members to the economy. He argues that indispensible forms of human activity — such as social reproduction — cannot be dismissed as unimportant or tangential to class analysis.

Static notions of workplace organization and job characteristics, an exclusive 'point of production' determinism in analyzing conditions which shape class relations, and a government statistics approach to classifying and counting the abstract individual wage-earner in isolation from family and social relationships are all problems in contemporary class analysis.

Rosalind Petchesky (1983) builds on Benenson's work. She places heavy emphasis on reproduction and fertility as determinants of female class position. Petchesky has proposed a class/work/fertility schema for analyzing different positions for women within traditionally defined class groupings. Her model points to distinct differences in experience, consciousness, and objective class position for "many if not most women" (1983: 232).

Both Benenson and Petchesky explore the way gender determines the experience of class, and vise versa. Age at the birth of first child, age at marriage, and number of children, for instance, are identified as variables in class position of females. Early marriage, early childbearing, and high fertility can lock young women into "a pattern of lifetime exclusion (from the labor force) which is established very early on" (Benenson, 1980: 188). On the other hand, the consequences of early marriage, early childbearing, and high fertility are quite different for middle-class professional men's wives than for working-class women who have similar fertility patterns.

This work, like Game's and Pringle's, demonstrates that the interaction between gender and class is essential to understanding capitalism, work, and other spheres of existence. Much additional research on class and gender recognizes the need for reconceptualization and new theoretical orientation. While space does not allow a full review, the following is a list of some additional priorities which have been identified:

(1) the identification of specific varieties of forms of patriarchal relations under differing modes of production, and over time within a single mode of production (Hamilton, 1978; Humphries, 1977);
(2) the redefinition of 'the community of work' as necessarily involving more than paid wage laborers (Tilly, 1981; Hufton, 1971);
(3) the role of unions in institutionalizing gender-based conflict which divides the working class and discourages females from union activism (Cook, et. al., 1984; Milkman, 1980; Jameson, 1977; Nash, 1975);
(4) the causes/consequences of the failure of reform movements to recognize women's interests and address gender inequality (Benéria and Sen, 1983; Graham, 1977; Hufton, 1971; Thomas, 1967);
(5) recognition of the difference in material interests and motivations during class conflict for women and men and analysis of the consequences for the form, content, and outcome of collective action (Petchesky, 1983; Goldberg, 1983; Jameson, 1977; Nash, 1977; Scott, 1974);
(6) analysis of 'class struggles of the marketplace' and their importance in class conflict along with analysis of the importance of women's roles as administrators of wages (Humphries, 1977; Rapp, 1982; Tilly, 1981; Tilly and Scott, 1978).

Empirical, historical research is required to suggest new directions scholars need to explore in order to develop a more successful understanding of the central features and history of contemporary capitalism (Burris, 1982; Barrett, 1980; Young, 1980; Seccombe, 1980).

Class, gender, and collective protest

In my own research I am exploring the connection between production, reproduction, and collective protest. In particular, I am looking at the gender context of two labor disputes in the early 1970s which mobilized large numbers of rural, working-class women in central Appalachia: (1) a strike for union recognition at a Pike County, Kentucky hospital where over two hundred non-professional hospital employees (five out of six of whom were women) maintained a twenty-four hour picket line for over two years; (2) a mining strike in Harlan County, Kentucky, which led to the formation of a militant women's auxiliary on behalf of one hundred eighty male miners striking for over fourteen months for union recognition.

The question of such a high degree of involvement by women in these coalfield community disputes underlies my research. The objective is to use the two cases of activism to explore factors which may help explain it. An intensive case study approach provides the opportunity to read back into the objective situations and motivations underlying collective protest.

As indicated above, recent research suggests the need to look at family situations to understand how women will react to political action, union organizing efforts, and strike activities. A central question of my research is the degree to which relationships inside households — not just relationships in the workplace — affect women's responses to work and their attitudes toward labor organizing.

The research involves an attempt to elaborate new analytic tools to study the class and gender intersection. In particular, theoretical priority is placed on the concept of *household economy* as a set of complex processes structured by *gender*, shaping different objective conditions for different members of a household, and thereby mediating the way individuals experience social *class*.

In order to empirically study household economy, I am developing profiles on the composition and operation of households for a sample of women involved in each strike. These profiles include information such as: the number of people living in each home and their kin or non-kin relationships; incomes, savings, and sources of non-cash support available to households; marriage and fertility characteristics; consumption patterns and debts; paid work experiences of all household members; division of labor regarding housework, child care, and the elderly; age and education; condition of the housing unit itself; and networks among women which link households.

I am also looking at variations in the ways women participated in the strikes. I am collecting data on the degree and form of women's involvement, women's perceptions and leadership roles, and the duration of involvement. I am particularly interested in discovering whether or not household patterns are related to protest involvement, the central empirical question of the research.

The two strike contexts permit comparison across an important dimension — relationship to the wage economy. In Pike County, women organized to protect their own wages and to control their own work situations. In Harlan County, women organized to protect wages earned by other members of the household and crucial to family survival. If household economy does influence women's collective protest within each case, it will be important to see if those patterns hold when women's relationships to waged labor vary. If patterns do not hold across cases, the breakdown of differences will be drawn out for theoretical speculation and the development of hypotheses for further research.

Conclusions

Recent theoretical and empirical work on class and gender raises questions about concepts and perspectives which inform Appalachian research. While important new scholarship on work, community, class divisions, and collective protest has greatly improved our understanding of the region, it is important that Appalachian scholars respond to challenges raised by innovations in class and gender analysis.

Attention to gender relations as they are historically constructed under contemporary capitalism suggests the need to redefine definitions of the composition of the workforce, bases of employment patterns, consequences of economic processes, the unit of and boundries of analysis of class relations, and the historical construction of work relations in the region. A more elaborate and differentiated definition of community structure and history is called for, as is a more complex approach to divisions within classes and family structure. The study of quiescence and rebellion becomes even more complex when new theoretical perspectives are applied to class, community, and family composition. These new perspectives help pave the way for more adequate incorporation of such social dimensions of class as age, race, and ethnicity.

The implications of recent work on class and gender for academic scholarship are substantial. They are equally important for those interested parxis of political activity. Efforts to challenge management control of the work process and production, efforts to build viable community organizations, efforts to address the state and advocate for human rights or peace all require an understanding of gender relations as historically constructed under capitalism.

Finally, the road to academic and practical reconsideration of basic assumptions about gender relations is difficult. Scholars and activists face much resistance in attempting to analyze or address gender-based inequality. The intellectual excitement that comes when conceptual blinders are lifted and more adequate understandings of our lives and histories begin to emerge is just reward for the effort. A new vision of a future family, work, community life based on human dignity and respect depends on incorporating an understanding of forces which divide and degrade people, including gender inequality.

REFERENCES

Banks, Alan
    1983-84   Coal miners and firebrick workers: the structure of work relations in two eastern Kentucky communities. Appalachian Journal 2 (Autumn-Winter): 85-102.

Barrett, Michele
    1980   Women's Oppression Today: Problems in Marxist Feminist Analysis. London: New Left Books.

Benenson, Harold
    1980   The Theory of Class and Structural Developments in American Society: A Study of Occupational and Family Change, 1945-1970. Ph.D. dissertation, New York University.

Benéria, Lourdes, and Gita Sen
    1983   Women's role in economic development: practical and theoretical implications of class and gender inequalities. Pp. 243-59 in Swerdlow, Amy and Hanna Lessinger (editors). Class, Race, and Sex: the Dynamics of Control. Boston: G.K. Hall.

Braverman, Harry
    1974   The Degradation of Work in the Twentieth Century, New York: Monthly Review Press.

Burawoy, Michael
    1979   Manufacturing Consent: Changes in the Labor Process Under Monopoly Capitalism. Chicago: University of Chicago Press.

Burris, Val
    1982   The dialectic of women's oppression: notes on the relation between capitalism and patriarchy. Berkeley Journal of Sociology 27: 51-74.

Chodorow, Nancy
    1978   The Reproduction of Mothering; Psychoanalysis and the Sociology of Gender. Berkeley: University of California Press.

Cook, Alice H., Val R. Lorwin, Arlene K. Daniels (editors)
    1984   Women and Trade Unions in Eleven Industrialized Countries. Philadelphia: Temple University Press.

Corbin, David Alan
    1981   Life, Work, and Rebellion in the Coal Fields: the Southern West Virginia Miners, 1880-1922. Chicago: University of Illinois Press.

Dalla Costa, Mariarosa and Selma James
    1979   The Power of Women and the Subversion of the Community. Bristol, England: Falling Wall Press.

Edwards, Richard C.
　　1979　　Contested Terrain: the Transformation of the Workplace in the Twentieth Century. New York: Basic Books.

Eller, Ronald D.
　　1982　　Miners, Millhands, and Mountaineers: Industrialization of the Appalachian South, 1880-1930. Knoxville, Tennessee: The University of Tennessee Press.

Game, Ann and Rosemary Pringle
　　1983　　Gender at Work. London: George Allen and Unwin.

Gaventa, John
　　1980　　Power and Powerlessness: Quiescence and Rebellion in an Appalachian Valley. Chicago: University of Illinois Press.

Goldberg, Roberta
　　1983　　Organizing Women Office Workers: Dissatisfaction, Consciousness, and Action. New York: Praeger.

Graham, Ruth
　　1977　　Loaves and liberty: women in the French Revolution. Pp. 236-54 in Renate Bridenthal and Claudia Koonz (editors). Becoming Visible: Women in European History. Boston: Houghton Mifflin Company.

Hamilton, Roberta
　　1978　　The Liberation of Women. London: Allen and Unwin.

Hartmann, Heidi
　　1979　　The unhappy marriage of marxism and feminism: towards a more progressive union. Capital and Class 8 (summer).

Hufton, Olwen
　　1971　　Women in revolution. Past and Present 53 (November): 90-108.

Humphries, Jane
　　1977　　Class struggle and the persistence of the working-class family. Cambridge Journal of Economics 1 (September): 241-58.

Jameson, Elizabeth
　　1977　　Imperfect unions: class and gender in Cripple Creek, 1894-1904. Pp. 166-202 in Milton Cantor and Bruce Laurie (editors). Class, Sex, and the Woman Worker. Westport, Connecticut: Greenwood Press.

Kaplan, Temma
　　1982　　Female consciousness and collective action: the case of Barcelona, 1910-1918. Signs 7 (spring): 545-566.

Kessler-Harris, Alice
　　1982　　Out to Work: A History of Wage-Earning Women in the United States. New York: Oxford University Press.

Lerner, Gerda
　　1976　　Placing women in history: a 1975 perspective. Pp. 349-67 in Carroll, Berenice A. (editor). Liberating Women's History: Theoretical and Critical Essays. Urbana: University of Illinois Press.

Lewis, Jane
    1981   Women lost and found: the impact of feminism on history. Pp. 55-72 in Spender, Dale (editor). Men's Studies Modified: the Impact of Feminism on the Academic Disciplines. New York: Pergamon Press.

Loof, David H.
    1977   Assisting Appalachian families. Pp. 102-12 in Williamson, J.W. (editor). An Appalachian Symposium: Essays Written in Honor of Cratis D. Williams. Boone, North Carolina: Appalachian Consortium Press.

    1971   Appalachia's Children: the Challenge of Mental Health. Lexington, Kentucky: University Press of Kentucky.

MacKinnon, Catharine A.
    1982   Feminism, marxism, method, and the state: an agenda for theory. Signs 7 (summer): 515-44.

Maggard, Sally Ward
    1984   The Roots of Social Action: Women, the Industrial Experience and the Land in Central Appalachia. Paper presented at the Southern Sociological Society's 47th Annual Meeting. Knoxville, Tennessee. April 19.

Milkman, Ruth
    1980   Organizing the sexual division of labor: historical perspectives on 'women's work' and the American labor movement. Socialist Review 49 (January-February): 95-150.

Nash, June
    1975   Resistance as protest: women in the struggle of Bolivian tin-mining communities. Pp. 261-71 in Ruby Rohrlich-Leavitt (editor). Women Cross-Culturally: Change and Challenge. The Hague: Mouton Publishing.

Petchesky, Rosalind Pollack
    1983   Reproduction and class division among women. Pp. 221-41 in Swerdlow, Amy and Hanna Lessinger (editors). Class, Race, and Sex: the Dynamics of Control. Boston: G.K. Hall.

Rapp, Rayna
    1982   Family and class in contemporary America: notes toward an understanding of ideology. Pp. 168-87 in Thorne, Barrie with Marilyn Yalom (editors). Rethinking the Family: Some Feminist Questions. New York: Longman.

Rapp, Rayna, Ellen Ross, and Renate Bridenthal
    1979   Examining family history. Feminist Studies 5 (spring): 174-200.

Scott, Joan Wallach
    1974   The Glassworkers of Carmaux: French Craftsmen and Political Action in a Nineteenth-Century City. Cambridge: Harvard University Press.

Seccombe, Wally
    1980   Domestic labor and the working class household. In Fox, Bonnie (editor). Hidden in the Household. Toronto: The Women's Press.

Thomas, Edith
    1967   The Women Incendiaries. London: Secker and Warburg.

Tilly, Louise A.
    1981   Paths of proletarianization: organization of production, sexual division of labor, and women's collective action. Signs 6 (winter): 400-17.

Tilly, Louise A. and Joan W. Scott
    1978   Women, Work and Family. New York: Holt, Rinehart and Winston.

Weller, Jack
    1965   Yesterday's People: Life in Contemporary Appalachia. Lexington, Kentucky: University Press of Kentucky.

Whisnant, David
    1980   Modernizing the Mountaineer: People, Power, and Planning in Appalachia. New York: Burt Franklin.

Young, Iris
    1980   Socialist feminism and the limits of dual systems theory. Socialist Review 50/51 (March-June): 169-88.

Beyond the "Traditional Mountain Subculture": A New Look At Pre-Industrial Appalachia

by
Mary Beth Pudup

"Let us now come to the Highlands—a land of promise, a land of romance, and a land about which, perhaps, more things are known that are not true than of any part of our country."

John C. Campbell
The Southern Highlander and His Homeland

Introduction

Appalachian Scholars are fond of quoting John Campbell on the persistent misunderstanding of the region, and indeed much recent scholarship has had the explicit goal of setting the historical record straight. This paper attempts a critical, yet friendly reading of this work, arguing that despite its significant achievements, certain aspects of Appalachia's economic and social history remain poorly understood. The central problem identified is a simplistic view in preindustrial Appalachia.

While the region's twentieth century industrial history has been carefully analyzed, the preindustrial era largely remains a *terra incognita* surrounded by dense thickets of "invented tradition." Analysis of both preindustrial economic activities and social class formation has been effectively precluded by adherence to romantic notions of a traditional mountain subculture. The net result has been a static portrayal of preindustrial Appalachia as a halcyon backdrop to the region's harsh industrialization experience. This paper takes a new look at the preindustrial era. It argues that during the nineteenth century, local economic and social pre-conditions were established which propelled the region along a path of dependent capitalist development. The term dependent is used specifically to denote Appalachia's historic reliance on absentee capital financing of industrial development, and how such development took place to satisfy non-local resource demands.

The paper is divided into two parts. In the first section, I attempt to demonstrate the continuity between old and new visions of preindustrial

Appalachia as a regional subculture. I then discuss how this essentially cultural definition of the era has obscured some of the structural processes underlying the region's economic develoment trajectory. In the second section, I make similar arguments concerning preindustrial social processes. I suggest the search for appropriate models of Appalachian regional development has proceeded at the expense of concrete historical analysis. As a result, a social relations internal to the region have been made to conform *a priori* with a variety of frameworks, prohibiting the region's history from "speaking for itself." In the conclusion I suggest some priorities for future regional historical research.

A few caveats are in order. By openly criticizing the definition of the "traditional mountain subculture," I do not wish to imply that preindustrial Appalachia — or the present-day region for that matter — somehow lacks culture. Indeed there is considerable evidence to the contrary, although rarely is it enunciated in terms of a coherent concept of culture. Second, by structurally linking the preindustrial and industrial economics, I am not suggesting they represent a teleological path of development. What happened in Appalachia at the turn of the century was the conjunction of several historically constituted processes which are the subject of the author's dissertation (Pudup forthcoming). Finally, this paper raises issues specific to research on the central Appalachian coal fields, although it bears relevance for the study of non-coal dominated areas of the region as well.

Beyond the "Traditional Mountain Subculture"

A commonplace assertion voiced at the turn of the twentieth century held that Appalachia was a region where nothing much had changed since the earliest years of its settlement. Freeholding households cultivated small subsistence plots in 1900 just as they had during the 1820's, using the most rudimentary implements of tillage. Appalachians engaged in little commercial intercourse among themselves and, taken together provided few commercial links between Appalachia and the rest of the nation. Since transportation routes followed meandering creek beds, movement on foot and horseback was plagued by either mud or dust, depending on the season. The various waves of immigration that had broken on American shores throughout the nineteenth century had largely bypassed the region. Settled principally by persons of Scotch-irish, German, and English extraction, these groups mutiplied and divided among themselves, lending Appalachia a rather distinct and coherent social and cultural identity.

These perceived conditions captured the imagination of many contemporary observers of the American scene. In scholar journals and popular literary magazines of the day, Appalachia became identified with melancholy, bucolic notions of a traditional American past. As self-subsisting tillers of the soil, the region's people seemed to have preserved much that was considered intrinsically American: rugged individualism and a dogged determination to survive. From this identification of place with time, what Henry Shapiro has called the "invention of Appalachia," emerged a vision of Appalachia as a regional subculture — at once part of and apart from America. This powerful vision has of late received extensive critical scrutiny, most notably by Shapiro himself (1978) and David Whisnant (1983).

Shapiro's and Whisnant's books, *Appalachian On Our Mind* and *All That Is Native And Fine,* respectively, concern material and ideal aspects of a preindustrial Appalachian culture. They question the veracity of our understanding of that culture, given the ways it has been perceived by and for us. Both have been enormously influential in re-interpreting the historical development of Appalachian regional identity, which, as they demonstrate, has been consistently defined by people and institutions located outside the region. In this sense, both have been much-needed palliatives to the seemingly endless stream of literature depicting Appalachia as a region where "time stood still," inhabited by "yesterday's people."

So, too, are they part of a wider recent effort to re-interpret the actual economic and social history of the region. This history has been written most frequently as an isolated and backward subculture becoming, in essence, ever more backward and isolated. Through an extraordinary interpretive leap, the region once celebrated as a traditionally American subculture became condemned as a culture of poverty. Historical accounts singled out Appalachia's social and economic isolation as the root cause of all its problems.

Recent scholarship has turned this historical argument on its head (e.g. Lewis, et. al. 1978; Gaventa 1980; Eller 1982). Chronic regional poverty, it is argued, has resulted not from isolated but from the very opposite: Appalachia's particular form of integration into the United States economy and society. A rather glaring light is cast on the irony that Appalachia's subsistence economy was "discovered" and codified as traditionally American at precisely the time it was being undermined by capitalist development. The agents of disruption were absentee capitalists who flocked to the region and gained control over its natural resources. In doing so, they exerted a form of colonial domination, forever altering the intimate relationship between the land and the people. Since then, the argument goes, the region has been subject to national and international economic fluctuations over which it has had no control. The Appalachian people have derived few of the benefits which can accompany capitalist development. A new and equally powerful vision thus emerged from recent scholarship: that of a region suffering cultural, economic, and social deprivation at the hands of outsiders.

This new vision of Appalachia substantially incorporates the one put forth at the turn of the century. Both share an idealized view of the preindustrial era. In fact, although recent scholarship has been highly critical of the invention of Appalachia as a regional subculture, it has breathed new life into melancholy stereotypes. This suggests certain blind spots persist in "corrective" scholarship. I would argue these blind spots are two: the identification of Appalachia's preindustrial economy solely as a subculture; and a failure to analyze the region's history as continuous process. I would argue further that the latter problem follows rather directly from the former.

Historian Ronald Eller's work renders well the continuity with early idealizations of preindustrial Appalachia. He begins his book *Miners, Millhands, and Mountaineers* (1982:3) thusly:

> "Few areas of the United States in the late nineteenth century more closely exemplified Thomas Jefferson's vision of a democratic society than did the agricultural communities of the southern Appalachians. Long after the death of Jefferson and long after the nation as a whole had turned down the Hamiltonian path toward industrialism, the southern Appalachian Mountains remained a land of small farms and scattered open-country villages.... Nowhere did the self-sufficient family farm so dominate the culture and social system as it did in the Appalachian South."

In Eller's view, one more generally shared by regional scholars, the preindustrial era was governed by the "traditional mountain subculture." This subculture was characterized by a set of material practices surrounding subsistence production (and reproduction) of individual households (e.g. farming and home manufacturing), and related *mentalite* emphasizing strong kinship affiliations, individualism, and traditionalism (cf. Knipe and Lewis 1971:26-27). Perhaps the most frequently claimed element of the traditional mountain subculture is the deep attachment the Appalachian people developed with the land on, and from which they lived. To quote Eller again at length (1979:85):

> "Perhaps more than in other rural areas, the physiography of the land itself shaped the development of culture and social patterns in the mountains. Each community occupied a distinct cove, hollow, or valley and was separated from its neighbors by the rim of mountains or ridges.... Economic and social activities were largely self-contained within these geographic "bowls," with individual households relying upon themselves or their neighbors for both the necessities and pleasures of life. The land was such a dominant factor in mountain culture that neighborhoods often drew their names from the creeks or branches which penetrated the settlement..."

Rather than merely attack the obvious romanticism of Eller and his counterparts, it is important to emphasize that their view of the traditional mountain subculture is not simply an intellectual one, but a profoundly political one as well. After decades of scholarship depicting Appalachia as a culture of poverty, a new generation of scholars, many with roots in the region, clearly perceived the need to assert a new view of Appalachia which re-claimed for its people a role as rational human agents. Moreover, eulogizing a benevolent mountain subculture helped this generation of scholars carve into sharp relief the economic and social dislocations accompanying capitalist development in the region.

My criticism of this view of preindustrial Appalachia is that it fails to recognize that the material practices which formed part of the region's subculture were *also* the structural bases of the region's preindustrial economy. Preindustrial economic activities, like subsistence farming, are frequently described but rarely analyzed as such. One is given the distinct impression that the region lacked an economy until the twentieth century. The problem bears directly upon and is perhaps best illustrated by a further problem: the failure to consider Appalachia's economic development as a continuous historical process.

Appalachian economic history, as written, is polarized between subsistence agriculture (nineteenth century) and natural resource extractive industrial development (twentieth century). A decade or two of absentee capital investment in resources and transportation is the bridge spanning the two eras. Historians correctly signal absentee capital penetration as the harbinger of change. But they seem to accept uncritically that industrial development would be dependent upon absentee capital financing. The entire process of industrialization in Appalachia is analyzed consistently as a response to raw material demands existing outside the region. Scholars have rarely asked why such demands did not exist locally, or why investment in extractive industries was not financed by local capital. So quick to affirm the deleterious relationship between absentee capital and Appalachia's people and resources, they have not yet explored what alternative development path the region's economy might have followed.

Implicit acceptance of the necessary role played by absentee capital suggests that the preindustrial economy has not been examined, in dynamic terms, for its self-generating development potential. For this reason, there exists little ostensible continuity between the preindustrial and industrial eras of economic history. A more correct view, I believe, is that the preindustrial economy failed to generate demands for the region's raw material resources. By the same token, it failed to generate capital locally which might have been invested in industrial development. National demands for raw materials and absentee capital filled these local vacuums, In this view, absentee capital and demand are not just the historical bridges spanning the preindustrial and industrial economies, but are the structural bridges as well.

In his attempt to advance regional debates beyond the colonial hypothesis, Richard Simon has been the only scholar to point to this structural relationship, although he does so only in passing. Simon's work analyses the "development of underdevelopment" in southern West Virginia, has wider applicability throughout the coal fields. He claims:

> "...it was inevitable that in the undeveloped West Virginia economy in 1880 resources would be developed by absentee owners for export....There was no internal market in which manufacturing could be developed and from which commodities could be exported or coal consumed. The only market for West Virginia's resources was in the industrial northeast" (1981:190).

A complex argument is made by Simon, one part of which is that West Virginia lacked the capacity for developing its own resources. But for what reason? As Simon continues:

> "...there was little financial capital in West Virginia with which to build the railroads and open the mines... In the southern part of the state, which had remained agricultural, almost the entire initial investment had come from outside capital" (1981:180-181).

Thus Simon relates "inevitable" absentee capital investment to the fact that southern West Virginia had "remained agricultural." He does not specify, however, just what it was about the area's agriculture that forged this relationship.

The need for such specification becomes apparent in light of the historical development of other regions in the United States (and world) whose economies were also governed by agricultural production (cf. Moore 1966; Brenner 1976). For different forms of agriculture can, and indeed have precipitated, distinct patterns and processes of industrialization, depending on such things as the social organization of agriculture, the extent to which it is integrated into markets, and the particular structure of the markets themselves. In the midwest, for example, a highly competitive and commercialized household agriculture gave rise to industries both supplying farm inputs and processing farm outputs. Such industries developed in tandem with agriculture, through investments made by independent classes of merchants and manufacturers. Midwestern agriculture was both a source of capital and a market for manufacturing in the region. By contrast, in the south, plantation slavery was the predominant form of commercial agriculture. The plantation system fettered that region's industrial development during the antebellum era. Its social and economic legacies contributed to the narrowly-based, and highly repressive nature of subsequent southern industrialization (cf. Post 1982; Billings 1979, 1982).

The historical differences between the midwest and the south illustrate some of the ways in which agricultural production has profoundly shaped regional industrialization. This general point holds for the central

Appalachian region. Coal industry development in Appalachia did not result solely from the unfolding of some inexorable geographic logic of the industry, or of the larger economy of which it formed a part. Although the coal industry arouse to satisfy demands existing many hundreds of miles away from the region, its specific timing and investment patterns were largely governed by prevailng conditions of the local preindustrial economy.

However quaint or picturesque it appears in hindsight, the preindustrial economy has exactly that — an economy — and as such possessed its own internal logic. Subsistence production practices satisfied most demands of the local population. The household was not only a "unit of production and consumption" as in the midwest, but more specifically, the household was the unit of consumption for most of what it produced. This resulted in a shallow, if not non-existent social division of labor in the mountains which was manifest in the lack of an internal commercial market for goods and services. Thus, industries which might have tapped the region's raw material base, like farm implement manufacture, did not develop. Local market conditions delayed industrialization until external demand for coal and timber penetrated the region.

This same set of conditions also had implications for the pattern of investment in resource-based industries. Households did produce surpluses, but these were strictly what remained after subsistence needs were met. Surplus items were traded with local merchants, but local commerce took place on barter terms, effectively prohibiting either trading party from accumulating much in the way of liquid capital assets. These barriers to local capital accumulation generated a chronic local shortage of money capital. The net effect was that absentee capital was the principal source of investment in the region's resource industries and transportation infrastructure.

From the Region as Class to Classes with the Region

A related set of issues will now be raised concerning how regional scholarship has treated social class in preindustrial Appalachia. There seem to be two main currents in its treatment. The first derives from the colonial model and thus treats the region *tout court* as a class exploited by outsiders. The second equivocates, to the extent that it suggests class distinctions might have existed during the preindustrial era but didn't matter, and what really matters is the class structure created by capitalist development. The argument in this section is that both share an idealized view of preindustrial Appalachia, which fails to account for how the preindustrial class structure left "openings" for the entrance of an absentee capitalist class. Furthermore, although the importance of a "local elite" is often hinted at, the composition and actions of this elite are rarely specified.

A spirited debate among regional scholars took place during the 1970's over what new theoretical framework would best explain Appalachia's relationship with the rest of the United States (and world). Scholars sought to remove the stigma of isolation attached to culture of poverty theories, and demonstrate how Appalachia's endemic poverty had resulted from the opposite condition. A variety of frameworks were advanced, including the dependency model (Arnett 1978); the world system (core-periphery) model (Conti 1979; Walls 1978); the uneven development model (Simon 1978); and the internal colonialism model (Lewis and Knipe 1978). The last of these has exerted the most pervasive influence on regional scholarship.

Indeed, the colonial model has gained such currency that its central tenets need not be reviewed here. Owing to its undeniable appeal, the model single-handedly re-directed regional research. It underpins John Gaventa's pivotal study *Power and Powerlessness* (1980) as well as Ronald Eller's *Miners, Millhands, and Mountaineers* (1982). The colonial model provided the raison d'etre for the monumental work of the Appalachian Land Ownership Task Force (1983), and a host of other works too numerous to mention.

To be sure, the colonial model has been dealt its fair share of criticism. David Walls, (1978:326) in particular, has found the model "strained at some key points—" especially on the issue of forced, involuntary entry. Richard Simon has been perhaps the most vociferous critic of the colonial model. He concedes that it transcends merely blaming the victims of poverty. But he suggests the model implies absentee capitalists behave in a manner inherently different from local caipitalists (Simon 1981). Furthermore, it imputes a degree of self-conscious, cohesive action to absentee capitalists belied by historical evidence.

But perhaps most important for Simon, the colonial model reifies the idea that Appalachia has been exploited by outsiders. The region is assigned a one-to-one correspondence with social relations of exploitation and domination, and thus is portrayed as a class in itself (Simon 1983-84). In doing so, the colonial model fails on its own terms in explaining at least one central feature of the so-called "colonialization complex." This failure stems from its grossly over-simplified view of social life in the mountains prior to capital penetration. Somewhat ironically, then, the colonial model actually perpetrates some of the very same stereotypes it sets out to quash.

An unabashedly romantic view of preindusrial Appalachia is the fulcrum on which the colonial model rests. The colonial model necessarily endorses this view, since its entire analysis centers on the violence done to the traditional mountain subculture by outside agents of industrialization. Such romanticism enforces a simplified view of preindustrial social life. Preindustrial Appalachia is likened to a "society approximating an Asian or African country" and its people described as "natives" and "illiterate, simple mountain farmers" (Knipe and Lewis 1978). There is a double irony here. By imputing social simplicity to African and Asian countries, which in fact has been shown otherwise, the colonial model evinces a racism akin to that it bemoans. Furthermore, the colonial model helps to immortalize the commonplace stereotype of a region inhabited by illiterate natives.

But much more than irony is at stake. An essential role in establishing and maintaining the "colonialization complex" is given to "the natives who became colonizers of their own people" (Knipe and Lewis 1978:22). Local colonizers are dependent upon absentee capitalists and thus ally themselves with outsiders. Yet the colonial model does not account for the emergence of the local colonizers themselves. In fact, with its elementary social view of preindustrial Appalachia, it cannot do so. To the extent that it presupposes a region populated by simple country folk, one is left to wonder exactly who the local colonizers could have been.

What is clearly missing from the colonial interpretation of Appalachian regional development is an understanding of actual local social conditions during the preindustrial era. The need to formulate such an understanding can be found, took, in other regional scholarship which departs from the colonial model. Its point of departure lies in explicitly assigning to "local elites" a significant role in capitalist development. Since it shares a common set of themes, this scholarship need not be reviewed in its entirety. Only the central tenets of the argument will be discussed here.

The common starting point is that social class divisions were virtually absent or unimportant to preindustrial Appalachia. Statements to the effect that "we're all kin" are taken as evidence of scant social differentiation among the population. Thus, kinship displaced class, while the preindustrial economy itself exerted a levelling effect on class differentiation. Once this egalitarian view is asserted, however, it is usually followed by a somewhat sheepish admission that while class was sublimated, class distinctions did exist, and eventually became very important. To quote Eller (1982:11-12):

> "The dominance of a democratic ethos, however, did not mean the absence of a class structure in nineteenth century Appalachia....Class distinctions did exist in the larger community, county and region...The southern mountain country contained a minority of wealthier, landed families whose economic power and political influence set them off as elite group...these wealthier families provided the political leadership in the mountains and often controlled local commercial enterprises...their political influence, access to resources, and contacts with the outside placed mountain elites in a strategic position to benefit from economic change."

According to this argument, class remained a latent source of social division in the mountains until the late nineteenth century, when absentee capitalists began taking notice of the region's resources. Only then was it made manifest. The question then turns to what role the local elite performed during capitalist development. The consensus here is that local elites were followers rather than leaders, merely riding the development bandwagon drawn by outsiders. Citing evidence from local newspaper editorials, Arnett (1978:36) states "many of the citizens of the area— especially merchants, professionals, and real estate agents— welcomed capitalists, whatever their nationality, with open arms." Eller echoes this view (1982:57): "native middle class entrepenuers served as effective brokers for absentee investors and as energetic missionaries of the new industrial faith." In doing so, Conti (1979-80:52) claims "this local leadership pursued essentially a 'modernizing' role, diffusing change from the American metropolis to the Appalachian hollers." Only Batteau (1971:32) has assigned to local elite a more provocative role: "in every form of major development...the pioneering enterpreneurs were not outsiders, but locally born and raised entrepeneurs from such towns as Hazard and Paintsville."

In large measure, this argument surrounding the role of local elites is founded on a few well-worn examples of local tycoons like John C.C. Mayo, C. Bascom Slemp, and Floyd Day. Nonetheless, these men, particularly Paintsville native John Mayo, are treated as the exception rather than the rule (cf. Caudill 1982; Turner and Traum 1984). Thus, although scholarship admitting the existence and importance of local elites represents a saluatory departure from the strictly colonial interpretation of Appalachian development, a number of issues remained unresolved by it.

One may ask first whether Batteau is correct in asserting members of the local elites were actually the "pioneering entrepeneurs"— that is, leaders rather than followers. If so, this would certainly destroy more than a few shibboleths within the domain of Appalachian studies. But more important, one may ask what, if any, was the "typical" situation in the mountains. Did each county have its own local elite, or was the elite "really" only a handful of prominent individuals region-wide? Existing scholarship identifies an elite in nearly every county, but, because such work paints the picture in broad strokes only, it tells little about the actual composition of the elite at the local level, and the routine detail of their activities both before and during Capitalist development. Finally, to the extent that the local elite is accorded economic and political power and prestige, one may ask why its members did not oppose absentee capital penetration, and pursue industrial development by themselves. Local demand for the region's raw materials might have been scarce, but external demand was mounting. Why then did local elites not rise to meet this demand?

The task of resolving these issues, I would argue, must begin with an understanding of the social class structure that had emerged in preindustrial Appalachia in tandem with its economy. This economy had been governed by a subsistence logic, with little extra-household commerce or industry. Limited surplus production generated little local capital accumulation. In social terms, this meant there had developed a large class of direct producers and only a small commercial class. Dependent as it was on the vagaries of household surplus production, the mountain commercial class did not, and indeed could not become the vanguard capitalist class in the region. Thus, the issue of whether a local merchant-centered elite were leaders or followers is rendered moot. There existed very real barriers to its collective ability to accumulate capital on a large enough scale to finance industry or infrastructure investments. Its relatively weak economic position, in turn, created space in the local social structure for an absentee class of investors. Only when Appalachian regional development is viewed as a continuous historical process, in its economic *and* social dimensions, does this become apparent.

I would argue further that such a "long view" is necessary for understanding precisely what roles local elites did perform in capitalist development. For by suggesting that they could not become the vanguard capitalist class, I do not wish to negate their importance. One critical reason why so much equivocation has surrounded "who they were" and "what they did" is that regional scholars have been wont to define and explain mountain elites in terms of pre-determined models. Thus for Arnett, (1978) they are part of the "infrastructure of dependency"; for Conti, (1979) they are Sicilian-like "broker capitalists"; and for a large number of scholars, they remain "local colonizers."

No systematic attempt has yet been made to study the preindustrial mountain elites in a specific place, through time, in order to permit them to define and perhaps even explain themselves. And, it might be added, to illuminate the "typical" situation. In this regard, one is wise to heed the words of historian Edward Thompson (1963:11). Although written in another context, they bear direct relevance for the Appalachian case:

> "The question of course, is how the individual got to be in this 'social role', and how the particular social organization (with its property rights and structure of authority) got to be there. And these are historical questions. If we stop history at a given point, then there are no classes but simply a multitude of individuals with a multitude of experiences. But if we watch these men over an adequate period of social change, we observe patterns in their relationships, their ideas, and their institutions. Class is defined by men as they live their own history, and, in the end, this is its only definition."

Conclusion

Three years ago David Whisnant sounded a call for a "a second level of Appalachian historical analysis and writing" with "more tolerance for abiguity, irony, paradox, and contradiction" (1982:117). This paper represents a preliminary move toward that goal. In reviewing the main currents of recent Appalachian historical scholarship, three overlapping research priorities have emerged: the development of appropriate comparative frameworks; the need for micro-level analysis; and the use of "new" information sources. Each of these will be discussed briefly.

The Appalachian region is frequently compared with other so-called underdeveloped areas of the world, particularly with nations of the third world. Although such comparisons— especially those between different coal fields— have often been quite fruitful, I believe historical research must begin with comparisons a bit closer to home. Appalachian regional scholarship as a whole presupposes a process of regional formation which itself must be explained. The most elemental historical forms of social and economic differentiation took place within the boundaries of the various states which comprise the Appalachian region. Thus, before we begin to study Appalachia as a region possessing some set of common characteristics, we must first explain, for example, how the east Kentucky mountain area became differentiated from the rest of the state of Kentucky (and so on for the mountains of western North Carolina, eastern Tennessee, northern Georgia, etc.).

One issue around which an intra-state comparative focus becomes critical is internal improvements, like transportation. During the nineteenth century, most internal improvement programs were undertaken by state governments, owing to the reluctance on the part of the federal government to become involved in ostensibly local development projects. Since the Appalachian region was notoriously lacking in improved transportation infrastructure until the twentieth century, we must ask how and why state policies discriminated against the mountains. Another issue is the promotional campaigns organized by many states to attract outside industrial investors. To what extent, if any, did mountain politicians participate in these campaigns? These, and other questions pertaining to intra-state differentiation can lead to a second level of comparative work much needed in Appalachian studies: among different areas of the mountains (e.g. western North Carolina and eastern Kentucky). Finally, they can provide a firm basis upon which larger-scale comparative research can be undertaken: between Appalachia and other U.S. and world regions.

The second priority for regional historical research concerns the need for micro-level analyses in Appalachia. Thanks to the pioneering work of the past decade, we now have a rather clear outline of the contours of Appalachian social and economic history. Yet as this paper has tried to show, we still know relatively little about the content of this history at the local level. Aside from processes governing social class formation, there is work to be done on the intersection of class and kinship, demographic history, inheritance practices, land use, and local-level politics. This leads directly to the third research priority: the use of "new" information sources.

To the extent that the transmission of social "information"; during the preindustrial era in Appalachia was governed by oral tradition, regional historical research can not make use of the common set of qualitative tools used by economic and social historians (such as diaries, letters, mercantile account books, newspapers). Owing to this very real problem of historical recovery, which is more than a scholar's methodological dilemma, we may never know certain things about the region's past. Yet this does not foreclose the possibility of meaningful historical research. A variety of public records, maintained at the county, state, and national levels, can be used to address many historical problems. A few examples will make clear the potential abundance of historical information that does exist.

Tax assessments were made on an annual basis in most counties. These assessment books, many of which have been placed in permanent storage in state archives, detail the ownership of a variety of forms of real and personal property. Not only do these records permit cross-sectional analyses of property ownership, but longintudinal ones as well. Deed records of course contain information on real estate transfers. But based on evidence from east Kentucky, deed books were also used to record many other economic transactions, such as loans and tenancy arrangements. Finally, county court order books permit a reading of the conduct of local politics.

The three research priorities identified here are by no means exhaustive, but they will help to fulfill the challenging agenda of a "second-level" of Appalachian historical research.

BIBLIOGRAPHY

Appalachian Land Ownership Task Force, 1983. *Who Owns Appalachia? Landownership and Its Impact.* Lexington, Ky.: The University Press of Kentucky

Arnett, Douglas, 1978. *Eastern Kentucky: The Politics of Dependency and Underdevelopment.* Unpublished PH.D. Dissertation, Duke University

Ball, Richard, 1968. "A Poverty Case: the Analgesic Subculture of the Southern Appalachians" *American Sociological Review* 33 pp. 885-895

Batteau, Allen, 1971., "The Contradictions of a Kingship Community" in Robert L. Hall and Carol B. Stack, eds. *Holding Onto The Land And The Lord; Kinship, Ritual, Land Tenue And Social Policy In The Rural South.* Athens: University of Georgia Press

Billings, Dwight, 1979. *Planters And The Making Of A "New South"; Class, Politics And Development In North Carolina.* Chapel Hill: University of North Carolina Press

Billings, Dwight, 1982. "Class Origins of the 'New South': Planter Persistence an Industry in North Carolina" in Michael Burawoy and Theda Skocpol, eds. *Marxist Perspectives.* Chicago: University of Chicago Press

Brenner, Robert, 1976., "Agrarian Class Structure and Economic Development in Pre-Industrial Europe". *Past and Present* No. 70 pp. 30-75

Campbell, John C., 1921. *The Southern Highlander And His Homeland.* New York: The Russell Sage Foundation

Caudill, Harry M., 1982. "The Strange Career of John C.C. Mayo". *Filson Club Quarterly* 56 pp. 258-289

Conti, Eugene, 1979. *Mountain Metamorphosis: Culture and Development In East Kentucky.* Unpublished Ph.D. dissertation, Duke University.

Conti, Eugene, 1979-80. "The Cultural Role of Local Elites in the Kentucky Mountains: A Retrospect Analysis". *Appalachian Journal 7* pp. 51-68.

Eller, Ronald D., 1979. "Land and Family: An Historical View of Preindustrial Appalachia". *Appalachian Journal* 6 pp. 83-109

Eller, Ronald D., 1982. *Mines, Millhands and Mountaineers: Industrialization of the Appalachian South,* 1880-1930. Knoxville: University of Tennessee Press.

Gaventa, John, 1980. *Power and Powerlessness: Quiescence and Rebellion in an Appalachian Valley.* Urbana: University of Illinois Press.

Knipe, Edward E. and Helen M. Lewis, 1971. "The Impact of Coal Mining on the Traditional Mountain Subculture" in J. Kenneth Moreland, ed., *The Not So Solid South: Anthropological Studies in a Regional Subculture.* Athens: University of Georgia Press pp. 25-37.

Lewis, Helen, et al., eds., 1978. *Colonialism in Modern American: The Appalachian Case.* Boone, NC: Appalachian Consortium Press.

Lewis, Helen and Edward Knipe, 1978. "The Colonialism Model: The Appalachian Case" in Lewis, et. al., eds., 1978. pp. 9-31.

Moore, Barrington, Jr., 1966. *Social Origins of Dictatorship And Democracy.* Boston: Beacon Press.

Post, Charles, 1982. "The American Road to Capitalism". *New Left Review* No. 133 pp. 3-51.

Pudup, Mary Beth, forthcoming, *Land, Class, and Rural Transformation: The East Kentucky Coal Fields,* 1870-1920. Ph.D. dissertation in progress, University of California, Berkeley.

Shapiro, Henry D., 1978. *Appalachia On Our Mind: The Southern Mountains and Mountaineers in the American Consciousness,* 1870-1920. Chapel Hill: University of North Carolina Press.

Simon, Richard, 1981. "Uneven Development and the Case of West Virgina: Going Beyond the Colonialism Model". *Appalachian Journal* 8 pp. 165-186.

Simon, Richard, 1983-84. "Regions and Social Relations: A Research Note". *Appalachian Journal* 11 pp. 23-31.

Turner, Carolyn Clay and Carolyn Hay Traum, 1983. *John C.C. Mayo; Cumberland Capitalist.* Pikeville, Ky.: Pikeville College Press.

Walls, David, 1978. "Internal Colony or Internal Periphery? A Critique of Current Models and an Alternative Formulation" in Lewis, et. al., eds., 1978 pp. 319-349.

Walls, David, 1978. *Central Appalachia in Advanced Capitalism: Its Coal Industry Structure and Coal Operator Associations.* Unpublished Ph.D. dissertation, University of Kentucky.

Whisnant, David, 1982. "Second-Level Appalachian History: Another Look at Some Fotched-On Women". *Appalachian Journal* 9 pp. 115-123.

Whisnant, David, 1983., *All That is Native and Fine; The Politics of Culture in an American Region.* Chapel Hill: University of North Carolina Press.

ETHNICITY AND MOBILITY
  Convenor: Elizabeth Barrett, Appalshop
Blacks: An Invisible Institution in Appalachia?
  Wilburn Hayden, Jr., Western Carolina University
Moving On: Recent Patterns of Appalachian Migration
  Philip J. Obermiller, Northern Kentucky University
  Robert Oldendick, University of Cincinnati
Long Journey Home
  Elizabeth Barrett, Appalshop

Blacks: An Invisible Institution in Appalachia?

by
Wilburn Hayden, Jr.

ABSTRACT

The institution of black invisibility is defined and discussed in terms of its impact on the social-economic status of blacks in the Region. Using counties with close to 4000 or more blacks, 20 concentrated areas were identified. These concentrations center around the following conditions: I. Coal-Industrial Site; II. Major University or Military Base; III. Urban Center; IV. Combination of I and III; and V. Combination of II and III.

Seventy five (75) percent of all blacks in the Region were in the 63 counties while only 37% of whites. The third concentration and the two (2) combintion concentrations (the combinations included urban) accounted for 15 of the 20 concentrations, 74.4%. The paper identifies high urbanization of blacks as a factor that contributes to the institution of black invisibility. Thus, as a group, the black experience compared to whites as a group is very different in the Appalachian Region.

The concept of "black Appalachia invisibility" was first put in print and defined by Clarence Wright in 1973.[1] Ed Cabbell's article[2] seven years later provided support for the concept through an informal survey of blacks in the Region. Cabbell identifies two myths that are useful in understanding the concept: (1) "...the number of black people in the mountains is inconsequential."[3] and (2) "...Appalachia is a land of 'poor white hillbillies' beset solely with 'white problems' and not the 'color problems' that plague the rest of America."[4] He further concludes that these myths have resulted in the failure of scholars and analysts of the Region to focus on the existence and plight of black Appalachians, thus causing blacks to be a neglected minority within a neglected minority (people of Appalachia).[5]

Black invisibility as an institution within the Region will be defined as the view of Appalachia as a white Region justifying the formal and informal collections of customs, practices, beliefs and attitudes that lead (led) to ignoring the plight, contributions and experiences and to unequal social and economic conditions of blacks as a group. There are two constructs which are important to understanding the definition: *view* and *group*. View is the holding to and acting on an unsubstantiated judgment or opinion.

Turning now to the construct group, when there are few minority individuals or when a majority member develops a close friendship with a minority individual, the individual in the majority group may see the minority individual or friend as separate from the minority group. As one moves throughout the region it is clear that individual blacks appear to escape unequal treatment by whites. Both blacks and whites have learned to accept the institution of black invisibility which creates the appearance of a high level of tolerance for the individual(s). The tolerance level quickly shifts to unequal treatment when the institution is challenged. For example (this example is to illustrate a point and does not negate the many exceptions) even today there are hollows, communities or counties that demonstrate and maintain that blacks are not welcome. The white residents of these hollows, communities or counties may work daily alongside a black individual and develop a positive relationship. The non-work association is maintained in a neutral setting or in the black community. Seldom is the black allowed social contact within the white residents' setting. If the black raises the issue, the friendship begins to shift. The white resident now sees the black individual as a member of a group—visible—desiring to be an equal.

The invisible institution of blacks is seen by some as a positive factor. This perspective sees invisibility as important to the lack of racial tension and the perception of greater freedom in the region for blacks. By being invisible, blacks are (were) not singled out as a significant threat to the order of the white domain, thus able to co-exist. But with this perspective, many blacks suffered discrimination as individuals. The invisibility meant that blacks could be ignored by the institutions of the region (particularly employment). The invisibility of blacks may well be singled out as a major cause for the high degree of poor housing, higher proportion of poverty and unemployment, lack of ownership of large holdings of land, a small voice in the political and governmental decisions or services, and a lesser social status.

An examination of the 1980 census data will be presented to determine how the extent black invisibility is more than a view about blacks as a group. The census identifies 1,575,368 blacks living in 397 counties in the region. The total population for the region is 21,019,681. The black population is 7.8% of the region which is about 4% less than the percentage of blacks (11.8%) in the country as a whole. Table I is a distribution by race for the 13 states. American Indians represented 0.1% of the region numbering 29.373. Others represented 0.5% and numbering 110,146 which are primarily individuals who failed to be identified by race.

TABLE 1

STATE POPULATION DISRIBUTION
IN THE APPALACHIAN REGION AS DEFINED BY THE ARC

STATES AND PERCENTAGES	TOTAL	WHITES	BLACKS	AMER. INDS.	OTHERS
Alabama	2,448,121	1,926,125	486,438	2,721	32,837
Percentage	100.0	78.7	19.9	0.1	1.3
Georgia	1,104,081	1,027,236	71,048	2,387	3,410
Percentage	100.0	93.0	6.5	0.2	0.3
Kentucky	1,078,076	1,056,048	18,394	809	2,852
Percentage	100.0	98.0	1.7	0.1	0.3
Maryland	220,132	212,358	6,419	171	1,184
Percentage	100.0	96.5	2.9	0.1	0.5
Mississippi	481,717	346,080	133,569	654	1,414
Percentage	100.0	71.8	27.8	0.1	0.3
New York	1,082,794	1,053,887	15,592	3,950	9,365
Percentage	100.0	97.3	1.5	0.3	0.9
North Carolina	1,217,514	1,094,682	112,137	7,041	3,654
Percentage	100.0	89.9	9.2	0.6	0.3
Ohio	1,262,503	1,229,540	26,715	1,944	4,304
Percentage	100.0	97.4	2.1	0.2	0.3
Pennsylvania	6,103,923	5,741,637	332,121	4,608	25,557
Percentage	100.0	94.1	5.4	0.1	0.4
South Carolina	835,095	654,155	176,481	675	3,784
Percentage	100.0	78.3	21.2	0.1	0.4
Tennessee	2,090,517	1,955,618	120,775	2,506	11,618
Percentage	100.0	93.5	5.9	0.1	0.5
Virginia	505,487	493,412	10,618	352	1,098
Percentage	100.0	97.6	2.1	0.1	0.2
West Virginia	1,929,122	1,853,437	65,061	1,555	9,069
Percentage	100.0	96.0	3.,4	0.1	0.5
TOTAL	20,359,082	18,644,215	1,575,368	29,373	110,146
PERCENTAGE	100.0	91.6	7.8	0.1	0.5

Alabama has the largest number of blacks at 486,438 and third largest percentage of 19.9%. The largest percentage is 27.8% from Mississippi with the fourth largest black population of 133,569. The state with the smallest percentage was New York at 1.5% and the eleventh largest population of 15,592. The state with the smallest number of blacks was Maryland at 6,419. Table 2 is the ranking of each state by the number and percentage of population.

Table 2. Ranking for Each State by Number and Percentage of Blacks.

States	Number	Percentage
Alabama	1	3
Georgia	7	5
Kentucky	10	12
Maryland	13	9
Mississippi	4	1
New York	11	13
North Carolina	6	4
Ohio	9	10
Pennsylvania	2	7
South Carolina	3	2
Tennessee	5	6
Virginia	12	10
West Virginia	8	8

For most scholars and people in the region these numbers are no surprise, yet blacks as an invisible institution remains. WHY? A closer look at the census data provides some light to the question.

Table 3. Number of Concentrations and Counties for Each State

States	Number of Concentrations	Number of Counties
Alabama	2	19
Georgia	1	6
Kentucky	0	0
Maryland	1	1
Mississippi	2	9
New York	1	1
North Carolina	3	4
Ohio	1	1
Pennsylvania	3	7
South Carolina	1	6
Tennessee	2	2
Virginia	0	0
West Virginia	3	6
TOTAL	20	62

The mean number of blacks per county was computed at 3,968. County maps for each state were used to plot counties with near or more than 3,968 blacks. Twenty (20) concentrations consisting of 62 of the 397 counties were plotted. These counties were 15.6% of the total counties. Kentucky and Virginia were the only states to have all of its regional counties with less than 4,000 blacks. Table 3 is the number of concentrations and number of counties. Table 5 are the counties for the 20 concentrations.

The concentrations resulted from three conditions and two combinations of the three: (I) Coal or Industrial Site; (II) a Major University or Military Base; (III) an Urban Center; (IV) Combination of I and III; and (V) Combination of II and III.

Five (5) of the 20 concentrations of 23.8% were in the first two conditions. Twelve (12) or 57.1% concentrations were from Urban Environments. The three remaining concentrations were combinations with an urban setting. Thus 74.4% of the counties were urban (see Table 4).

Table 4. Number of Concentrations by the Five Factors for Each State

States	I	II	III	IV	V
Alabama	1				1
Georgia			1		
Kentucky (none)					
Maryland	1				
Mississippi		1	1		
New York			1		
North Carolina		1	1		
Ohio			1		
Pennsylvania			2		1
South Carolina		1		1	
Tennessee			2		
Virginia (none)					
West Virginia			2		
TOTAL	2	3	11	1	2

The total number of blacks in these concentrations was 1,157,986. This number represents 73.5% of the total number of blacks. Thirty-six point six percent (36.6%) of all whites were found in the counties that formed the 20 concentrations. According to an Appalachian Regional Commission report, 74% of the 1980 U.S. population lives in an urban environment while 48% of the total Appalachian population lives in an urban environment.[6] The conclusion was made "...that Appalachia remains essentially a region of small towns and rural areas."[7] The conclusion, though accurate for white Appalachia, is not the case for black Appalachia. The ARC report falls to the fate of the institution of black invisibility. Black Appalachians live in urban environments. For twenty-six point five percent (26.5%) of the blacks,

TABLE 5
COUNTIES FOR THE TWENTY CONCENTRATIONS FOR EACH STATE

ALABAMA
Concentration: 1
Lauderdale
Lawrence
limestone
Madison
Morgan

Concentration: 2
Pickens
Tuscaloosa
Walker
Jefferson
St. Clair
Etowah
Calhoun
Talladega
Shelby
Randolph
Tallapoosa
Cambers
Coosa
Elmore

GEORGIA
Concentration: 3
Floyd
Bartow
Polk
Carroll
Gwinnett
Hall

MARYLAND
Concentration: 14
Washington

MISSISSIPPI
Concentration: 5
Marshall

Concentration: 6
Chickasaw
Clay
Kemper
Lee
Lowndes
Noxub ee
Oktibbeha

NEW YORK
Concentration: 7
Chemung

NORTH CAROLINA
Concentration: 8
Buncombe

Concentration: 9
Forsyth

Concentration: 10
Rutherford
Burke

OHIO
Concentration: 11
Jefferson

PENNSYLVANIA
Concentration: 12
Erie

Concentration: 13
Mercer

Concentration: 14
Allegheny
Beaver
Fayette
Washington
Westmoreland

SOUTH CAROLINA
Concentration: 15
Anderson
Cherokee
Greenville
Oconee
Pickens
Spartanburg

TENNESSEE
Concentration: 16
Knox

Concentration: 17
Hamilton

WEST VIRGINIA
Concentration: 18
Fayette
McDowell
Mercer
Raleigh

Concentration: 19
Cabell

Concentration: 20
Kanawha

the report is accurate, and the case of the institution of black invisibility may be argued, especially since non-urban black Appalachians are a sub-minority of a minority *of a minority.*

Realizing that blacks in the region are found in the same environments as most blacks in the nation, it is not difficult to see why the institution of black invisibility exists. The social and economic conditions for blacks in the region are very different from whites. To acknowledge and respond to the difference requires the visibility of blacks in the region. By not ignoring the difference, black individuals as a group may be able to do in the region what has not occurred in the rest of the nation — move toward equal treatment. This means shifting some of the analysts, resources and services to the urban struggle, life, and social and economic conditions of the visible black Appalachian.

One final note that can be concluded from this study that speaks to the region as a whole is the increasing urbanization of the region. With 48% of the region living in urban environments in 1980, it is clear that by 1990 the majority of Appalachia will be living in urban centers. Thus, the focus of Appalachian Studies and resources may need to include the urban invisible Appalachian.

POPULATION DISTRIBUTION BY RACE FOR THE TWENTY CONCENTRATIONS OF BLACK APPALACHIAN IN COUNTIES WITH 3,990 OR MORE BLACKS

ALABAMA

Concentration: 1	Total People	Whites	Blacks	Amer. Indian	Others
Lauderdale	80,546	72,375	7,845	99	227
Lawrence	30,170	23,013	5,074	40	2,043
Limestone	46,005	39,351	6,539	36	79
Madison	196,966	154,782	39,069	439	2,676
Morgan	90,231	81,131	8,816	98	186
Region Total	433,918	370,652	67,343	712	5,211
Percentage	100.00	83.5	15.2	.2	1.1
Concentration: 2					
Pickens	21,481	12,451	8,978	12	40
Tuscaloosa	137,541	99,335	37,405	101	700
Walker	68,660	63,547	4,839	98	176
Jefferson	671,324	444,426	223,759	520	2,619
St. Clair	41,205	36,935	4,128	51	91
Etowah	103,057	88,806	13,809	121	321
Calhoun	119,761	97,313	21,074	215	1,159
Talladega	73,831	50,922	22,745	45	119
Shelby	66,298	58,982	6,947	106	263
Randolph	20,075	15,173	4,869	10	23
Tallapoosa	38,676	28,096	10,451	13	116
Chambers	39,191	25,222	13,894	14	61
Coosa	11,377	7,411	3,950	08	08
Elmore	43,390	33,585	9,655	28	122
Regional Total	1,455,867	1,062,204	386,503	1,342	5,818
Percentage	100.00	73	26.5	.1	.4
State Total	1,899,785	1,432,856	453,846	2,054	11,029
Percentage	100.00	75.4	23.9	.1	.6

GEORGIA

Concentration: 3					
Floyd	79,800	69,305	10,237	89	169
Bartow	40,760	35,889	4,720	96	55
Polk	32,386	27,518	4,832	—	36
Carroll	56,346	46,484	9,679	59	124
Gwinnett	166,903	161,144	4,154	295	1,310
Hall	75,649	68,461	6,762	143	283
Region Total	451,844	408,801	40,384	682	1,977
Percentage	100.00	90.5	8.9	.2	.4

MARYLAND

Concentration: 4					
Washington	113,086	107,150	5,049	89	798
Percentage	100.0	94.7	4.5	.1	.7

MISSISSIPPI

Concentration: 5					
Marshall	29,296	13,598	15,577	39	82
Percentage	100.0	46.4	53.2	.1	.3

	Total			Amer.	
Concentration: 6	People	Whites	Blacks	Indian	Others
Chickasaw	17,853	11,393	6,434	22	04
Clay	21,082	10,482	10,540	05	55
Kemper	10,148	4,592	5,512	44	—
Lee	57,061	45,224	11,645	09	183
Lowndes	57,304	37,224	19,601	94	385
Monroe	36,404	25,560	10,827	07	10
Noxubee	13,212	4,629	8,534	47	02
Okitibbeha	36,018	23,305	12,355	12	346
Region Total	249,082	162,409	85,448	240	985
Percentage	100.0	65.2	34.3	.1	.4
State Total	278,378	176,007	101,025	279	1,067
Percentage	100.0	63.2	36.3	.1	.4

NEW YORK

Concentration: 7					
Chemung	97,656	92,629	3,957	224	846
Percentage	100.0	94.9	4.1	.2	.8

NORTH CAROLINA

Concentration: 8					
Buncombe	160,801	146,125	13,943	193	540
Percentage	100.0	90.9	8.7	.1	.3
Concentration: 9					
Forsyth	243,683	182,647	59,403	451	1,182
Percentage	100.0	75	24.4	.2	.4
Concentration: 10					
Rutherford	53,787	47,159	6,534	20	74
Burke	72,504	66,953	5,213	95	243
Region Total	126,291	114,112	11,747	115	317
Percentage	100.0	90.4	9.3	.1	.2
State Total	530,775	442,884	85,093	759	2,039
Percentage	100.0	83.4	16	.2	.4

OHIO

Concentration: 11					
Jefferson	91,564	85,956	5,000	123	484
Percentage	100.0	93.9	5.5	.1	.5

PENNSYLVANIA

Concentration: 12					
Erie	388,780	265,589	121,135	384	1,672
Percentage	100.0	68.3	31.2	.1	.4
Concentration: 13					
Mercer	128,299	122,258	5,521	106	414
Percentage	100.0	95.3	4.3	.1	.3
Concentration: 14					
Alleghany	1,450,085	1,288,989	150,077	1,104	9,915
Beaver	204,441	191,964	11,644	169	664
Fayette	159,417	153,093	5,844	137	343
Washington	217,074	208,957	7,324	256	537
Westmoreland	392,294	383,903	6,527	267	1,597
Region Total	2,423,311	2,226,906	181,416	1,933	13,056
Percentage	100.0	91.9	7.5	.1	.5
State Total	2,940,390	2,614,753	308,072	2,423	15,142
Percentage	100.0	88.9	10.5	.1	.5

SOUTH CAROLINA

Concentration: 15	Total People	Whites	Blacks	Amer. Indian	Others
Anderson	133,235	109,823	22,895	109	408
Cherokee	40,983	32,800	7,988	37	158
Greenville	287,913	235,210	50,842	227	1,584
Oconee	91,811	43,656	48,037	43	75
Pickens	79,292	72,794	5,849	73	576
Spartanburg	201,861	159,872	40,870	136	983
State Total	835,095	654,155	176,481	675	3,784
Percentage	100.0	78.3	21.2	.1	.4

TENNESSEE

Concentration: 16					
Knox	320,494	288,675	28,806	426	2,587
Percentage	100.0	90.1	9.	.1	.8
Concentration: 17					
Hamilton	287,740	229,976	55,840	308	1,616
Percentage	100.0	80.	19.4	.1	.5
State Total	608,234	518,651	84,646	734	4,203
Percentage	100.0	85.3	13.9	.1	.7

WEST VIRGINIA

Concentration: 18					
Fayette	57,863	53,276	4,321	41	225
McDowell	49,899	42,401	7,378	25	95
Mercer	73,932	68,483	5,030	65	354
Raleigh	86,821	79,408	6,862	59	492
Region Total	268,515	243,568	23,591	190	1,166
Percentage	100.0	90.7	8.8	.1	.5
Concentration: 19					
Cabell	106,815	101,627	4,488	70	630
Percentage	100.0	95.1	4.2	.1	.6
Concentration: 20					
Kanawha	231,414	215,953	13,776	155	1,530
Percentage	100.0	93.3	6	.1	.5
State Total	606,744	561,148	41,855	415	3,326
Percentage	100.0	92.5	6.9	.1	.5

STATE POPULATION DISTRIBUTION
IN THE APPALACHIA REGION AS DEFINED BY THE ARC

STATES AND PERCENTAGES	Total	Whites	Blacks	Amer. Indian	Others
Alabama	2,448,121	1,926,125	486,438	2,721	32,837
Percentage	100.0	78.7	19.9	0.1	1.3
Georgia	1,104,081	1,027,236	71,048	2,387	3,410
Percentage	100.0	93.0	6.5	0.2	0.3
Kentucky	1,078,076	1,056,048	18,394	809	2,852
Percentage	100.0	98.0	1.7	0.1	0.3
Maryland	220,132	212,358	6,419	171	1,184
Percentage	100.0	96.5	2.9	0.1	0.5
Mississippi	481,717	346,080	133,569	654	1,414
Percentage	100.0	71.8	27.8	0.1	0.3
New York	1,082,794	1,053,887	15,592	3,950	9,365
Percentage	100.0	97.3	1.5	0.3	0.9
North Carolina	1,217,514	1,094,682	112,137	7,041	3,654
Percentage	100.0	89.9	9.2	0.6	0.3
Ohio	1,262,503	1,229,540	26,715	1,944	4,304
Percentage	100.0	97.4	2.1	0.2	0.3
Pennsylvania	6,103,923	5,741,637	332,121	4,608	25,557
Percentage	100.0	94.1	5.4	0.1	0.4
South Carolina	835,095	654,155	176,481	675	3,784
Percentage	100.0	78.3	21.2	0.1	0.4
Tennessee	2,090,517	1,955,618	120,775	2,506	11,618
Percentage	100.0	93.5	5.9	0.1	0.5
Virginia	505,487	493,412	10,618	352	1,098
Percentage	100.0	97.6	2.1	0.1	0.2
West Virginia	1,929,122	1,853,437	65,061	1,555	9,069
Percentage	100.0	96.0	3.4	0.1	0.5
TOTAL	20,359,082	18,644,215	1,575,368	29,373	110,146
PERCENTAGE	100.0	91.6	7.8	0.1	0.5

ALABAMA—Counties in Appalachia

Population State Total 1980	2,448,121	1,926,125	486,438	2,721	32,837

Total of Counties in Appalachia	Total Persons	Whites	Blacks	Amer. Indian	Others
1. Bibb	15,725	12,029	3,675	02	19
2. Blount	36,459	35,761	598	56	44
3. Calhoun	119,761	97,313	21,074	215	1,159
4. Chambers	39,191	25,222	13,894	14	61
5. Cherokee	18,760	17,185	1,550	13	12
6. Chilton	30,612	26,942	3,633	09	28
7. Clay	13,731	11,424	2,268	04	35
8. Cleburne	12,595	11,925	647	04	19
9. Colbert	54,519	42,209	9,146	68	3,096
10. Coosa	11,377	7,411	3,950	08	08
11. Cullman	61,642	60,928	528	69	117
12. De Kalb	53,658	52,538	939	90	91
13. Elmore	43,390	33,585	9,655	28	122
14. Etowah	103,057	88,806	13,809	121	321
15. Fayette	18,809	16,378	2,396	07	28
16. Franklin	28,350	26,991	1,301	22	36

ALABAMA con't

Total of Counties in Appalachia	Total Persons	Whites	Blacks	Amer. Indian	Others
17. Jackson	51,407	48,990	2,150	188	79
18. Jefferson	671,324	444,426	223,759	520	2,619
19. Lamar	26,453	14,457	,975	11	10,010
20. Lauderdale	80,546	72,375	7,845	99	227
21. Lawrence	30,170	23,013	5,074	40	2,043
22. Limestone	46,005	39,351	6,539	36	79
23. Madison	196,966	154,782	39,069	439	2,676
24. Marion	30,041	29,250	701	35	55
25. Marshall	645,622	64,444	1,016	62	100
26. Morgan	90,231	81,131	8,816	98	186
27. Pickens	21,481	12,451	8,978	12	40
28. Randolph	20,075	15,173	4,869	10	23
29. St. Clair	41,205	36,935	4,128	51	91
30. Shelby	66,298	58,982	6,947	106	263
31. Talladega	73,831	50,922	22,745	45	119
32. Tallapoosa	38,676	28,096	10,451	13	116
33. Tuscaloosa	137,541	99,335	37,405	101	700
34. Walker	68,660	63,547	4,839	98	176
35. Winston	29,953	21,818	69	27	8,039
Percentage	100.0	78.7	19.9	0.1	1.3

GEORGIA—Counties in Appalachia
Population
State Total

1980	1,104,081	1,027,236	71,048	2,387	3,410

Total of Counties in Appalachia	Total Persons	Whites	Blacks	Amer. Indian	Others
36. Banks	8,702	8,240	450	12	—
37. Barrow	21,354	18,139	3,189	20	06
38. Bartow	40,760	35,889	4,720	96	55
39. Carroll	56,346	46,484	9,679	59	124
40. Catoosa	36,991	36,683	228	18	62
41. Chattooga	21,856	19,929	1,892	10	25
42. Cherokee	51,699	50,406	1,041	41	211
43. Dade	12,333	12,076	192	22	43
44. Dawson	4,774	4,614	—	160	—
45. Douglas	54,573	51,348	2,966	96	163
46. Fannin	14,748	14,638	36	44	30
47. Floyd	79,800	69,305	10,237	89	169
48. Forsyth	27,958	27,628	05	288	37
49. Franklin	15,185	13,631	1,529	19	06
50. Gilmer	11,110	11,071	14	23	02
51. Gordon	30,070	28,794	1,185	63	28
52. Gwinnett	166,903	161,144	4,154	295	1,310
53. Habersham	25,020	23,658	1,266	35	61
54. Hall	75,649	68,461	6,762	143	283
55. Haralson	18,422	17,103	1,305	—	14
56. Heard	6,520	5,402	1,118	—	—
57. Jackson	25,343	22,528	2,739	12	64
58. Lumpkin	10,762	10,170	222	336	34
59. Madison	17,747	15,788	1,942	08	09
60. Murray	19,685	19,596	36	41	12
61. Paulding	26,104	25,005	1,041	21	37
62. Pickens	11,654	11,346	292	04	12
63. Polk	32,386	27,518	4,832	—	36

GEORGIA con't

Total of Counties in Appalachia	Total Persons	Whites	Blacks	Amer. Indian	Others
64. Rabun	10,466	10,345	80	32	09
65. Stephens	21,763	19,021	2,646	48	48
66. Towns	5,638	5,624	—	02	12
67. Union	9,381	9,336	—	34	11
68. Walker	56,470	54,021	2,320	60	69
69. White	10,120	9,669	401	22	28
70. Whitfield	65,789	62,626	2,529	234	400
Percentage	100.0	93.0	6.5	0.2	0.3

KENTUCKY—Counties in Appalachia

Population State Total 1980					
	1,078,076	1,056,048	18,394	809	2,852

Total of Counties in Appalachia	Total Persons	Whites	Blacks	Amer. Indian	Others
71. Adair	15,233	14,682	524	08	19
72. Bath	10,025	9,696	319	02	08
73. Bell	34,330	33,352	858	39	81
74. Boyd	55,513	54,259	1,078	45	131
75. Breathitt	17,004	16,923	43	17	21
76. Carter	25,060	25,022	07	12	19
77. Casey	14,818	14,768	22	04	24
78. Clark	28,322	26,489	1,789	08	36
79. Clay	22,752	22,357	347	08	40
80. Clinton	9,321	9,302	10	01	08
81. Cumberland	7,289	6,893	388	—	08
82. Elliott	6,908	6,908	—	—	—
83. Estill	14,495	14,472	—	07	16
84. Fleming	12,323	12,086	237	—	—
85. Floyd	48,716	48,440	230	46	—
86. Garrard	10,853	10,221	620	—	12
87. Green	11,043	10,600	441	—	02
88. Greenup	39,132	38,933	133	04	62
89. Harlan	41,889	39,782	1,927	99	81
90. Jackson	12,000	11,984	—	04	12
91. Johnson	685,004	24,362	5	38	27
92. Knott	17,945	17,799	128	08	10
93. Knox	30,239	29,847	322	17	53
94. Laurel	39,982	38,588	309	22	1,063
95. Lawrence	14,121	14,061	31	17	12
96. Lee	7,754	7,712	35	02	05
97. Leslie	14,882	14,858	06	12	06
98. Letcher	30,687	30,306	302	25	54
99. Lewis	14,545	14,499	29	10	07
100. Lincoln	19,053	18,259	762	12	20
101. McCreary	15,634	15,366	195	62	11
102. Madison	53,352	49,712	3,185	46	409
103. Magoffin	13,525	13,493	01	12	19
104. Martin	13,962	13,897	07	10	48
105. Menifee	5,117	5,050	51	02	14
106. Monroe	12,353	11,979	358	09	07
107. Montgomery	20,046	18,955	1,063	14	14
108. Morgan	12,103	12,057	21	15	10
109. Owsley	5,709	5,699	05	02	03
110. Perry	33,763	33,068	639	09	47

KENTUCKY con't

Total of Counties in Appalachia	Total Persons	Whites	Blacks	Amer. Indian	Others
111. Pike	81,123	80,631	320	37	135
112. Powell	11,101	10,970	106	15	10
113. Pulaski	45,803	45,131	564	23	85
114. Rockcastle	13,973	13,935	03	13	22
115. Rowan	19,049	18,657	293	23	76
116. Russell	13,708	13,581	109	05	13
117. Wayne	17,022	16,612	365	22	23
118. Whitley	33,396	33,109	205	19	63
119. Wolfe	6,698	6,686	02	04	06
Percentage	100.0	98.0	1.7	0.1	0.3

MARYLAND—Counties in Appalachia
Population State Total 1980

	Total Persons	Whites	Blacks	Amer. Indian	Others
	220,132	212,358	6,419	171	1,184

Total of Counties in Appalachia	Total Persons	Whites	Blacks	Amer. Indian	Others
120. Allegany	80,548	78,841	1,315	50	342
121. Garrett	26,498	26,367	55	32	44
122. Washington	113,086	107,150	5,049	89	798
Percentage	100	96.5	2.9	0.1	.5

MISSISSIPPI—Counties in Appalachia
Population State Total 1980

	Total Persons	Whites	Blacks	Amer. Indian	Others
	481,707	346,080	133,569	654	1,404

Total of Counties in Appalachia	Total Persons	Whites	Blacks	Amer. Indian	Others
123. Alcorn	33,036	29,443	3,427	44	122
124. Benton	8,153	5,066	3,087	—	—
125. Chickasaw	17,853	11,393	6,434	22	04
126. Choctaw	8,991	6,459	2,530	02	—
127. Clay	21,082	10,482	10,540	05	55
128. Itawamba	20,518	19,055	1,333	16	114
129. Kemper	10,148	4,592	5,512	44	—
130. Lee	57,061	45,224	11,645	09	183
131. Lowndes	57,304	37,224	19,601	94	385
132. Marshall	29,296	13,598	15,577	39	82
133. Monroe	36,404	25,560	10,827	07	10
134. Noxubee	13,212	4,629	8,534	47	02
135. Oktibbeha	36,018	23,305	12,355	12	346
136. Pontotoc	20,918	17,600	3,278	—	40
137. Prentiss	24,025	21,379	2,579	58	09
138. Tippah	17,739	14,744	2,978	08	09
139. Tishomingo	18,434	17,651	681	85	17
140. Union	21,741	18,688	3,000	38	15
141. Webster	10,300	8,267	2,014	08	11
142. Winston	19,474	11,721	7,637	116	—
Percentage	100.0	71.8	27.8	0.1	0.3

NEW YORK—Counties in Appalachia
Population

State Total 1980	1,082,794	1,053,887	15,592	3,950	9,365
Total of Counties in Appalachia	Total Persons	Whites	Blacks	Amer. Indian	Others
143. Allegany	51,742	51.080	173	229	260
144. Broome	213,648	207,921	3,266	411	2,050
145. Cattaragugus	85,697	83,088	580	1,723	306
146. Chautauqua	146,925	142,757	2,021	433	1,714
147. Chemung	97,656	92,629	3,957	224	846
148. Chenango	49,344	48,848	277	68	151
149. Cortland	48,820	48,263	236	127	194
150. Delaware	46,824	46,210	254	106	254
151. Otsego	59,075	58,230	431	103	311
152. Schoharie	29,710	29,207	230	72	201
153. Schuyler	17,686	17,412	96	66	112
154. Steuben	99,217	97,553	984	195	485
155. Tioga	49,812	49,032	413	53	314
156. Tompkins	86,638	81,657	2,674	140	2,167
Percentage	100.0	97.3	1.5	0.3	0.9

NORTH CAROLINA—Counties in Appalachia
Population

State Total 1980	1,217,514	1,094,682	112,137	7,041	3,654
Total of Counties in Appalachia	Total Persons	Whites	Blacks	Amer. Indian	Others
157. Alexander	24,999	23,250	1,668	25	56
158. Alleghany	9,587	9,367	203	3	14
159. Ashe	22,325	22,097	182	15	31
160. Avery	14,404	14,276	90	38	—
161. Buncombe	160,801	146,125	13,943	193	540
162. Burke	72,504	66,953	5,213	95	243
163. Caldwell	67,746	63,739	3,874	47	86
164. Cherokee	18,933	18,304	395	196	38
165. Clay	6,619	6,553	54	12	—
166. Davie	24,599	21,959	2,556	47	37
167. Forsythe	243,683	182,647	59,403	451	1,182
168. Graham	7,217	6,837	—	376	4
169. Haywood	46,495	45,495	790	80	130
170. Henderson	58,580	56,296	2,008	126	150
171. Jackson	25,811	22,839	507	2,418	47
172. McDowell	35,126	33,391	1,549	64	122
173. Macon	20,178	19,763	339	28	48
174. Madison	16,827	16,627	159	21	20
175. Mitchell	14,428	14,270	30	34	94
176. Polk	12,984	11,735	1,187	32	30
177. Rutherford	53,787	47,159	6,534	20	74
178. Stokes	33,086	30,574	2,373	34	105
179. Surry	59,449	56,321	2,929	56	143
180. Swain	10,283	7,676	101	2,493	13
181. Transylvania	23,417	22,071	1,240	32	74
182. Watauga	31,666	31,098	425	22	121
183. Wilkes	58,657	55,681	2,804	56	116
184. Yadkin	28,439	26,969	1,354	13	103
185. Yancey	14,884	14,610	227	14	33
Percentage	100.0	89.9	9.2	0.6	0.3
Total without Forsythe	973,831	912,035	52,734	6,590	2,472
Percentage	100.0	93.7	5.4	0.7	0.2

OHIO—Counties in Appalachia

Population State Total 1980	1,262,503	1,229,540	26,715	1,944	4,304

Total of Counties in Appalachia	Total Persons	Whites	Blacks	Amer. Indian	Others
186. Adams	24,328	24,255	25	27	21
187. Athens	56,399	53,719	1,644	134	902
188. Belmont	82,569	80,616	1,631	39	283
189. Brown	31,920	31,463	353	50	54
190. Carroll	25,598	25,413	89	22	74
191. Clermont	128,483	127,153	835	108	387
192. Coshocton	36,024	35,354	464	46	160
193. Gallia	30,098	28,882	956	98	162
194. Guernsey	42,024	41,236	577	48	163
195. Harrison	18,152	17,617	496	18	21
196. Highland	33,477	32,611	729	93	44
197. Hocking	24,304	24,045	152	16	91
198. Holmes	29,416	29,330	08	50	28
199. Jackson	30,592	30,305	230	25	32
200. Jefferson	91,564	85,956	5,000	123	484
201. Lawrence	63,849	62,120	1,470	163	96
202. Meigs	23,641	23,355	225	36	25
203. Monroe	17,382	17,366	05	05	06
204. Morgan	14,241	13,631	514	53	43
205. Muskingum	83,340	79,390	3,642	123	185
206. Noble	11,310	11,275	—	29	06
207. Perry	30,978	30,927	06	10	35
208. Pike	22,805	22,380	240	104	81
209. Ross	65,004	61,280	3,327	95	302
210. Scioto	84,541	81,684	2,447	186	224
211. Tuscarawas	84,614	83,539	750	144	181
212. Vinton	11,584	11,552	08	11	13
213. Washington	64,266	63,086	892	87	201
Percentage	100.0	97.4	2.1	0.2	0.3

PENNSYLVANIA—Counties in Appalachia

Population State Total 1980	6,103,923	5,741,637	332,121	4,608	25,557

Total of Counties in Appalachia	Total Persons	Whites	Blacks	Amer. Indian	Others
214. Allegheny	1,450,085	1,288,989	150,077	1,104	9,915
215. Armstrong	77,768	76,755	888	27	98
216. Beaver	204,441	191,964	11,644	169	664
217. Bedford	46,784	46,556	148	39	41
218. Blair	136,621	135,166	1,039	76	340
219. Bradford	62,919	62,605	97	39	178
220. Butler	147,912	146,512	845	108	447
221. Cambria	183,263	179,282	3,508	71	402
222. Cameron	6,674	6,648	10	09	07
223. Carbon	53,285	53,051	43	25	166
224. Centre	112,760	109,376	1,704	79	1,601
225. Clarion	43,362	42,918	256	35	153
226. Clearfield	83,578	83,096	276	67	139
227. Clinton	38,971	38,675	162	18	116

PENNSYLVANIA con't

Total of Counties in Appalachia	Total Persons	Whites	Blacks	Amer. Indian	Others
228. Columbia	61,967	61,640	214	17	96
229. Crawford	88,869	87,342	1,063	146	318
230. Elk	38,338	38,238	03	09	88
231. Erie	388,780	265,589	121,135	384	1,672
232. Fayette	159,417	153,093	5,844	137	343
233. Forest	5,072	5,030	09	22	11
234. Fulton	12,842	12,707	107	11	17
235. Greene	40,476	39,920	420	51	85
236. Huntingdon	42,253	41,170	926	55	102
237. Indiana	92,281	91,009	903	74	295
238. Jefferson	48,303	48,105	43	51	104
239. Juniata	19,188	19,143	08	06	31
240. Lackawanna	227,908	225,763	1,072	62	1,011
241. Lawrence	107,150	103,790	3,101	64	195
242. Luzerne	343,079	339,744	2,101	113	1,121
243. Lycoming	118,415	116,000	1,699	122	594
244. McKean	50,635	50,271	102	114	148
245. Mercer	128,299	122,258	5,521	106	414
246. Mifflin	46,908	46,690	110	24	84
247. Monroe	69,409	68,145	822	24	418
248. Montour	16,675	16,557	20	25	73
249. Northumberland	100,381	100,046	96	83	156
250. Perry	35,689	35,608	21	17	43
251. Pike	18,271	18,138	57	12	64
252. Potter	17,726	17,564	62	22	78
253. Schuylkill	160,630	159,715	335	52	528
254. Snyder	33,584	33,334	124	33	93
255. Somerset	81,243	80,982	66	49	146
256. Sullivan	6,349	6,290	43	06	10
257. Susquehanna	37,876	37,687	19	73	97
258. Tioga	40,973	40,695	149	35	94
259. Union	32,870	31,751	875	34	210
260. Venago	64,444	63,832	305	59	248
261. Warren	47,449	47,297	21	83	48
262. Washington	217,074	208,957	7,324	256	537
263. Wayne	35,951	35,806	70	30	45
264. Westmoreland	392,294	383,903	6,527	267	1,597
265. Wyoming	26,432	26,235	107	14	76
Percentage	100.0	94.1	5.4	0.1	0.4

SOUTH CAROLINA—Counties in Appalachia

Population State Total	Total Persons	Whites	Blacks	Amer. Indian	Others
1980	835,095	654,155	176,481	675	3,784

Total of Counties in Appalachia	Total Persons	Whites	Blacks	Amer. Indian	Others
266. Anderson	133,235	109,823	22,895	109	408
267. Cherokee	40,983	32,800	7,988	37	158
268. Greenville	287,913	235,210	50,842	277	1,584
269. Oconee	91,811	43,656	48,037	43	75
270. Pickens	79,292	72,794	5,849	73	576
271. Spartanburg	201,861	159,872	40,870	136	983
Percentage	100.0	78.3	21.2	0.1	0.4

TENNESSEE—Counties in Appalachia

Population State Total 1980	2,090,517	1,955,618	120,775	2,506	11,618
Total of Counties in Appalachia	Total Persons	Whites	Blacks	Amer. Indian	Others
272. Anderson	70,256	64,043	2,594	164	3,455
273. Bledsoe	9,478	9,125	320	08	25
274. Blount	77,770	74,859	2,582	99	230
275. Bradley	67,547	64,392	2,668	168	319
276. Campbell	34,923	34,643	170	57	53
277. Cannon	10,234	10,022	187	06	19
278. Carter	50,205	49,647	426	42	90
279. Claiborne	24,595	24,202	314	46	33
280. Clay	7,676	7,545	112	08	11
281. Cocke	28,792	28,020	668	25	79
282. Coffee	38,311	36,725	1,340	29	217
283. Cumberland	28,676	28,600	06	22	48
284. DeKalb	13,589	13,282	268	09	30
285. Fentress	14,826	14,795	02	11	18
286. Franklin	31,983	29,587	2,279	21	96
287. Grainger	16,751	16,595	136	08	12
288. Greene	54,422	53,010	1,233	53	126
289. Grundy	13,787	13,772	02	05	08
290. Hamblen	49,300	46,747	2,341	67	145
291. Hamilton	287,740	229,976	55,840	308	1,616
292. Hancock	6,887	6,833	38	03	13
293. Hawkins	43,751	42,778	826	61	86
294. Jackson	9,398	9,367	21	01	09
295. Jefferson	31,284	30,259	922	46	57
296. Johnson	13,745	13,623	86	08	28
297. Knox	320,494	288,675	28,806	426	2,587
298. Loudon	28,553	28,055	421	32	45
299. McMinn	41,878	39,629	2,043	68	138
300. Macon	28,700	27,745	888	11	56
301. Marion	24,416	23,262	1,102	25	27
302. Meigs	7,431	7,279	138	08	06
303. Monroe	28,700	27,745	888	11	56
304. Morgan	16,604	16,430	118	17	39
305. Overton	17,575	17,493	44	28	10
306. Pickett	4,358	4,340	01	16	01
307. Polk	13,602	13,566	05	13	18
308. Putman	47,690	46,359	768	42	521
309. Rhea	24,208	23,458	611	45	94
310. Roane	48,425	46,731	1,526	34	134
311. Scott	19,259	19,161	06	69	23
312. Sequatchie	8,605	8,548	18	17	22
313. Sevier	41,418	41,112	162	46	98
314. Smith	14,935	14,308	600	12	15
315. Sullivan	143,968	140,855	2,607	145	361
316. Unicoi	16,362	16,300	04	18	40
317. Union	11,707	11,689	—	16	02
318. Van Buren	4,728	4,714	04	04	06
319. Warren	32,653	31,351	1,199	30	73
320. Washington	88,755	85,269	3,004	89	393
321. White	19,567	19,097	431	09	30
Percentage	**100.0**	**93.5**	**5.9**	**0.1**	**0.5**

VIRGINIA—Counties in Appalachia
Population
State Total
1980

	Total Persons	Whites	Blacks	Amer. Indian	Others
	505,480	493,412	10,618	352	1,098

Total of Counties in Appalachia	Total Persons	Whites	Blacks	Amer. Indian	Others
322. Alleghany	14,333	13,923	356	12	42
323. Bath	5,838	5,284	553	01	—
324. Bland	6,349	6,131	198	09	11
325. Botetourt	23,270	22,093	1,124	13	40
326. Buchanan	37,989	37,839	21	14	115
327. Carroll	27,270	27,126	94	09	41
328. Craig	3,946	3,938	08	—	—
329. Dickerson	19,806	19,673	94	03	36
330. Floyd	11,563	11,152	384	06	21
331. Giles	17,810	17,400	354	05	51
332. Grayson	16,579	16,002	550	10	17
333. Highland	2,937	2,919	06	03	09
334. Lee	25,956	25,804	89	44	19
335. Pulaski	35,229	33,211	1,867	52	99
336. Russell	31,761	31,412	300	28	21
337. Scott	25,068	24,887	157	14	10
338. Smyth	33,366	32,669	594	22	81
339. Tazewell	50,511	48,990	1,304	39	178
340. Washington	46,487	45,555	798	19	115
341. Wise	43,890	42,863	857	38	132
342. Wythe	25,522	24,541	910	11	60
Percentage	100.0	97.6	2.1	0.1	0.2

WEST VIRGINIA—Counties in Appalachia
Population
State Total
1980

	Total Persons	Whites	Blacks	Amer. Indian	Others
	1,929,122	1,853,437	65,061	1,555	9,069

Total of Counties in Appalachia	Total Persons	Whites	Blacks	Amer. Indian	Others
343. Barbour	16,639	16,416	154	22	47
344. Berkeley	46,775	44,764	1,701	45	265
345. Boone	30,447	30,064	297	16	70
346. Braxton	13,964	13,795	75	11	83
347. Brooke	31,126	30,792	248	20	66
348. Cabell	106,815	101,627	4,488	70	630
349. Calhoun	8,250	8,187	12	04	47
350. Clay	11,265	11,246	04	03	12
351. Doddridge	7,433	7,406	04	08	15
352. Fayette	57,863	53,276	4,321	41	225
353. Gilmer	8,334	8,256	37	19	22
354. Grant	10,210	10,059	121	05	25
355. Greenbrier	37,665	35,992	1,539	25	109
356. Hampshire	14,867	14,714	107	10	36
357. Hancock	40,418	39,183	1,035	38	162
358. Hardy	10,030	9,816	203	08	03
359. Harrison	77,710	76,384	1,014	45	267
360. Jackson	25,794	25,711	16	15	52
361. Jefferson	30,302	27,389	2,733	40	140
362. Kanawha	231,414	215,953	13,776	155	1,530
363. Lewis	18,813	18,673	61	09	70
364. Lincoln	23,675	23,632	04	14	25

WEST VIRGINIA con't

Total of Counties in Appalachia	Total Persons	Whites	Blacks	Amer. Indian	Others
365. Logan	50,679	48,290	2,149	40	200
366. McDowell	49,899	42,401	7,378	25	95
367. Marion	65,789	63,186	2,263	91	249
368. Marshall	41,608	41,198	247	29	134
369. Mason	27,045	26,799	135	11	100
370. Mercer	73,932	68,483	5,030	65	354
371. Mineral	27,236	26,334	804	24	74
372. Mingo	37,336	36,162	1,100	11	63
373. Monongalia	75,024	72,270	1,536	82	1,136
374. Monroe	12,873	12,611	204	17	41
375. Morgan	10,711	10,583	104	08	16
376. Nicholas	28,126	28,051	03	15	57
377. Ohio	61,364	58,051	2,126	44	1,143
378. Pendleton	7,910	7,713	171	04	22
379. Pleasants	8,256	8,207	25	01	23
380. Pocahontas	9,919	9,814	70	15	20
381. Preston	9,952	9,814	55	45	38
382. Putman	38,089	38,012	52	25	—
383. Raleigh	86,821	79,408	6,862	59	492
384. Randolph	28,734	28,385	216	37	96
385. Ritchie	11,442	11,422	04	08	08
386. Roane	15,952	15,806	25	67	54
387. Summer	15,875	14,634	1,097	23	121
388. Taylor	16,584	16,411	109	29	35
389. Tucker	8,675	8,648	08	07	12
390. Tyler	11,320	11,297	03	04	16
391. Upshur	23,427	23,245	91	18	73
392. Wayne	46,039	45,920	21	22	76
393. Webster	12,245	12,228	—	09	08
394. Wetzel	21,874	21,800	05	13	56
395. Wirt	4,936	4,905	13	01	17
396. Wood	93,648	92,510	823	49	266
397. Wyoming	35,993	35,504	382	34	73
Percentage	**100.0**	**96.0**	**3.4**	**0.1**	**0.5**

NOTES

1. Clarence Wright. "Black Appalachian Invisibility—Myth or Reality?" *Black Appalachian Viewpoints*, 1 (August 6, 1978) pp. 1-3
2. Edward J. Cabbell. "Black Invisibility and Racism in Appalachia: An Informal Survey." *Appalachian Journal*, 16 (Autumn 1980) pp. 48-54.
3. Ibid., p. 48
4. Ibid.
5. Ibid.
6. ARC Staff. "Appalachia: The Economic Outlook Through the Eighties." *Appalachia*, 16 (December 1984) p. 5.
7. Ibid.

Moving On: Recent Patterns of Appalachian Migration

by
Phillip J. Obermiller
and Robert Oldendick

Although European mapmakers and explorers designated Appalachia as a graphic area as early as the sixteenth century, the notion of Appalachia as the locus of a particular culture, social structure, and political economy evolved much later, principally in the era following the Civil War (Shapiro, 1978; Walls, 1977). Local-color writers, educators, church people, and others used the purported physical and social isolation of Appalachia to explain the cultural uniqueness and lack of economic development of the region (Shapiro, 1977, 1978). By the turn of the century Appalachia and its people had been labeled as "different" and "deficient"; as a consequence, Appalachia was defined clearly as a major social problem by the beginning of the twentieth century (U.S. Department of Agriculture, 1935; Vance, 1962).

Such a problem must be defined before it can be treated. This step in the process requires the gathering and analysis of data; in the case of a large geographic "problem area" like Appalachia, researchers often seek information about the basic demographic processes of the area, including rates of fertility, mortality, and migration. The decline in fertility in Appalachia which began at the turn of the century and intensified in the 1950s, has been well documented (Ford and DeJong, 1963; Murdock and McCoy, 1974). Mortality rates for what was then called "The Allegheny Region" were compared with those of other regions of the country as early as 1860 (Walls, 1977). According to at least one demographic historian, significant outmigration from the mountains had already begun in the 1830s (Barron, 1977). The study of Appalachian migration patterns provides the most useful demographic approach for understanding not only the problems but also the social and economic dynamics of the region. Migration has been a key factor in both the early growth and the later loss of population in Appalachia (Belcher, 1962; Brown 1972). It serves as a clear indicator of the economic conditions prevailing in Appalachia and its subregions at any given time (Brown and Hillery, 1962; Peoples Appalachian Research Collective, 1972).

Moreover, theories of Appalachian cultural uniqueness and social isolation can be tested readily through studies of inmigrants and return migrants (Anglin, 1983; Garkovich, 1982), through studies of outmigrants (Schwarzweller, Brown, and Mangalam, 1971; Philliber, 1981), through comparisons of migrants with nonmigrants (Uhlenberg, 1975), and through international comparisons of Appalachian migrants with similar groups (Marger and Obermiller, 1983).

Although migration studies make an important and useful contribution to our understanding of the Appalachian experience, patterns of recent Appalachian migration have been neglected. No effort has been made to compare current (1980) Appalachian migration patterns with previously collected data on earlier Appalachian migration patterns, nor have recent Appalachian migration flows been compared with national migration trends. In this paper, we will attempt to update the study of Appalachian migration.

We will begin by examining the principal studies of Appalachian migration, and will describe the data set used in the current study. Next, we will present an overview of Appalachian migration for the period 1980-81, including a brief analysis of migration flows at the state level. This discussion will be followed by a description of current migration streams to selected urban areas, along with the change in migration to these areas that occurred between the late 1960s and the early 1980s. We will summarize these findings with a survey of recent patterns of net Appalachian migration by national regions, census divisions, states, and selected urban areas. To illustrate the underlying dynamics of these general migration patterns, we will examine two case studies, outmigration from Appalachia to Harris County (Houston), Texas, and inmigration into the Appalachian counties of Eastern Kentucky. In conclusion, we will discuss these findings both in light of the changes and continuity in Appalachian migration patterns over time and in terms of the relationship between these patterns and national migration trends.

PREVIOUS STUDIES

The field of regional studies has identified two basic economic options that affect migration: the distribution of economic opportunities to regional populations primarily through the creation of jobs, which inhibits migration, or the distribution of regional populations to external areas of economic opportunity, which encourages migration (Cumberland, 1973). Carter Goodrich and his associates (1936) recommended the later option as a result of a study they made in the mid-1930s, which included eight-four coal-producing counties in the Cumberland Plateau. The study advocated that the number of farmers and miners in this area be reduced through the outmigration of more than a quarter of the area's population (Goodrich et. al., 1936: 122-123).

Brown and Hillery (1962) documented the fact that many persons did, in fact, leave the southern Appalachian region during the twenty-year period between 1940 and 1960. Although a great deal of movement took place within the region, southern Appalachia also experienced a net loss of over thirteen percent of its population between 1940 and 1950, and a net loss of nineteen percent between 1950 and 1960 (Brown and Hillery, 1962: 59, Table 9). In his review of the 1970 census data, James S. Brown (1972) notes that between 1960 and 1970, outmigration from southern Appalachia continued at a considerably lower rate, resulting in a net loss by migration of five percent for the decade (Brown, 1972: 138). During the 1960s, the metropolitan areas within southern Appalachia increased by nearly eight percent, principally through inmigration, since natural increase had declined significantly during this period; with the exception of those in Georgia, the nonmetropolitan counties in each of the ten states with Appalachian areas experienced an overall loss due to net migration (Brown, 1972: 135-138).

Paralleling national trends in rural-to-urban migration, the majority of Appalachian migrants moved to large, industrialized metropolitan areas. Clyde B. McCoy and James S. Brown (1981) have documented in some detail the migration stream systems from southern Appalachia into major metropolitan areas of the country. Their study identifies the thirty top-ranking metropolitan destinations for southern Appalachian migrants, as well as the particular migration stream systems between West Virginia and Kentucky and the ten metropolitan focal areas for these systems (McCoy and Brown 1981). Although the rate of outmigration decreased over the thirty-year period ending in 1970, McCoy and Brown, find a great deal of consistency in the direction and proportions of Appalachian migration to the metropolitan focal areas they have identified.

The major finding of the Apalachian Regional Commission's Report to Congress on Migration (1979) is the turn around in net Appalachian migration. An analysis of the Social Security Administration's continuous work history sample for 1965, 1970, and 1975 indicates that Appalachian migration changed from a net loss to the region in the period of 1965-70 to a net gain in the period 1970-75. The pattern of outmigration also changed: while Northern states remained the destination of the greatest number of Appalachian migrants, states in the South showed the largest gain in the percentage of Appalachian migrants received (Appalachian Regional Commission, 1979b: Tables 11-3 and 11-4). The report concludes that most outmigrants enjoy greater incomes than they experienced while in Appalachia, and quickly gain income parity with workers in the areas where they settle (Appalachian Regional Commission, 1979b: 15).

THE CURRENT STUDY

The data for this study were compiled by the Bureau of the Census for the Internal Revenue Service (IRS) from the Individual Master File, which includes a record of every individual income tax return form 1040 and 1040A for 1980 and 1981. The Area-to-Area Migration Flow Data were developed by matching the social security numbers (SSNs) on returns filed in each year. When identical social security numbers were found, the counties of residence on each return were compared to see whether they matched. A match in county of residence was counted as an instance of nonmigrant; when the counties did not match, the taxpayer was considered an outmigrant from the county of residence in the base year, and an inmigrant to the county of residence in the subsequent year. The final step in the process was to tally the exemptions on all subsequent year forms which had identical SSNs with the base year, and to categorize them as either nonmigrant, inmigrant, or outmigrant. (See Notes 1,2, & 3.)

The figures derived from the IRS Area-to-Area Migration Flow Data have several limitations which should be noted so that the data presented here may be evaluated properly. Individuals who fail to file tax returns, those who are not required to file returns, and those who inflate the number of exemptions on their returns all detract from the representativeness of the data. In addition, the IRS has applied rules for suppression and aggregation to the data set in order to make it manageable and to protect the anonymity of individual taxpayers. (See Note 4.) These characteristics of the data set make it impossible to calculate the exact volumes of migration or to describe the social characteristics of the migrants.

The IRS data set, however, does have attributes not found in other sources of migration data such as the decennial census, the current population survey, or the Census Bureau's annual population estimates (Rogerson and Plane, 1985). First of all, it is inclusive: taxpayers and their dependents include ninety percent of the population. (See Note 5.) Also, it is timely: the IRS data allow the tracking of annual fluctuations in migration. It is specific: the IRS data can be analyzed at specific regional, subregional, state, and county levels for particular years and series of years. Finally, it is extensive: the IRS data allow the tracking of inmigrants and outmigrants, as well as county to county migration flows.

Other characteristics of this study were also worth noting. The definition of the Appalachian region and the definitions of metropolitan, urban, and rural counties within the Appalachian region employed in this study follow those used by the Appalachian Regional Commission (Appalachian Regional Commission, 1979a). (See Notes 6 & 7.) The "urban areas" referred to throughout the study are actually the counties in which the cities named are located; these areas are not necessarily congruent with the commonly used designations of urban places, urbanized areas, or metropolitan statistical areas (Weller and Bouvier, 1981). In addition, the data present migration flows for one year only; estimates for more extensive period cannot be extrapolated accurately from this small base.

In spite of these limitations, however, the data presented in the following sections of this report provide a current and fairly accurate picture of Appalachian migration patterns. Morever, these patterns can, with reasonable confidence, be compared with previously established patterns of Appalachian migration and with recent trends in U.S. internal migration.

THE FINDINGS

In the twelve months covered by this study, slightly more individuals left the Appalachian region than entered it. Table 1 shows that the leading sources of outmigrants were the metropolitan counties in Appalachia. These counties, which had 49 percent of the region's 1980 population, accounted for 55 percent of the outmigrants. The urban counties had 25 percent of the population and 24 percent of the outmigrants; the rural counties, which had 26 percent of the population, contributed 21 percent of the outmigrants. We found similar percentage distributions among metropolitan (54%), urban (23%), and rural (23%) Appalachian counties for the flow of migrants into the region.

TABLE 1.

1980-81 Appalachian migration by county type.[1]

	Destination			
Origin	Metropolitan	Urban	Rural	Out of Region
Metropolitan	119,418	35,147	22,831	289,752
Urban	34,699	22,262	29,475	127,870
Rural	22,157	30,452	41,365	114,123
Out of Region	281,845	119,830	119,671	—

1980-81 Net Migration —10,399

[1]For county typology see Appalachian Regional Commission, 1979.
Source: IRS Area-to-Area Migration Flow Data.

Internal migration flows within Appalachia indicate that rural counties are the most frequent destinations for those who leave rural counties; of all rural-county outmigrants 44 percent moved to other rural counties, 32 percent to urban counties, and 24 percent to metropolitan counties. Similarly, metropolitan counties are the most popular destination for those who leave metropolitan counties; of all metropolitan county outmigrants, 67 percent moved to other metropolitan counties, 20 percent to urban counties, and 13 percent to rural counties. Residents of urban counties, however, tend to move to either rural or metropolitan counties, with a preference for the latter. In the period 1980-81, 40 percent of all urban county outmigrants moved to metropolitan counties, 34 percent to rural counties, and only 26 precent to other urban counties.

Table 2a shows the non-Appalachian states with the most significant migration flows during the period under study. When we compared inmigrant flows with outmigrant flows, it became apparent that reciprocal flows exist between Appalachia and California, Florida, Illinois, New Jersey, and Texas. The flows from Indiana and Michigan to Appalachia are substantially one-way streams; few migrants move to these states from the region. The flows from Appalachia to Arizona and Massachussetts are also substantially one-way, but in the opposite direction: few migrants from these states move to Appalachia.

TABLE 2a.

Migration flows to and from the Appalachian region for selected states, 1980-81.[1]

Migrants to Appalachia (N)	State	Migrants from Appalachia (N)	State
5,135	Florida	10,734	Florida
2,136	Illinois	10,465	Texas
2,122	New Jersey	4,849	California
1,946	California	2,207	Arizona
1,836	Michigan	1,141	Illinois
1,724	Texas	525	Massachusetts
1,266	Indiana	431	New Jersey

TABLE 2b.

Net Appalachian migration for selected states, 1980-81.[1]

Net Gains	State
8,741	Texas
5,599	Florida
2,903	California
1,795	Arizona

Net Losses	State
−995	Illinois
−1,266	Indiana
−1,691	New Jersey
−1,784	Michigan

[1]Tables do not include states with Appalachian counties.
Source: IRS Area-to-Area Migration Flow Data.

The non-Appalachian states that show the most significant net gains in migrants from the region were Texas, Florida, California, and Arizona, in that order. Those showing the most significant net losses are Michigan, New Jersey, Indiana, and Illinois.

Table 3 presents a more precise view of recent Appalachian migration. The table includes those non-Appalachian counties that had a net gain or loss of 200 or more migrants from the Appalachian region in 1980-81. Since the counties are invariably metropolitan, the name of the chief city in each county is used to designate the "urban area."

TABLE 3.

Selected urban areas ranked by net Appalachian migration, 1980-81.[1]

Urban Area	Net Migration	From Appalachia	To Appalachia
Houston	6,570	7,883	1,313
Nashville	3,140	5,314	2,174
Tampa/St. Pete.	2,992	3,684	692
Phoenix	1,635	2,047	412
Dallas	1,537	1,658	121
Los Angeles	1,482	2,851	1,369
Lexington	940	2,745	1,805
W. Palm Beach	838	1,126	288
Columbus	691	4,365	3,674
Jacksonville	623	948	325
Anaheim	593	643	50
Charlotte	576	2,033	1,457
Ft. Lauderdale	492	2,163	1,671
Mobile	401	1,162	761
Jackson	345	554	209
San Diego	320	767	447
Washington	221	331	110
Roanoke	207	860	653
Louisville	-243	300	543
Indianapolis	-258	-0-	258
Dayton	-463	395	858
Cleveland	-630	1,616	2,246
New York	-632	813	1,445
Chicago	-1,024	1,112	2,136
Miami	-1,046	644	1,690
Detroit	-1,420	52	1,472
Cincinnati	-1,933	4,366	6,299
Atlanta	-5,670	9,995	15,665

[1]Table excludes urban areas in the Appalachian region.
Source: IRS Area-to-Area Migration Flow Data.

Houston and its environs had the largest net gain in migrants from Appalachia of any non-Appalachian urban areas in the United States: it had over twice as many migrants as the second and third highest-ranked urban areas, Nashville and Tampa/St. Petersburg, and well above three times as many as Phoenix, Dallas, and Los Angeles, which ranked fourth, fifth, and sixth respectively.

Atlanta was the chief among those urban areas that sent more migrants to the Appalachian region than they gained, and had by far the highest combined Appalachian in- and outmigration. These facts must be interpreted with caution, however, since the county in which the city of Atlanta is located, Fulton County, shares common boundaries with five Appalachian counties. Similar conditions exist for the counties in which Cincinnatti, Lexington, Roanoke, and Montgomery are located. Although these areas are likely to have high rates of exchange with neighboring counties, a situation that fulfills the technical definition of migration, their position in the ranking becomes somewhat ambiguous when compared with urban areas much more distant from Appalachia.

Table 4 presents a comparison of the thirty top-ranked metropolitan destinations for Appalachian migrants for the periods 1965-70 and 1980-81. Nine of the destinations found in the earlier ranking—Washington, Detroit, Baltimore, Columbia, Dayton, Norfolk, Richmond, New York, and Louisville—have been replaced in the more recent ranking by Houston, Lexington, Montgomery, Ft. Lauderdale, Phoenix, Dallas, Mobile, West Palm Beach, and Jacksonville. The positions of Atlanta, Birmingham, Chattanooga, Knoxville, and Philadelphia have remained fairly constant in each order, while Chicago and Cleveland rank significantly lower in 1981 than in the previous order. Pittsburgh, the Winston-Salem/Highpoint/Greensboro area, Charleston, and Greenville have all moved to substantially higher positions in the 1981 ranking.

TABLE 4.

Top-ranking metropolitan destinations for migrants from Southern Appalachia, 1965-70[1] and for migrants from the Appalachian region, 1980-81[2].

Rank	1965-70	1980-81
1	Atlanta	Pittsburgh*
2	Washington	Atlanta
3	Detroit	Birmingham*
4	Birmingham*	Houston
5	Knoxville*	Knoxville*
6	Chicago	Chattanooga*
7	Chattanooga*	Nashville
8	Cleveland	Greenville*
9	Los Angeles	Cincinnati
10	Nashville	Columbus
11	Huntington*	Tampa/St. Pete.
12	Huntsville*	Charleston*
13	Baltimore	Winston-Salem*/Highpoint/Greensboro
14	Columbus	Huntsville*
15	Tuscaloosa*	Huntington*
16	Cincinnati	Los Angeles
17	Greenville*	Lexington
18	Charlotte	Montgomery
19	Charleston*	Ft. Lauderdale
20	Columbia	Phoenix
21	Tampa	Charlotte
22	Dayton	Tuscaloosa*
23	Norfolk	Dallas
24	Richmond	Cleveland
25	New York	Mobile
26	Louisville	W. Palm Beach
27	Roanoke	Chicago
28	Winston-Salem*/Highpoint/Greensboro	Jacksonville
29	Pittsburgh*	Philadelphia
30	Philadelphia	Roanoke

*Located in the Appalachian Region.
Table excludes urban areas in the Appalachian region.
[1]Source: McCoy and Brown, 1981.
[2]Source: IRS Area-to-Area Migration Flow Data.

TABLE 5.

Net Appalachian migration to selected urban areas by census regions and divisions, 1980-1981.

Census Region	Census Division	Urban Area	Net Migration	Division Totals	Region Totals
South					9,420
	South Atlantic			-2,174	
		Tampa/St. Pete., Fl.	2,992		
		West Palm Beach, Fl.	838		
		Jacksonville, Fl.	623		
		Charlotte, N.C.	576		
		Ft. Lauderdale, Fl.	492		
		Washington, DC	221		
		Roanoke, Va.	207		
		Columbia, S.C.	63		
		Greensboro, N.C.	36		
		*Huntington, W.V.	19		
		Baltimore, Md.	-37		
		*Charleston, W.V.	-434		
		Miami, Fl.	-1,046		
		*Greenville, S.C.	-1,054		
		Atlanta, Ga.	-5,670		
	East South Central			3,487	
		Nashville, Tn.	3,140		
		Lexington, Ky.	940		
		Mobile, Al.	401		
		Jackson, Mi.	345		
		*Huntsville, Al.	267		
		*Knoxville, Tn.	256		
		*Tuscaloosa, Al.	168		
		Montgomery, Al.	-101		
		Louisville, Ky.	-243		
		*Chattanooga, Tn.	-503		
		*Birmingham, Al.	-1,183		
	West South Central			8,107	
		Houston, Tx.	6,570		
		Dallas, Tx.	1,537		
West					4,030
	West Pacific			2,395	
		Los Angeles, Ca.	1,482		
		Anaheim, Ca.	593		
		San Diego, Ca.	320		
	West Mountain			1,635	
		Phoenix, Az.	1,635		
Northeast					-2,421
	Middle Atlantic			-2,421	
		New York, N.Y.	-632		
		*Pittsburg, Pa.	-1,789		
North Central					-5,037
	East North Central			-5,037	
		Columbus, Oh.	691		
		Indianapolis, In.	-258		
		Dayton, Oh.	-463		
		Cleveland, Oh.	-630		
		Chicago, Il.	-1,024		
		Detroit, Mi.	-1,420		
		Cincinnati, Oh.	-1,933		

*Indicates urban area in Appalachian region.
Source: IRS Area-to-Area Migration Flow Data.

As elsewhere, we advise caution in examining this table because two different geographic definitions were used in constructing the rankings (see note 6). In the later ranking, the definition of Appalachia includes counties in the states of New York, Pennsylvania, and Ohio, while the earlier definition excludes counties in these states. This difference, for example, could be the principal reason behind the radical change in the ranking of the Pittsburgh area between one period and the other.

When net migration figures for selected urban areas are categorized by census regions and regional divisions (Table 5), a clear pattern emerges. For 1980-81 the urban areas in the Northeast and North Central regions show losses in Appalachian migration—2,421 and 5,037 respectively—while Western states show a net gain of 4,030. Urban areas in the South have a regional net gain of 9,420 migrants from Appalachia.

At the divisional level, net losses occur in urban areas located in the South Atlantic states despite substantial net gains in Florida, in East North Central states (5,037), and in the Middle Atlantic states (2,421). Net gains are recorded for urban areas located in the states of the East South Central (3,487), West South Central (8,107), West Pacific (2,395), and West Mountain (1,635) divisions.

In Table 6, which depicts the case study of Appalachian migration flows to the Houston urban area, it is evident that nearly three-fifths of the Appalachian migrants to Houston come from the Northern Appalachian subregion, slightly over two-fifths from Southern Appalachia, and a negligible number from Central Appalachia. These proportions parallel closely the distribution of the donor counties by subregion. In relation to total regional population, Southern Appalachia is proportionately represented in the Houston migration flow, Northern Appalachia is overrepresented, and Central Appalachia is underrepresented.

All the states with Appalachian counties with the exception of Virginia contributed to the Houston area migration flow. Pennsylvania and Alabama are overrepresented in this migration flow, both in number of donor counties and in proportion of the regional population. The numbers of migrants to Houston from Tennessee, West Virginia, New York, and Ohio are roughly proportionate to their respective states share of the regional population, but underrepresented in number of donor counties. Houston, in contrast is attracting Appalachian migrants from metropolitan counties in quantities vastly disproportionate to the number and total population of those counties. Only one in five of the migrants to Houston came from urban counties within the region; only three out of every hundred came from rural Appalachian counties.

Table 7 summarizes the case study of inmigration to the Appalachian counties of Eastern Kentucky. In 1980-81 22,535 persons moved into Kentucky's Appalachian counties, and about one-fifth of these came from major areas. The figures indicate that most of the movers in this area are internal

TABLE 6

1980-81 Appalachian migration to Harris County, Texas,
by Appalachian subregion, donor state, and county type.[1]

	Donor counties to Harris Co.		1980 Population of subregions, states, and donor counties[2]		Migrants to Harris Co.	
	(N)	(%)	(N)	(%)	(N)	(%)
SUBREGIONS						
Northern	57	55%	10,123,604	50%	4,453	56%
Southern	41	39%	7,995,784	40%	3,231	41%
Central	6	6%	2,114,947	10%	199	3%
Totals:	104	100%	20,234,335	100%	7,883	100%
STATES						
PA	26	25%	5,995,097	30%	2,921	37%
AL	18	17%	2,427,024	12%	1,772	22%
TN	14	13%	2,073,647	11%	869	11%
WV	11	11%	1,949,644	10%	589	7%
NY	8	8%	1,083,266	5%	467	6%
OH	12	11%	1,262,558	6%	462	6%
GA	5	5%	1,103,941	5%	269	3%
SC	2	2%	791,587	4%	158	2%
NC	3	3%	1,217,723	6%	156	2%
MS	3	3%	482,712	2%	145	2%
KY	1	1%	1,077,095	5%	40	1%
MD	1	1%	220,132	1%	35	1%
VA	0	0%	549,909	3%	0	0%
Totals:	104	100%	20,234,335	100%	7,883	100%
COUNTY TYPES						
*Metropolitan	56	54%	9,901,104	49%	6,018	76%
Urban	41	39%	5,107,839	25%	1,678	21%
Rural	7	7%	5,225,392	26%	187	3%
Totals:	104	100%	20,234,335	100%	7,883	100%

[1]For subregional definitions and county typology, see Appalachian Regional Commission, 1979.
[2]Source: Pickard, 1981a. All other figures are from IRS Area-to-Area Migration Flow Data.

migrants; that is, they moved from one county to another within Eastern Kentucky. The rest of the local moves are split fairly even between non-Appalachian Kentucky counties and counties in the Appalachian areas of West Virginia, Ohio, Tennessee, and Virginia.

Inmigrants to Eastern Kentucky come principally from urban areas in Kentucky and Ohio, followed by Michigan, Indiana, West Virginia, and Illinois. The chief urban donor areas include Lexington, Cincinnati, Louisville, Detroit, and Columbus.

DISCUSSION

Although the evidence is incomplete, the much remarked-upon "migration turnaround" of the 1970s which saw the first net gain in migration to Appalachia in five decades, may have come to an end in the early 1980s (Picard, 1981a, 1981b). This finding would correspond to a national trend detected in the early 1980s, in which the flow of migrants to rural America

TABLE 7

1980-81 migration into Kentucky Appalachian counties from selected donor areas.

			(N)	(%)
From Contiguous State Areas			17,783	79%
	(N)	(%)		
Kentucky (App. Cos. to App. Cos.)	15,129	85%		
*Kentucky (Non-App. Cos. to App. Cos.)	1,279	7%		
*West Virginia	528	3%		
*Ohio	422	2%		
Tennessee	320	2%		
Virginia	105	1%		
		(100%)		
From Urban Areas by State			4,752	21%
	(N)	(%)	(N)	(%)
Kentucky			2,312	49%
Lexington	1,805	78%		
Louisville	507	22%		
		(100%)		
Ohio			1,341	28%
Cincinnati	542	40%		
Columbus	307	23%		
Dayton	240	18%		
Hamilton/Middletown	214	16%		
Mansfield	38	3%		
		(100%)		
Michigan			440	9%
Detroit	401	91%		
Battle Creek	39	9%		
		(100%)		
Indiana			354	7%
Indianapolis	221	62%		
Ft. Wayne/Elkhart/So. Bend	133	38%		
		(100%)		
West Virginia			155	3%
Huntington	119	77%		
Charleston	36	23%		
		(100%)		
Illinois			150	3%
Chicago	150	100%		
		(100%)	(100%)	
Total inmigrants			22,535	100%

*Less inmigrants from urban areas in these states.
Source: IRS Area-to-Area Migration Flow Data.

decreased notably from that of the mid-1970s (Agresta, 1985; Population Reference Bureau, 1982). Within Appalachia, however, the migrants' preference for rural counties over urban counties continued from the 1970s into the 1980s, but the flow of internal migrants away from metropolitan counties appears to have ended (Picard, 1981b). the most frequent destinations for internal migrants in this study were metropolitan counties, while the least frequent were the formerly popular urban counties.

Appalachian migrants also reflect national preference in their choices of which states to enter and which states to leave. The 1980 census data document a preference for destinations in Texas, Florida, California, and Arizona and a disinclination to stay in Illinois, Indiana, New Jersey, and Michigan (Robey and Russell, 1983). The national migration flows to states in the South and West and away from the North and East are paralleled by the Appalachian migration patterns presented in this study (Rogerson and Plane, 1985).

In their choice of urban destinations, migrants from Appalachia go where jobs are available, but probably encounter intense competition from other migrants upon arrival. Eight of the top-ranked urban destinations of Appalachian migrants are among the twelve urban areas projected to have the greatest population growth between 1980 and 2000: Houston, San Diego, Dallas, Los Angeles, Phoenix, Anaheim, Ft. Lauderdale, and Tampa/St. Petersburg (Holdrich, 1984). Similarly, six of the top-ranked urban destinations of Appalachian migrants are among the twelve urban areas projected to have the greatest gain in employment between 1980 and 2000: Houston, Los Angeles, Anaheim, Dallas, San Diego, and Phoenix (Holdrich, 1984).

Although recent Appalachian migration patterns parallel national patterns of migration, they diverge significantly from historic patterns of Appalachian migration. Brown and McCoy (1981) found high correlations among the rankings for the metropolitan destinations of Appalachian migrants in the 1950s, 1960s, and 1970s. Despite some inconsistency in the way the data were gathered for the 1965-70 study and the 1980-81 study, we noted a substantial change in the pattern of migrant destinations in the 1980s. The change is clear and consistent throughout the county, state, and regional levels of analysis. The focus of Appalachian migration has shifted from the cities and states of the Northeast and Midwest, and has now turned toward the cities and states of the South, Southwest, and West.

The study of outmigration from Appalachia to the Houston area provides some insight into the nature of these migration flows. A sizeable portion (24%) of the migrants in the Houston flow came from nonmetropolitan counties. About one in two came from Northern Appalachia, more than one in three from Pennsylvania, and one in six from the Pittsburgh area. This migration stream is likely to be a mixture of upwardly mobile urban business people and professionals seeking career advancement in Houston; unemployed blue-collar workers from the declining manufacturing industries in Northern Appalachia; entry-level job seekers leaving areas of small population and few opportunities; retirees seeking a better climate; and relatives of members of each of these groups. The composition of this stream, as far as it can be accurately characterized, may serve to approximate the other streams of outmigrants identified in this study.

The immigration to Eastern Kentucky adds another aspect to the migration picture. The migration flows into this area come almost exclusively from the North, with only two lateral flows, Louisville/Lexington and Charleston/Huntington. These migrants are likely to be return migrants, with social and cultural roots in Appalachian Kentucky (Anglin, 1983).

Although some may be retirees, they are younger on the whole than the networks of kin and acquaintances who drew them back (Garkovich, 1982). They may be looking for work in the coal industry or in service jobs that wax and wane with the fortunes of the coal business. Others are visitors, biding their time and accumulating whatever resources they can for the next move in search of work.

CONCLUSION

Three major conclusions can be reached on the basis of this study. First, it appears that patterns of outmigration from Appalachia changed substantially between the 1960s and 1970s and the early 1980s. The urban areas that serve as the focal points for current Appalachian migration flows are now more likely to be found in the Southern and Western states than in those of the Midwest or Northeast. Second, it appears that patterns of internal migration within Appalachia have changed between 1970 and 1980. Migrants within the region are moving to metropolitan counties at higher rates in the 1980s than in the previous decade. Third, outmigrants from the Appalachian region move in a fashion quite similar to other internal migrants in the United States. Current Appalachian migration streams flow toward the same general receiving areas as do the larger national migration streams. In their patterns of "moving on," recent Appalachian migrants are less similar to earlier migrants from Appalachia than to their contemporaries in other parts of the country.

NOTES

1) Only the returns in which the SSN in 1980 matched the SSN in 1981 were included. Reasons for nonmatches include errors in entering or reading the SSN, individuals marrying and having the second SSN on a joint return, deaths, failure to file, and falling outside the guidelines for filing.

2) Some reasons for differences in the number of exemptions between matching 1980 and 1981 returns are births, deaths, marriages, and dependents leaving the status of dependent. Since the 1981 data are the most recent, they have been interpreted as being the best indication of the actual number of exemptions.

3) Exemptions for blindness and age were not included in the final tally.

4) When the number of returns indicating movement from one county to another were ten or less, they were aggregated into the appropriate larger category: "same state" or one of the four census regions. The present study makes no allocation of the exemptions in these categories.

In addition, if county-to-county migration did not account for at least 0.5% of the migrants to the county of destination on the inmigration data set or at least 0.5% of the migrants from the county of origin on the outmigration data set, this information was not presented by county but included in a larger geographical category. This resulted in roughly one-third to two-fifths of the data being reported on a higher geographical level than the county-to-county level. Consequently, the figures presented in this study for county-to-county migration are quiet conservative.

Finally, since different aggregation rules may be in effect for inmigration and for outmigration data, the results produced from the two data sets are not necessarily symmetrical. An example may help to illustrate the discrepancies this may cause. In the inmigration data, where Elk County, PA, is the county of destination, the records show that 21 returns were filed by people who migrated from Allegheny County (Pittsburgh), PA. The outmigration data, in which Allegheny County is the county of origin, have no separate record for these 21 returns that indicate relocation in Elk County, but have them aggregated with other "same state" movers. These returns represent four percent of the returns for migrants into Elk County, and accordingly they are listed individually in the inmigration data; however, they account for less than 0.5% of the returns for migrants from Allegheny County, and therefore are aggregated in the "same state" category in the outmigration data. This aggregation procedure causes underestimates of the county-to-county migration into counties with large populations and underestimates of the county-to-county migration out of these counties. With this in mind, we have used the outmigration data set when counties with large populations were the place of destination, and the inmigration data set when these counties were the place of origin.

5) The 1980 census was conducted on April 1, 1980, and the data for the base year in this study were collected on April 15, 1980. The total exemptions for a random sample of Appalachian counties averaged 83 percent of the total census population for these counties. The difference between the national average (90 percent of census totals) and the Appalachian average may be attributed in part to the region's high incidence of poverty, which may place many individuals below the minimum income requirement for filing a tax return (Appalachian Regional Commission, 1982a, 1982b).

6) Consensus is lacking on a geographic definition of the region. In 1894 William G. Frost defined "the Mountain Region of the South" as consisting of 194 counties (Walls, 1977); John C. Campbell (1921) included 254 counties in the "Southern Highlands"; the U.S. Department of Agriculture (1935) variously designated 205 or 236 counties as the "Southern Appalachians"; Brown and Hillery (1962) define "Southern Appalachia" as 190 counties; McCoy and Brown (1981) employ four different definitions of the region, one of which includes 303 counties; Philliber (1981) includes 396 counties in his study of Appalachian migrants; and the Appalachian Regional Commission (1979a) defines the region as 397 counties. This study adopts the most inclusive definition in order to obtain the greatest range of comparability with similar research.

7) The working lists of metropolitan, urban, and rural counties used by the Appalachian Regional Commission were revised in light of the 1980 census data. The county lists used in this study follow the ARC revisions of June 30, 1983.

REFERENCES

Agresta, Anthony
    1985. "The Migration Turnaround: End of a Phenomenon?" *Population Today*, 13:6-7.

Anglin, Mary.
    1983. "Experiences of In-Migrants in Appalachia." Pp 227-238 in Allen Batteau, ed., *Appalachia and America: Autonomy and Regional Independence*. Lexington: The University Press of Kentucky.

Appalachian Regional Commission.
    1984a. "Appalachian Unemployment, November, 1983." (Map) *Appalachia*, 17:2

    1984b. "Projects Funded in Distressed Counties in FY 1983." (Map) *Appalachia*, 17:6.

    1982a. "Appalachian Population and Per Capital Money Income. (Table) *Appalachia*, 16: 22-23.

    1982b. "Poverty Status of Household Population in Appalachia." (Table) *Appalachia*, 16: 24-25.

    1979a. *Appalachia—A Reference Book*. Washington, D.C.: Appalachian Regional Commission.

    1979b. *A Report to Congress On Migration* Washington, D.C.: Appalachian Regional Commission.

Barron, Hal Seth.
    1977. "A Case for Appalachian Demographic History." *Appalachian Journal*, 4: 208-215.

Belcher, John C.
  1962. "Population Growth and Characteristics." Pp 37-53 in Thomas R. Ford, ed., *The Southern Appalachian Region: A Survey.* Lexington: University of Kentucky Press.

Brown, James S.
  1972. "A Look at the 1970 Census." Pp. 130-144 in David S. Walls and John B. Stephenson, eds., *Appalachia in the Sixties: A Decade of Reawakening.* Lexington: The University Press of Kentucky.

Brown, James S., and George A. Hillery.
  1962. "The Great Migration, 1940-1960." Pp 54-78 in Thomas R. Ford, ed., *The Southern Appalachian Region: A Survey.* Lexington: University of Kentucky Press.

Campbell, John C.
  1921. *The Southern Highlander and His Homeland.* New York: The Russell Sage Foundation.

Cumberland, John H.
  1973. *Regional Development: Experiences and Prospects in the United States of America.* Second edition. The Hague: Mouton.

Ford, Thomas R., and Gordon F. DeJong.
  1963. "The Decline of Fertility in the Southern Appalachian Mountain Region." *Social Forces,* 42:89-96.

Garkovich, Lorraine.
  1982. "Kinship and Return Migration in Eastern Kentucky." *Appalachian Journal,* 10: 62-70.

Goodrich, Carter, Bushrod W. Allin, C. Warner Thornthwaite, et al.
  1936. *Migration and Economic Opportunity: The Report of the Study of Population Redistribution.* Philadelphia: University of Pennsylvania Press.

Holdrich, Martin K.
  1984. "Trends: Prospects for Metropolitan Growth." *American Demographics,* 6:33-37.

Longino, Charles F., Jr.
  1984. "Migration Winners and Losers." *American Demographics,* 6: 27-45.

Marger, Martin N., and Phillip J. Obermiller.
  1983. "Urban Appalachians and Canadian Maritime Migrants: A Comparative Study of Emergent Ethnicity." *International Journal of Comparative Sociology,* 24: 229-243.

McCoy, Clyde B., and James S. Brown.
  1981. "Appalachian Migration to Midwestern Cities." P; 35-78 in Wm. W. Philliber and Clyde B. McCoy, eds., *The Invisible Minority: Urban Appalachians.* Lexington: The University Press of Kentucky.

Murdock, Steven H., and Clyde B. McCoy.
  1974. "A Note on the Decline of Appalachian Fertility, 1930-1970." *Growth and Change,* 5, 39-42.

Peoples Appalachian Research Collective.
  1972. "Urban Migrants: Industrial Heartland Refugees." Special Issue. *Peoples Appalachia,* Vol. 2, No. 7, (July).

Philliber, William W.
  1981. *Appalachian Migrants in Urban America: Cultural Conflict or Ethnic Group Formation?* New York: Praeger.

Pickard, Jerome.
    1981a.   "A Decade of Change in Appalachia." *Appalachia*, 14: 1-9.

    1981b.   "Appalachia's Decade of Change = A Decade of Inmigration." *Appalachia*, 15: 24-28.

Population Reference Bureau.
    1982.   "U.S. Population: Where We Are; Where We Are Going." *Population Bulletin*, Vol. 37, No. 2, (June).

Robley, Bryant, and Cheryl Russell.
    1983.   "Trends: Altered States." *American Demographics*, 5: 34-36.

Rogerson, Peter A., and David A. Plane.
    1985.   "Monitoring Migration Trends." *American Demograpics*, 7: 27-47.

Schwarzweller, Harry K., James S. Brown, and J.J. Mangalam.
    1971.   *Mountain Families in Transition*. University Park, PA: The Pennsylvania State University Press.

Shapiro, Henry D.
    1977.   "Appalachia and the Idea of America: The Problem of the Persisting Frontier." Pp. 43-55 in J.W. Williams, ed., *An Appalachian Symposium*. Boone, NC: Appalachian State University Press.

    1978   *Appalachia on Our Mind*. Chapel Hill, NC: The University of North Carolina Press.

Uhlenberg, Peter.
    1975.   "Noneconomic Determinants of Nonmigration: Sociological Considerations for Migration Theory." *Rural Sociology*, 38: 296-311.

U.S. Department of Agriculture.
    1935.   *Economic and Social Problems and Conditions of the Southern Appalachians*. Miscellaneous Publication No. 205.

Vance, Rupert B.
    1962.   "The Region: A New Survey." Pp 1-8 in Thomas R. Ford, ed., *The Southern Appalachian Region: A Survey*. Lexington: University of Kentucky Press.

Walls, David S.
    1977.   "On the Naming of Appalachia." P. 56-76 in J.W. Williamson, ed., *An Appalachian Symposium*. Boone, NC: Appalachian State University Press.

Watts, Ann DeWitt.
    1981.   "Cities and Their Place in Southern Appalachia." *Appalachian Journal*, 8: 105-118.

Weller, Robert H., and Leon F. Bouvier.
    1981.   *Population: Demography and Policy* New York: St. Martin's Press.

White, Stephen E.
    1983.   "Return Migration to Appalachian Kentucky: An Atypical Case of Nonmetropolitan Migration Reversal." *Rural Sociology*, 48: 471-491.

FREE AT LAST?: THREE VIEWS OF APPALACHIAN HISTORY
  Convenor: Judi Jennings, Kentucky Humanities Council
The Significance of Ingle's Ferry in the Settling of the Appalachian Region
  Laura Binder, Radford University
Impact of the Company Town on Traditional Life
  Dean Herrin, University of Delaware
Whitfield County, Georgia: Slavery Politics on the Edge of Appalachia
  Derrell C. Roberts, Dalton Junior College

Impact of the Company Town on Traditional Life

by
Dean Herrin

In October of 1897, the Big stone Gap *Post*, of Wise County, Virginia, reflected on recent change in the county:

> Two years ago, along the banks of Callahan creek...was a gloomy wilderness... The advent of the railroad, breaking the stillness of this grand and wild mountain district, was not more wonderful to the ordinary native than the sudden springing into existence of Stonega.[1]

The "gloomy wilderness" had been replaced by a mining town, which was soon to become the base of operations for the Virginia Coal and Iron Company. Labor recruited from the mountains was supplemented with immigrants from southern Europe and southern Blacks. Houses, churches, mine structues, and roads all appeared where once only a few isolated cabins had stood. A physical transformation had taken place on the banks of the Callahan, a transformation that occured many times throughout Appalachia around the turn of the twentieth century. The story seemed to be the same everywhere: traditional, agricultural patterns of life were disrupted and replaced by the industrial rhythms and structures of mine camps. Farming the land gave way to mining the earth as the primary occupation of the region. Many native Appalachian mountaineers fled this industrial invasion, moving further into the mountains to re-establish the way of life they knew best. Others, however, saw in the coal camps opportunity, excitement, money, or a host of other real and imagined enticements. Mountain cabins, plows, and seasonal work rhythms were given up for company housing, coal cars, and industrial whistles. But the break with tradition was never complete. Older cultural patterns were drawn upon to help in the adjustment to newer patterns. Tradition informed and guided innovation. This study of one particular coal camp, Stonega, Virginia, will focus on life in these camps, on the patterns of associations formed by those who lived in the camps, and on the preservation of tradition.

Tradition was not easily preserved. Coal camps were perceived by some as not only the active agents in the physical transformation of Appalachia, but as agents in the transformation of traditional Appalachian society. The establishment of coal camps and the subsequent rise in the population of Appalachia were welcomed by many observers of the mountain region as solutions to its "community problem." Unaware or unimpressed by the communalism afforded by court days, or the local church, or through shared farm labor, the sociologist Edward Alsworth Ross wrote in *The New Republic* in 1924:

> In the mountains between Pennsylvania and Georgia are pocketed three million old-line Americans who illustrate the social effects of isolation as vividly as Albania or the Caucasus.[2]

Others also pointed to the supposed lack of community in the mountains. "Lack of good roads has caused an undue isolation, has prevented cooperative activity and the realization of the ideals of a modern community life...", wrote one journalist. Another suggested that an "over-developed individualism" had resulted because "there is no cohesive community life..."[3] Samuel Tyndale Wilson, in his mission-study text of 1906, *The Southern Mountaineers*, believed that:

> The industrial invasion will introduce much evil, but it will, in part at least, prepare the way for better things. It will break up the isolation. Shiftlessness will disappear if the awards of labor are forthcoming. The days of no trade and no money are passing away. The mountaineer sees it, dreads it, and will profit by it.[4]

Whether or not mountaineers who moved into Stonega "profited" by it is beyond the scope of this paper, but they did form not simply a community, but several different types of community in the camp. By "community" I mean a shared set of values and interests that distinguishes one group from another. A recent study asserts that class consciousness was the primary definition of community among miners in southern West Virginia in the early part of this century.[5] Community based on class feeling was present but not dominant in Stonega before the 1930s, coexisting with other "communities" based on race, ethnicity, and such factors as religion and location in camp.

The physical structure of Stonega helped to determine community. Built largely in 1896 and 1897, the town was divided into various sections representing class, racial and ethnic divisions. The Immigration Commission, created by Congress in 1908 to investigate the living conditions of immigrants in American industry, reported that mining camps in Wise County were segregated "principally because of the desire of the employees themselves for segregation."[6] Whether the coal company named the various sections of Stonega is unknown, but the names are indicative of the social ordering in the camp. Black laborers were housed in Red Row, Slavetown, Creek Row, Smokey Row, and Possum Trot, locations near the coke ovens. Immigrants, mostly Hungarians and Poles, lived in Hunk Town. The rest of the camp was made up of native white Americans, some from the Appalachian region and others brought to Stonega from nearby states. They lived in such areas as Quality Row, Avondale, and Church Hill. Employees may have preferred living in segregated parts of the camp, as the Immigration Commission reported, but the coal company most clearly maintained this segregation in the assignment of houses. In a letter describing the condition of vacant houses in two other Stonega Coke and Coal Company* camps in Wise County, a company official ranked them in the following order:

1) For First-Class Americans
2) For Low-Class Americans
3) For Foreigners
4) For First-Class Colored Labor
5) For Low-Class Colored Labor[7]

At the top of the housing scale were those houses intended for the supervisory personnel of the company, such as the superintendent of the camp, the company doctor, and other officials. These houses were large, three-story, fourteen to sixteen-room structures occupying the section of town known as the "Park", which simply by its name evokes a pastoral scene set apart from such sections as "Smokey Row" and "Possum Trot". Company clerks and store employees, and certain skilled employees, such as electricians were housed nearest the Park, in the section known as "Quality Row". These houses were two-story, and as with most other houses in Stonega, were semi-detached and intended for two families. Each unit in Quality Row houses had four rooms in its half. The most common type of house built in Stonega was the two-story, double-pen type, found in almost all sections of the camp, and occupied by all groups. The cheapest form of housing consisted of two-room shacks, built in the Possum Trot section and intended for Black labor. These houses were so identified with Black workers that one former resident of Stonega only remembered them as "colored people-shacks". The final house type constructed by the company was a one-story, four-room house, twenty-one of which were built in 1910 to house the workers of the com-

*The Virginia Coal and Iron Company's successor.

pany's carpentry shop.[8]

The segregated sections of Stonega and the selective assignment of houses were indicative of company attitudes toward miners. Since the development of the Stonega field, the native Appalachian population had been looked down upon by the intruders. When General John Daniel Imboden was first promoting the area in the 1880s, he commented once on how he had told a group of investors all about Wise County and,

> ...how nice it was ...and interested them so much that when our road is built they are coming out to see for themselves. They think it must be delightful to see and mingle with primitive people.[9]

Stonega Coke and Coal Company's annual report for 1917 referred to the Wise County natives who the company first encountered as "at least two hundred years behind the civilization of the more densely populated sections of the United States."[10] The Appalachian mountaineers were not simply culturally inferior; they were culturally deficient. A Stonega resident and office clerk who wrote a weekly news item for the Big Stone Gap *Post*, contributed the following in 1903:

> We rise to remark that the only thing Stonega needs to make it the most desirable place on the globe, is for the cultured people who come here to reside, to disseminate their culture by using their talents in reaching out and helping those who have not been so highly favored...[11]

Blacks and immigrants were also considered among those who had "not been so highly favored", with frequent disparaging remarks found in company reports, letters, and news items in the Big Stone Gap *Post*.[12] This attitude on the part of the company helped foster a class solidarity among the miners, a solidarity of "us" versus "them". But class solidarity of the miners was also tempered by divisions of race and ethnicity, divisions made more acute by the company's labor problems. The 1917 annual report for the Stonega Coke and Coal Company claimed that since the establishment of the coal industry in the Stonega area, the shortage of labor had been the most serious problem faced by the coal operators. As the mining and coking operations had increased at Stonega in the late 1890s, and as other mines opened in the region, the native population was unable to provide the necessary number of workers.[13] To obtain the necessary labor, large numbers of men were brought into the Stonega area "on transportation" between 1895 and 1920. In 1899, 1,000 men were imported to the region, while in 1900, the figure rose to 1,377. From 1915 to 1920, the Stonega Coke and Coal Company imported a yearly average of 2,260 workers.[14] Many of the workers imported into the region were either recently-arrived immigrants, or southern Blacks. The annual report for 1900 listed a monthly average of 1,405 workers on the company's payroll for that year. Of these men, 49.5 per cent were native whites, 31.8 per cent were Blacks, and 18.7 per cent were immigrants, mainly Hungarian.[15]

Many of these men brought in from outside the area did not stay long in Stonega, however. The usual procedure was for the company to pay the travel expenses of the worker to the mines, and then take out so much every month from the worker's paycheck until the transportation costs had been reimbursed. Upon arriving in Stonega, some workers left the camp and hired on with other local mine operators, thereby avoiding the transportation fee. Most of the coal companies in Wise County, including the Stonega Coke and Coal Company, were active in trying to lure workers away from one another. Others left because they did not like the work, or the area, or both. Transportation men who left the area in 1916 reported that they had to sneak away at night, as the company had guards who were watching them. For the period 1905 to 1915, 18.8 percent of all men brought into Stonega on transportation left without working.[16] Native workers also moved from camp to camp, to increase wages, to escape harsh conditions, or for a variety of other reasons. One might assume that the mobility of mine workers would have prohibited any formation of "community" in the coal fields, but as David Corbin has shown for West Virginia, miners' mobility led to the creation of a large community uniting isolated company towns.[17] Each company town afforded miners a sense of identification, whether derived from occupation, church membership, kinship ties, or ethnic affiliation. Most migrant miners found "communities" to fit into in each coal camp.

The different racial and ethnic communities in the coal camps helped to support and sustain the families of Stonega. Native whites, immigrants, and Blacks all occupied separate sections of Stonega, and maintained tight-knit communities around these sections. Each group had its own church, its own fraternal orders, and its own customs. Fraternal organizations in particular reflected both mutual support among the miners and ethnic and racial separation; five lodges were established for native white miners, two each for immigrant and Black miners, and one even for wives of white miners.[18]

Traditional values and preserved patterns of life were also instrumental in maintaining community. The immigrant population in Stonega was particularly adept at maintaining strong ties with the "old world". A Roman Catholic priest who served Stonega reported that at certain times of the year, such as First Holy Communion, Confirmation, or the consecration of a new church, one "would imagine to live for the time in a village of the former Austrian-Hungarian Empire."[19]

The occupation of mining itself enabled all groups in Stonega to uphold certain work traditions, particularly those associated with agriculture. The company complained in its 1902 annual report that "the insurmountable difficulty is to prevail upon the employees to work sufficient time to get the yield out of the plant equal to its capacity."[20] Part of the problem stemmed from the method of mining used in the early Stonega mines. Most miners were paid not by the hour, but by the amount of coal they loaded. The shift usually began about seven in the morning, but the miner was free to come and go as he pleased. He bought his own tools and blasting powder, and he decided when he had loaded enough coal. The distances between working places in the mines, and the small number of supervisors meant that most miners worked all day without seeing a boss. In a sense, the miner sold the coal to the company. The editor of *Coal Age* described mining as late as 1921 as similar to a "cottage industry, only the cottage is a room in the mines." The process was very similar to a tenant farmer "selling" his crops to the landlord, and many miners in Stonega had indeed been tenant farmers before coming to the camp. [21]

There were other ways in which miners maintained touch with their agricultural past. Many miners operated farms near Stonega and would leave the mines periodically throughout the year to tend to their crops. Many others in the camp maintained gardens and kept cows, chickens, and hogs. The company, of course, became frustrated with the seasonal work habits of the miners: "It is impossible to maintain the discipline necessary to get the efficient results desired and possible." The company began mechanizing their mines after 1915, but it encountered "prejudice against trying anything new" on the part of the miners. Jerry Bruce Thomas has reported that the tonnage system of mining persisted in the coal industry long after machinery made it obsolete.[22]

Besides maintaining a traditional work discipline, residents of Stonega resisted certain ideoilogical aspects of camp life, often in subtle ways. Freedom of choice was protected by the miners, who patronized peddlers and local stores, even though the company went so far as to fire employees who allowed competing salesmen into their company homes.[23] Traditional habits were maintained by the miners, who refused to drink piped water, even though the company warned of a contaminated water supply and threatened to fire workers who continued to drink well water.[24] Religious independence was claimed by the miners as evidenced by the complaint of the coal company in 1904 that attendance was very poor in the church it had built and continued to support.[25] Old customs of entertainment were still enjoyed by the miners, as they gambled and drank illegal whiskey and "layed off" work days after particularly boisterous weekends.[26] Residents of Stonega did not completely reject the capitalistic and industrial ideology sponsored by the coal company, but the adjustment to camp life was eased somewhat by the maintenance of traditional patterns of life.

The company was also able to use tradition to its advantage. When more workers were needed, Appalachian natives who were felt to be influential with mountaineers were asked to recruit workers from the hills. A Catholic priest was hired to attract immigrants to Stonega. Bake ovens were built behind some houses in Stonega, so that the company could "get some Hungarian families to locate there..." But as with work habits, most traditional patterns of behavior was considered by the company to be objectionable and "peculiar."[27]

Many miners saw each other as "peculiar" as well. Immigrants were subject to Americanization efforts. One local priest complimented the "foreigners" on their flag-raising during World War I, and claimed that they "bought liberty bonds until they had to borrow money to pay their regular bills."[28] Most buildings and events at Stonega were segregated into white and black sections, and many white Stonega residents recalled in interviews that "people knew their place." The different racial and ethnic groups at Stonega coexisted peacefully most of the time, but there were occasional outbreaks of violence. The Big Stone Gap *Post* for May, 1898, reported a fight in which "nearly all nationalities were represented."[29] A more typical pattern of interaction was described by a local priest, who related the trouble that Appalachian natives had with understanding the Roman Catholic faith of the immigrants:

> It is their conviction that the Catholics believe neither in Christ nor in the Bible, that they worship the Virgin and adore pictures, that they are a mixture of Mormons, Jews and Mohammedans, and that it is safer not to fool with them.[30]

Traditional cultural patterns were not destroyed in Stonega. In fact, each group's preservation of past cultural behavior was one factor that created boundaries between racial and etchnic groups in Stonega, and was a principal reason why class feeling and behavior was only one of several relationships formed by the miner in Stonega.

The transition from an individual farmstead to a coal camp thrust the Appalachian mountaineer into a new industrial environment in Wise County, Virginia. In the camp the miner belonged to various "communities" that further aided in the adjustment to an industrial setting. The miner was at any one time, a member of a certin social and economic class, a work group, a church, a lodge hall, a family, and perhaps other groups as well. The miner's membership in these communities and his adaptation of past cultural values to the coal camp gave the miner a sense of security and self-identity in a new environment.

NOTES

1. Big Stone Gap (Virginia) *Post*, 7 October, 1897.
2. Ronald D. Eller, *Miners, Millhands, and Mountaineers* (Knoxville: University of Tennessee Press, 1982) pp. 33-38; Margaret Ripley Wolfe, "Aliens in Southern Appalachia: Catholics in the Coal Camps, 1900-1940," *Appalachian Heritage*[6] (Winter 1978) :44.

3. Henry D. Shapiro, "Appalachia and the Idea of America: The Problem of the Persisting Frontier," in *An Appalachian Symposium: Essays Written in Honor of Cratis D. Williams*, ed. J.W. Williamson (Boone, N.C.: Appalachian State University Press, 1977), p. 51.

4. Henry D. Shapiro, *Appalachia on Our Mind: The Southern Mountains and Mountaineers in the American Consciousness* (Chapel Hill, N.C.: University of North Carolina Press, 1978) p. 159.

5. David Alan Corbin, *Life, Work, and Rebellion in the Coal Fields* (Urbana: University of Illinois Press, 1981).

6. U.S. Congress, Senate, *Reports of the Immigration Commission — Immigrants in Industries*, S. Doc. 633, 61st Congress, 2nd sess., 1911, Part 1, Vol. 2, "The Bituminous Coal Mining Industry in the South," p. 211.

7. E. Drennen to D.B. Wentz, 4 October 1915, Westmoreland Coal Company Collection, Hagley Museum and Library, Greenville, DE, Accession (Acc.) 1765, Series (Ser.) II, Box 385, Virginia File No. 17: "Houses and Buildings, 1914-1918."

8. D.B. Sayers to E. Drennen, 26 July 1915, Westmoreland, Acc. 1765, Ser. II, Box 385, Virginia File No. 17: "Houses and Buildings, 1914-1918"; *Stonega Coke and Coal Company Annual Report, 1917*, Westmoreland, Acc. 1765, Ser. II, Box 211, pp. 25-26, 39: Transcript No. 24, Interview with Joseph Tony, Big Stone Gap, Virginia (December 1972), Oral History Collection, Emory and Henry College, Emory, Virginia.

9. Eller, *Miners*, p. 49.

10. *Annual Report, 1917*, Westmoreland, p. 3.

11. Big Stone Gap *Post,*, 24 December 1903.

12. *Annual Report, 1917*, Westmoreland, p. 7; Big Stone Gap *Post*, 31 March, 1898: Big Stone Gap *Post*, 24 July, 1902.

13. *Annual Report, 1917*, Westmoreland, p. 3.

14. *Annual Reports, 1915-1920*, Westmoreland: "Virginia Coal and Iron Company: Annual Report of Operating Department (1899 and 1900),"Westmoreland, Acc. 1764, Ser. I, Box 4.

15. "Virginia Coal and Iron Company: Annual Report of Operating Department (1900)," Westmoreland.

16. E. Drennen to D.B. Wentz, 19 November 1913, Westmoreland, Acc. 1765, Ser. II, Box 385: A.H. Reeder to J.B. Newton, 5 July 1906, Westmoreland, Acc. 1765, Ser. II, Box 443, Virginia File No. 125: "Va. Iron, Coal & Coke Co. 1905-1923"; *Annual Report, 1915*, Westmoreland, p. 10.

17. Corbin, *Life, Work and Rebellion*, p. 42.

18. Big Stone Gap *Post*, 8 June, 1899: 9 October, 1902; 30 July, 1903; 6 August, 1903.

19. "Sacred Heart Church of Stonega and Missions," unpublished MS. (in author's possession), St. Bernard Abbey, Cullman, Alabama, p. 4.

20. "Annual Reports to the Stockholders (1902)," Westmoreland.,

21. United States, Department of Justice, "Memorandum (Earnest Randolph)," dated October 29, 1915, Straight Numerical File 182363, Record Group 60, National Archives; Richard M. Simon, "The Labor Process and Uneven Development: The Appalachian Coalfields, 1880-1930," *International Journal of Urban and Regional Research*[4] (March 1980): 55.

22. Jerry Bruce Thomas, "Coal Country: The Rise of the Southern Smokeless Coal Industry and Its Effect on Area Development, 1872-1910," (Ph.D. dissertation, University of North Carolina, 1971), p. 206; Big Stone Gap *Post*, 30 June, 1904; *Annual Report, 1918*, Westmoreland, p. 7; "Annual Reports to the Stockholders (1902)," Westmoreland; *Annual Report, 1916*, Westmoreland, p. 31.

23. Wise County Court Records, File No. 2285, Wise County Courthouse, Wise, Virginia.

24. D.B. Wentz to A.H. Reeder, 20 January 1909, Westmoreland, Acc. 1765, Ser. II, Box 416, Virginia File No. 9: "Small Pox at Stonega and Osaka 1904-1911."

25. A.H. Reeder to D.B. Wentz, 8 August 1904, Westmoreland, Acc 1765, Ser. II, Box 360, Virginia File No. 12: "Churches 1904-1909."

26. Transcript No. 24, Interview with Joseph Tony.

27. A.H. Reeder to D.B. Wentz, 8 July 1907, Westmoreland, Acc. 1765, Ser. 11, Box 416, Virginia File No. 9: "Small Pox at Stonega and Osaka 1904-1911"; C.G. Duffy to R.E. Taggert, 8 Apiril 1916, Westmoreland, Acc. 1765, Ser. II, Box 384, Virginia File No. 107: "Houses Leases 1915-1916"; Big Stone Gap *Post*, 24 July, 1902.

28. "Sacred Heart Church of Stonega and Missions," p. 4.

29. Big Stone Gap *Post*, 26 May, 1898.

30. Wolfe, p. 48.

REALITIES AND MYTHS: MOUNTAIN POLITICS
    Convenor: Ron Eller, Mars Hill College
Hubbard's Branch of Mill Creek—1964 and 1984:
Twenty Years After the War on Poverty
    Warren Brunner, Berea, Kentucky
    Tom Boyd, Berea College
Boss Hoggism—Fact or Fiction: The View from Eastern Kentucky
    Stuart Sprague, Morehead State University

Hubbard's Branch of Mill Creek —1964 and 1984: Twenty Years After the War on Poverty

by
Warren Brunner
and Tom Boyd

Introduction

What we attempt here is a naturalistic study of an occurrence. The goal is not the testing of an hypothesis about the cause of events; we don't even plan to defend any hypothesis. Our ambition in this work deals with awareness of things — consciousness. Brunner and Boyd have been working together — reasoning, arguing, and at times even agreeing — in order to capture a tiny part of an occurrence in American history. This capture, if successful, has as its goal a heightening of our awareness of social change. What we attempt for the next 15 minutes is a manipulation of perspective, an addition to the social construction of reality of The War on Poverty.

Our information comes from a variety of sources: Brunner's photographs taken in Mill Creek in 1964 and 1984, files and other information about the Appalachian Volunteer/Council of the Southern Mountains summer program, data about the area published between 1964 and 1984, visits with families that were the target of the program, and talks with some of the participants responsible for guiding the program. Photographers use image to make language. Sociologists use language (albeit at times jargon and numbers) to make image. Here we plan to make private worlds public to heighten the awareness of us all. Our presentation will be brief. We hope all will become sensitized to some reality of Hubbard's Branch and that the discussion of images and argument that follows will be the way we might begin to "make sense" out of Appalachian rural social change and The War on Poverty.

The Economic Opportunity Act of 1964 proclaimed its goal was "to eliminate the paradox of poverty in the midst of plenty". (Harrington, p. 3) In January, during his State of the Union Message, President Johnson declared "an unconditional war on poverty". The Office of Economic Opportunity, which was created to fight this war, received considerable attention and never cost the government even one-percent of the federal budget. (Harrington, p. 21) Besides community action, a number of other programs to alleviate problems of low-income citizens were started and live on today as Head Start, Food Stamps, Medicaid, and the like.

Today, awareness of this period of American history is often limited to the belief that such programs were gigantic, were handouts, and were unsuccessful. The Reagan administration's view seems to conform to this conventional belief in spite of other views. Even though the War on Poverty never got off the ground, it is blamed for some of the budget ills of the 1980's. As Michael Harrington puts it, "The savior that never was (has become) the scapegoat that is." (Harrington, p. 20) This assistance effort was not gigantic — America remains the Westernworld's most limited welfare state. (Harrington, p. 16) Such programs were not simply handouts — most required local aid and recipients had to demonstrate that they "earned" the amelioration of their problems. Finally, the efforts were not uniformly without impact — figures on life expectancy, levels of educational attainment, and nutrition crept up during the period after a variety of programs were put in place. As portrayed in the popular media and political pronouncements today, American awareness of The War on Poverty is a memory of events that never happened. (Harrington, p. 15)

We construct images of what did happen in one tiny place in the Appalachian region of America. Hubbard's Branch of Mill Creek—1964-1984.

The Appalachian Volunteer Summer Program: 1964

The Appalachian Volunteers started before the formation of the federal office of Economic Opportunity. The AV's earliest labors were in the Spring of 1964: these were work projects to improve school buildings using college students and local volunteer labor on Saturdays. In January 1964, the President's Appalachian Regional Commission sent a consultant to eastern Kentucky to investigate the feasibility of organizing and mobilizing a group of volunteers to work on the "grass roots" level of poverty in Appalachia. He focused on the Appalachian Volunteers of The Council of the Southern Mountains. (Conn, p. 10) During February, a lead article in *Newsweek* was titled "Poverty USA", and it had a special section on Appalachia. The description of Sargent Shriver's plans for OEO said that among other things, there were "...pilot programs on the drawing board (that) involve putting college students...to work as tutors for potential high school dropouts." (*Newsweek*, p. 36) Hubbard's Branch of Mill Creek in Clay County was possibly the earliest recipient of one of these programs.

From June 8 through August 7 in the summer of 1964, college students taught reading, writing, and arithmetic and organized recreational activities in this community. The people on Mill Creek had requested school renovation, but as stated in the project report, "since school renovation appeared unnecessary and since a number of students had offered to volunteer their services during the summer, the idea of a community summer school project gradually developed". "The need for a program that would teach the three R's but, more important, would motivate the children of Mill Creek to want to learn was obvious." (CSM, Mill Creek Project Report, p. 3)

The educational activities took place in the Hubbard Cemetery Missionary Baptist Church. The church voted to allow the use of the building for a summer school program. While on the project, the volunteers were given room and board by the Mill Creek residents. The proposal for funding said the college students would attempt to provide educational experiences for some 20 school age students and that this would bring to the community, "...a modern educational experience that goes far beyond anything that has been attempted in a similar eastern Kentucky community. (Project proposal, p. 1)

The daily school activities ran from 8:30 to 11:30 a.m. and from 1:00 to 4:00 p.m. The "curriculum" included movies, records, painting, music made by a rhythm band, and reading. Field trips included parents, and the group went to Cumberland Falls, Levi Jackson State Park, and the State Capitol Building at Frankfort. While in Frankfort, Governor Breathitt met with them in the Capitol Rotunda. An excited news release accompanied by photographs went out from the Commonwealth of the Kentucky Department of Public Information.

The budget for this summer school project was $775. It had $375 for supplies and field trips and $400 for living allowances and expenses of the volunteers. Equipment and books were borrowed from the Kentucky Extension Library Service and the Berea College Library. A basketball and goals were given by businessmen in Manchester, as was a car for the older boys to tear down and work on. All project documents stressed that the parents of the pupils assumed responsibility for providing meals and lodging for the volunteers.

The original college student volunteers were from New York City (Union College) Detroit (Harvard College) and St. Louis (Cumberland College). Two additional volunteers, one from Massachusetts and one from Tennessee, joined the project after the midpoint replacing two of the originals who left for health reasons.

Reports about the project say that, "For the first time, the children had become friends with someone whom they could admire and look up to who was not a school dropout..." One of the volunteers said the project goal was "not just to teach reading and writing, but to live with the people and to enter into their way of life". As officials described it, "The volunteer teachers became friends and possible symbols for what the children may try to become". The volunteer teacher taught the parents about the world and how 'outsiders' or formally educated people look at the world and life". (Project report, *passim*) At the end of the summer a VISA volunteer was assigned to Mill Creek to carry on other community work.

Upon the completion of this earliest AV summer school program the Sunday *Courier-Journal* ran an article using a Brunner's photographs. It was entitled "Students Bring Light to Mountain Children", and under the heading "Volunteers pioneer classes at Mill Creek" the author, after giving details of program, community, families, and education concluded, "the Appalachian Volunteers need money in order to continue the school renovation and summer teaching programs". *(Courier Journal,* section 4, p. 4)

The money did come in to support the Appalachian Volunteers: in 1965 the OEO came to play a major role in this support. Eight months after the completion of the project, in April 1965, the Coordinator of the CSM Education Projects wrote to the Director of the AV's about the Mill Creek project. He acknowledged that, "The Mill Creek project was one of the firm publicity and growth angles of the Appalachian Volunteers...". However, given this impact on the AV's, he wanted a better handle on the impact upon the families. "How are the residents of Mill Creek living now — as compared to conditions, human and environmental, before the project?" (CSM, letter April 16, 1965) The AV Director's response to the question included the facts that some students considered attending outside boarding schools, books were left behind for the one-room school, and the VISA worker was receiving community cooperation in a variety of efforts.

The Appalachian Volunteer development effort has been described as encompassing three different strategies — issue organizing, community organizing, and the self-help programs which began with the early "enrichment" efforts such as this one at Mill Creek. (Whisnant, pp. 195-197) With the passing of 20 years can we any better respond to the question of how residents of Mill Creek are living now after their encounter with such "enrichment"?

The Community

In 1964, as now, Hubbard's Branch of Mill Creek was a dispersed residential area 22 miles from the county-seat of Manchester and about four miles up the creek from the local post office and stores of the nearest crossroads community. Then, as now, community activities were centered around its hillside cemetery and the annual homecoming the second Sunday in August each year. Transportation in and out of the community was on a dirt road that had wooden flooring on the bridges criss-crossing the stream. Today, it is much the same except for the new cement bridges crossing the creek. The post office has left the store that formerly housed it, migrating about 300 yards onto the blacktop and that much closer to Manchester. Carried on by a different owner on the same site, what was formerly Mrs. Hubbard's store is still a commercial venture.

The summer school program was to assist the pupils that attended the Middle Mill Creek Elementry School — a structure that now is a family home. Education has migrated out of the community to the more modern consolidated elementry school about eight miles away and nearer the population concentrations. While some students in 1964 walked to the one-room elementary school others rode a bus out for more advanced education. Twenty years ago, according to the driver it was a 36 person bus, and today the same man drives a bus with a 65 child capacity.

In the early 1950's, the Rural Electric Cooperative brought electricity to the community. (correspondence with Flem Messer, Jan. 1985) For the census enumeration district of which Mill Creek is a part, by 1980 electricity as a fuel for cooking was up 55% from the 1970 figure to 84% of the households using it. Between 1970 and 1980, coal and wood as heating fuels went from 100% down to 68% usage. What the census calls "complete plumbing facilities" were found in 4% of the homes in 1970, and now they are found in 44% of the homes in the area. Forty-five percent of the households are estimated to have telephones, and among the families on Mill Creek this includes one having that necessary modern adjunct, an unlisted telephone number. Housing conditions have changed. Both assistance programs and individual prosperity have led to new siding on homes and weatherproofing. Trailers have been brought in for housing returned migrants, and some new homes are the result of the regional franchise effort 'Jim Walker Homes' replacing the much earlier custom of building with local materials.

The Mill Creek community in its physical and social aspects presents a face of stability in the continuation of the church, the cemetery and the annual homecoming celebration. It also demonstrates deep change in the transfer of institutions from local scope and size to county and regional ranges of taste and control. The community is within the Red Bird Purchase unit of the Daniel Boone National Forest, thus a major land owner is the federal government. Their policy for land use is not one promoting homesteads and family life. Private landholding within the forest area is common, and it is on that land that community life continues, but the National Forest is still a major force. When the husband in one of the four original households participating in the summer program died, the spouse sold the land and moved out of the community. The Forest Service later purchased this land and the homestead is gone. Federal ownership replacing private ownership is an important force of change that originates from outside the community and has a major impact upon it.

The Families

According to project records, six families and thirty-three children lived in this area of Mill Creek. Four of the families and twenty of the children participated in the summer school program. The project description said, "The families are related by geographical proximity, common church membership or association, and often by kinship". (Project description, p.1) These ties of horizontal or local level social interaction are found twenty years later in fascinating patterns. In 1964 of the four families in the program, one had seven members, two had nine members, and one had ten members. These four original households have become twenty-nine households encompassing the original generation and the new one. The original thirty-five persons have changed in group composition only slightly — three are now deceased, but there were also three additional births in the original families. Of all these persons, 49% (17) lived on Mill Creek in 1984. Eight people lived in nearby rural areas, seven in nearby county-seats, and three persons in 1984 lived away from eastern Kentucky. The program did open up the community to new experiences but, while one entire family group with descendants moved out of the community when the land was sold to the Forest Service, Mill Creek has not experienced the reduction in population found in other parts of Appalachia.

Between 1970 and 1980 the enumeration district surrounding Mill Creek had a 12% decline in the number of housing units, an 18% decline in the number of residents, and an 11% decline in the number of families. There was also a shift in the model size of households from six or more persons to three persons. Mill Creek defied this pattern and at the same time, took part in it.

Families still thrive on Mill Creek; children have moved away to stay, while others who left have returned to live near the original homeplaces, parents and siblings. One entire family-group, even though it moved over the ridge into the next county, keeps in touch through a variety of activities including the church homecoming. For the three resident and remaining family-groups, the first has gone from one to three households in the community, the second has gone from one to six households in the local area and the third from one to four households in Mill Creek. This change in twenty years, from four to thirteen households in this community, represents a 225% increase! At the same time, the family group that moved away plus "branches" of the other three make sixteen households living outside Mill Creek. Branches of Mill Creek stems are found as far away as Louisville, Arkansas and Illinois. Seventeen of the original thirty-five persons are still living today in this community, and the count of these plus their descendants and spouses makes a total of forty-six persons — a 31% rise in the population! At the same time, it differs in its family growth. Hubbard's Branch mirrors the surrounding enumeration area in one way — the model size of households. In 1964 model family size was 9 persons, and today it is three persons as in the rest of the area.

One of the summer project volunteers, the teacher, was quoted in the final report:

> Through me and the other volunteers (the parents) realized their need to send their children to school, the need to learn more themselves and the need to think about their children leaving the mountains for a new life. (The children were given)...inspiration, enthusiasm and a desire for something bigger and better, something reaching into the world they had known nothing about. The community as a whole began to realize that they were people that could and should want to be a part of the whole world. (Final report, p. 7-8)

Mill Creek families are now part of the wider world but at the same time, they have not rejected life in the community. Absence of participation in formal education does not explain this view of "home".

Participation in Formal Education

During the summer school, formal education in 1964 was described in these terms: "Given such a set of circumstances of isolation, limited communications and poor schools, it is not unreasonable to expect to find the adults with little if any formal education and their children extremely limited and retarded in their school achievement level. Only one parent on Mill Creek had gone to high school. Of those able to read and write, very few had reached the eighth grade. Nearly half of the 20 children participating in this program were behind in their grade level from two to five years". (report, p. 3) What has taken place in the 20 year interval?

Twenty-six children were alive in the four famiies at the time of the summer school with 20 of them attending "classes" in the church for nine weeks. The educational attainment for the 25 alive in 1984 was the following: ten had completed high school (38%), one completed high school and some college (4%), seven ended their education with some high school (27%) and eight ended their education with the eighth grade or less (31%). Of the adults in the four families in 1964 seven had only some elementary school and one had completed high school. Thus, in 1964 the adult model attainment of education was some elementary school, but for the children 20 years later, the model attainment of education is the completion of high school (42%).

In the enumeration district surrounding Mill Creek, from 1970 to 1980 there was an increase in the level of schooling for the population 25 years of age and older. For this group, 14% of the population had completed high school or gone further. However, the 25 Mill Creek summer project children and siblings 42% had attained this same level. Taking only the 11 Mill Creek children resident in the community today 27% (3) have completed high school. Focusing only on the fourteen program participants that are not presently resident in Mill Creek, 57% (8) have completed high school.

From these comparisons between generations inside the community and across the next generation comparing Mill Creek with the surrounding area, a greater participation in formal education is clearly seen. The claims made to questions of the impact of the program eight months after its completion were, "three students were considering going away to school", "the community for the first time is well-supplied with books", and there is "a greater awareness of the value and need for education on behalf of children and adults alike". (project report, pp. 11-12) In 1984, there is little evidence to the contrary.

Even one person who was an adult in the 1984 group, expanded participation in formal education. After the husband died and the family moved to the next county in 1971, she got her GED high school diploma while raising the remaining children. (interview with family A) In America today, formal education and employment are closely linked in claims for the efficacy of schooling; the "need" for formal education is most commonly justified in terms of employment. Only rarely is the connection with citizenship mentioned. How did the summer school participants fare in terms of employment?

Employment Patterns

In 1964, the project proposal said, "The only sources of employment in the community are subsistence farming or coal mining". (proposal, p.1) According to 1980 census figures the enumeration district had Agriculture Forestry and Mining as the most common industry with 39% of the total employment, retail trade was next with 25% and the third most common employment was educational services, 10%. Between 1970 and 1980, the mean income had gone up by 147% and there was a 24% decline in the number of families classified as "poverty status". While these figures are less easily comparable, the best estimate is that during the decade there was also a 13% increase in persons receiving public assistance. Connected with these issues of "poverty status" and public assistance is the record of labor force participation. For the enumeration district in 1980 63% of the population sixteen and over were not in the labor force. The fate of the people on Mill Creek had been a variation on this employment theme.

The twenty-five children that were program participants or siblings of participants have a deviant record of labor force participation, 15 (60%) are in the labor force and 10 (40%) are not in the labor force — a reversal of the enumeration district proportions. Adding the generation that were adults in 1964 gives a similar picture for the entire group of persons involved in some way with the program — 47% are not in the labor force and 53% are in the labor force.

Of the 15 persons not in the labor force, 8 (53%) are housewives, 4 (27%) are simply not working, and 3 (20%) are retired or disabled. For the seventeen persons in the labor force the most common employment was in some aspect of coal, 6 (35%). Then school system employment accounted for 4 jobs (24%). The remaining employment consists of two factory workers, a mechanic, a nurse, a person in retail trade, a person in services, and one woman in military service. Of course, some of these persons are members of branch households located outside Mill Creek. Looking only at those persons resident in the program site in 1984, 4 are employed in coal related work (23%), 4 are housewives (23%), 3 are working for the school system, 3 are retired or disabled, and 3 are without work.

The program evaluation in 1964 said, "The immediate result of the Mill Creek Project is readily observable to anyone who knew the community before the program began. As a result of the summer project, the community has had a good exposure to the 'outside' world (project report, p. 11). Using "outside" and "inside" as appropriate images for the situation in 1964 is open to considerable debate; its inappropriateness in 1984 should be evident! Mill Creek program participants make up the American world — both "inside" and "outside".

Remembrances: Two Versions

Hubbard's Branch of Mill Creek 20 years after the start of The War on Poverty has changed perhaps in order to remain the same. Participation had been transferred to institutions outside the community. Family remains strong today and there are branches of these stem families scattered around. Participation in formal education had changed as has employment. But what is remembered of the program? In this case, the remembrances have two versions. The volunteer teacher in an interview during the summer and reports about the project present one version of remembrances The other version is the recollections of participants now entering adulthood or in the ranks of the almost elderly in 1984.

1964: "These are healthy intelligent and enthusiastic children. They responded extremely well to the things I tried to teach them". (Courier Journal, 1964) *1984:* "I can remember me watching that film, that's me there". (child of family A, 1985) The most vivid recollection of the summer program was singing songs and playing games. (child of family B, 1985) Two of the participants from the same family who now still live in Mill Creek said the most important result of the AV program was the contact the children had with others of the community. They said they learned to get along with other children and learned about what was outside of Mill Creek.

1964: "Rice Motor Company has donated a 1955 car for the older boys to tear down and work on as they learned the names and spelling of the different parts". (project report, p. 4) *1984:* A young man who is a Honda mechanic with a GED and certificate from a welding school didn't remember much about learning, but he laughed and remembered the boys taking apart the car — they never got it back together again.

1964: "The parents were very cooperative". "They might not have understood the things I did, and sometimes they found them strange, but they were tolerant". (Courier Journal, 1964) *1984:* "Part of the time we had classes in a barn!" (child of family B, 1985 "I think the project helped the kids a lot. I know it did my kids. It was a great thing. It encouraged kids to go on to school, to do things". (interview of parent in family A, 1985)

1964: "The individual families have had strangers come into their homes and leave as close personal friends". (project report, p. 10) *1984:* "Everything is gone now. We had 100 apple trees when I sold the place. It's not the same. Everything changed". "I think about the good old days, when I was really happy up there. We didn't have anything, no money, but we had love and happiness." (parent in family A)

Conclusion:

The program evaluation in 1964 said, "Education and many of the expected material and cultural aspects of modern America are only abstractions to the average Mill Creeker". (project report, p.2) In 1984, it is very hard to make such a case. Material aspects of modern America are found in the community today such as Jim Walker homes, unlisted telephone numbers, and manufactured household furnishings to name a few. Branches of Mill Creek families engage in occupations as varied as nursing, military service, and factory labor receiving cultural and social messages as well as material benefits. Still some continuity is found. Families are close, they keep in contact, and where possible live near one another. Those who live away try to return each year for the homecoming in August. Even the stem family that moved out returns for this. Education varies and on the average is much greater than that found 20 years ago.

Is America a different place because of this also? The War on Poverty has come and gone in the direct sense of OEO and the placing of volunteers in communities. The Appalachian Volunteers did go on to use the Mill Creek program, and other "enrichment" programs, as examples of their work— "useful publicity and growth angles" as it was described. Mill Creek was visited, photographed, and in turn visited others. Did their opening up their lives enrich other lives in America? Could the Appalachian Volunteers have received their initial financial support without the help of communities such as Mill Creek?

As the August 1964 *Courier Journal* stated near its conclusion, "A project such as this is difficult to evaluate, partly since it produces few immediate tangible results. Its potential significance is long-range..." Results, tangible or intangible, for social events are not easily seen to come from one clear single source or even a few sources. Social life is much more complex than this search for a single cause will justify. We live in a world of interaction between numerous social, economic, and environmental forces.

Nonetheless, of all the material we discovered and sifted through, one result can be directly attributed solely to the program and the impact of the summer effort. This is an event simple in its action and profound in its meaning — as profound as anything can be in the dynamics of family and community in Appalachia. In Clay County, there is a young woman born long after the summer program was over. She is a high school graduate, married with one child of her own, and they live in a rural area near Mill Creek. She is named Connie after the woman, the idealistic and maybe naive college student, that spent part of the summer of '64 on Mill Creek. This naming may be all the explaining we can give.

TABLE 1: FAMILIES PARTICIPATING IN THE PROJECT IN 1964*

FAMILY A
Parents: Mr. and Mrs. A
Children:

Male	Age 13	Completed Grade 6
Male	Age 11	Completed Grade 4
Female	Age 10	Completed Grade 3
Female	Age 9	Completed Grade 3
Female	Age 7	Completed Grade 1
Male	Age 6	Will be in Grade 1
Male	Infant	

Family B
Parents: Mr. and Mrs. B
Children:

Female	Age 12	Completed Grade 2
Female	Age 10	Completed Grade 2
Female	Age 7	Completed Grade 1
Female	Age 4	
Female	Age 2	

Family C
Parents: Mr. and Mrs. C
Children:

Male	Age 13	Completed Grade 4
Male	Age 11	Completed Grade 4
Female	Age 9	Completed Grade 1
Male	Age 6	Will be in Grade 1
Male	Age 5	
Male	Age 4	
Male	Age 1	

Family D
Parents: Mr. and Mrs. D
Children:

Female	Age 18	Completed Grade 8
Male	Age 16	Completed Grade 3
Male	Age 14	Completed Grade 2
Female	Age 12	Completed Grade 4
Female	Age 10	Completed Grade 2
Male	Age 6	Will be in Grade 1
Male	Age 7	Schooling Not Possible
Male	Age 4	

*From project report (Names obscured by authors of this paper.)

Note at bottom of page: "There is another man on Mill Creek who has 4 or 5 children but we have not been able to get him involved in the community or get him to send his children to the school program. Aside from him there is only one other person on the creek with children but they have not reached school age."

TABLE 2: Original Plus Next Generation Households — 1984

Family A   No. Persons   Place of Residence
1. Mrs. A and 2 children   3 people   County Seat
2. Male and family   5 people   Nearby Rural
3. Male alone   1 person   Nearby Rural
4. Female and family   3 people   County Seat
5. Female and family   5 people   Nearby Rural
6. Female and family   5 people   Illinois
7. Male and family   2 people   Nearby Rural
8. Male and family   2 people   Nearby Rural

                                                    8 Households outside Mill Creek
                                                    0 Households on Mill Creek

Family B
1. Mr. and Mrs. B.   2 people   Mill Creek
2. Female and family   3 people   Mill Creek
3. Female and family   3 people   Mill Creek
4. Female   1 person   Arkansas
5. Female and family   3 people   County Seat
6. Male and family   3 people   Mill Creek

                                                    2 Households outside Mill Creek
                                                    4 Households on Mill Creek

Family C
1. Mr. and Mrs. C and 2 children   4 people   Mill Creek
2. Male's widow and family   3 people   Mill Creek
3. Male and family   5 people   Mill Creek
4. Female and family   5 people   Nearby Rural
5. Male and family   5 people   Nearby Rural
6. Male and family   2 people   County Seat
7. Female and family   3 people   Nearby Rural

                                                    2 Households outside Mill Creek
                                                    5 Households on Mill Creek

Family D
1. Mr. and Mrs. D   2 people   Mill Creek
2. Female and family   5 people   Mill Creek
3. Male and family   6 people   Mill Creek
4. Male and family   3 people   Mill Creek
5. Female and family   2 people   Louisville
6. Female and family   3 people   County Seat
7. Male and family   3 people   Mill Creek
8. Male and family   4 people   Mill Creek

                                                    2 Households outside Mill Creek
                                                    5 Households on Mill Creek

Source: Interviews with families, Fall 1984 and Winter 1985

TABLE 3: Demographic Change in Mill Creek 1964-1984

	1964	1984	% Increase or Decrease
Families on Mill Creek	4	13	+225%
Persons on Mill Creek	35	46	+31%
Mean Household Size	X=8.75 Persons	X=3.5 Persons	

1984 Residence of Persons on Mill Creek in 1964 Plus 3 Siblings

Mill Creek	17	49%
Nearby Rural	8	23%
County Seat	7	20%
Outside East Kentucky	3	8%
	35	

TABLE 4: Education of Program Participants and Siblings in 1984

Total Group
Some Elementary	7	28%
Some High School	7	28%
Completed High School	10	40%
Some College	1	4%

Group Resident in Mill Creek
Some Elementary	4	36%
Some High School	4	36%
Completed High School	3	27%
Some College	0	
	11	

Group Resident Outside Mill Creek
Some Elementary	3	21%
Some High School	3	21%
Completed High School	7	50%
Some College	1	7%
	14	

(Estimated Education in the Enumeration District — 1980 Census)
Some Elementary	72%
Some High School	14%
Completed High School	12%
Some College	2%

TABLE 5: Labor Force Participation for Program Participants: Siblings and Parents — 1984

Labor Force Participation		
Persons in Labor Force	17	53%
Persons Not In Labor Force	15	47%
Persons Not In Labor Force		
Retired/Disabled	3	20%
Housewife	8	53%
No Work	4	27%
Persons in Labor Force By Industry		
Coal	6	35%
Mechanic	1	
Nurse	1	
Operator	2	12%
School Employee	4	24%
Military	1	
Retail Trade	1	
Services	1	
(Estimated Labor Force Participation in the Enumeration District—1980)		
Persons in Labor Force		37%
Persons Not in Labor Force		63%

Sources and References

Interviews with Families in Mill Creek and elsewhere, 1984 and 1985.

1970 Census of the Population, Clay County, ED0016.

1980 Census of the Population, Clay County, ED0038.

Council of the Southern Mountains Papers, Berea College, Special Collections "Proposal to The Council of The Southern Mountains Educational Committee" no date.

"Mill Creek Project Report" no date

Letter from Coordinator Education Programs, CSM to Director of Appalachian Volunteers, April 16, 1965.

"Students Bring Light to Mountain Children" *The Courier Journal*, August 9, 1964, section 4, page 4. Jim Hampton.

Newsweek, "Poverty USA", Feb. 17, 1964, pp. 19-38.

Philip Conn, "Appalachian Volunteers: An Experiment in Community Development", unpublished thesis, Institute of Social Studies, The Hague, 1966.

Michael Harrington, *The New American Poverty,* New York (1984).

David Whisnant, *Modernizing the Mountaineers,* "One-Eye in the Land of the Blind: The Appalachian Volunteers" pp. 185-219, New York (1980).

www.ingramcontent.com/pod-product-compliance
Lightning Source LLC
Chambersburg PA
CBHW051055160426
43193CB00010B/1192